6/99

Colonel Abel Streight

The Lightning Mule Brigade

Abel Streight's 1863 Raid into Alabama

Robert L. Willett, Jr.
Author of *One Day of the Civil War*

With Foreword by Edward G. Longacre,
Author of *Mounted Raids of the Civil War*

Guild Press
Carmel, Indiana

ISBN# 1-57860-009-5 Hardcover
1-57860-025-1 Softbound

Library of Congress No. 99-71525

Cover Art by Edwin Forbes—#5 "The Supply Train"

To my three children, Leslie, Tom and Barbara,
who, sometimes in spite of their parents, successfully emerged
through childhood and adolescence into adulthood and became my
three best friends.

TABLE OF CONTENTS

FOREWORD

On rare occasions, an historical event will display all the elements of quality fiction: an engaging cast of characters, a swift-moving plot, a deft mix of comedy and high drama, an outcome held in suspense until the last minute, and an exciting denouement. Such are the ingredients of Streight's Raid across northern Alabama in the spring of 1863, one of the Civil War's lesser known but more entertaining episodes. The story features a plucky and determined hero, Colonel Abel D. Streight of Indiana; a wily foe, Brigadier General Nathan Bedford Forrest of Tennessee, the war's most brilliant cavalry commander; and a host of supporting characters, including 1,700 Union infantrymen mounted (through the perversity of nameless logisticians) on a herd of the most fractious and contrary mules in captivity. Riding more conventional mounts, Forrest's outnumbered command fought off a screening movement by another Federal force, then raced to overtake the "Mule Brigade" before it could cut a strategic railroad at Rome, Georgia.

Writing after the war, a Union cavalryman who set off on an expedition through Mississippi soon after Streight's people headed south from Nashville, Tennessee, observed that "a cavalry raid at its best is essentially a *game* of strategy and speed, with personal violence as an incidental complication. It is played according to more or less definite rules, not inconsistent, indeed, with the players killing each other if the game cannot be won in any other way. . . ." This man knew whereof he spoke: of the hundreds of raids launched in all quarters of the war zone between 1861 and 1865, the great majority featured hard riding and widespread destruction of enemy property but few pitched battles and a limited amount of bloodshed.

Streight's Raid, however, was a notable exception. Even with their long headstart, the slow-footed mules could not outdistance Forrest's gallopers; the result was a series of bloody clashes in the Alabama hill country that took a toll of raiders and pursuers alike and complicated Streight's efforts to gain his objective before he could be brought to bay. How the expedition ended is the stuff of Civil War legend; it has the power to surprise and impress today.

Robert L. Willett, Jr.'s account of Streight and Forrest, the first book-length treatment of their confrontation, has much to recommend it. Based on research among primary sources including numerous relevant and sometimes obscure first-person accounts, it features a fast-paced narrative, illuminating character studies and colorful prose. If it sometimes reads like a novel, this is a tribute to the skill of the author and to the captivating nature of the subject he has rescued from the shadows of history.

—Edward G. Longacre
Author of *Mounted Raids of the Civil War*

PREFACE

An unlikely group of four military commanders was destined to meet in a fiercely contested, physically exhausting, always confusing encounter in northern Alabama. None of the four had military training or experience prior to his Civil War service. All were successful commanders with varied battle experience during the first two years of the war.

One was a New York native: a corpulent, thirty-three-year-old publisher from Indianapolis.

One was born in Massachusetts: a thirty-two-year-old, college-educated civil engineer and railroad surveyor from Iowa.

One was a tall, slender, uneducated, forty-one-year-old slave-trader, businessman and farmer from Tennessee.

One was a thirty-seven-year-old unschooled tailor, sheriff and deckhand from Alabama.

One thing they all shared—the engineer, the publisher, the slave-trader and the tailor—was a firm belief in the rightness of his cause.

The purpose of the book is to recount the myriad of details that made up the causes of success or failure in this tragi-comic war episode called Streight's Raid. It still is a matter of debate whether its impact on the war as a whole was significant or simply another example of military strategy gone awry. Certainly it was one of the most interesting and engaging incidents, and is therefore proper for examination in a nation increasingly fascinated by the human drama of the Civil War.

By April 1863, after two years of war, there had been 878 "engagements" in the various theaters of the American Civil War.[1] One of these engagements was the raid of Union Colonel Abel D. Streight into north Alabama. The raid is of special interest because it exemplified the new, aggressive spirit of Union raiding and tested the ingenuity and the hardiness of both the Northern and Southern forces involved. It also illustrated the fact that, "In these days, on both sides, men were prepared to take boundless risks. Their hopes and not their fears were their guides."[2] This raid in particular let the hopes outpace reality. In a span of three weeks, it produced examples of the best and the worst of war. There was heroism and hardship on both sides, testing the endurance and skills of both men and officers. Virtually every recounting of the story expresses praise and admiration for its organizer and leader, Colonel Abel D. Streight. He was far from a well-known figure in the spring of 1863, compared to the man he would face, Nathan Bedford Forrest, already a legend in cavalry warfare. The raid is significant not only for the action itself, but because of the ground on which it took place, northern Alabama. All of these factors contributed to this highly charged little scene in the war.

It was, after all, human beings (and mules) who lived the story. We have tried to provide as many of the personal insights of those involved as possible, recognizing that time has claimed great quantities of material that existed at one time. There still remain vast numbers of official Civil War records; however, official records are written by the participants and tend to set forth those facts which glorify the teller and deal less with the shortcomings of the participants. Unfortunately, the South has lost a great many of its records, letters, diaries, journals and memoirs, compared to those remaining in the North. If the following pages seem to project more Northern viewpoints, that is simply because more of these records exist.

The mules who survived what has to be recognized as one of the extreme cases recorded of animal abuse either did not survive to tell the tale, or were mute on the subject.

In many cases there was a definite conflict in the narratives left by the troopers. This contradiction exists not only for Northern view versus Southern, but also for men from different regiments—they saw things differently. This is not surprising; in war, confusion is almost always present, and no one person sees everything. Many of the memoirs were written long after the events themselves, so the tales became more graphic, even heroic, over the passage of years. We have tried to present what seems to be the logical definition of an event, but in some cases, where discrepancies were severe, we included several versions. We do hope this is as accurate a description as possible of what one author has called one of the "Crucial moments of the Civil War."[3]

This is the tale of Colonel Streight, with as much detail and accuracy as our research can provide. We have traveled the roads of the colonel as he passed through Alabama and have been over the path of his screening force under Brigadier General Grenville Dodge across the corners of Mississippi and Alabama. We feel as close to this raid as if it had happened in our generation.

In pursuing our goal, we discovered that many strange factors influenced the outcome of the raid, and that the aftermath provided almost as much mystery and intrigue as the raid itself. The one factor that no research can ignore, or quantify, is the part played by pure luck. This raid had all kinds of luck, much of it bad, some of it good. But luck, whimsical and capricious, aided first one side, then the other. Some of the tales of the raid have a comic aspect, and the overall view of the raiders gives a chuckle at times, but it is difficult to laugh ultimately at anything that caused such agony and tragedy as Streight's Raid.

We have spent many hours in archives and libraries, visiting with personnel in many warehouses of knowledge, and express our sincere appreciation for all of the many who steered us toward areas we would have overlooked. While we cannot recognize everyone who helped, special thanks go to Marylin Bell Hughes, Archivist Public Services, Tennessee State Library and Archives. She is a special person. Stephen E. Towne, former Reference Archivist in the Indiana State Archives was another who went beyond the call of duty to supply us with knowledge and resource material we had no idea existed. Norton and Ingrid Martensson-Pereira were hosts who allowed us the time and comfort to pursue the National Archives and Library of Congress. As always, Leslie Mitchell gave us computer advice and comfort and deserves our thanks. Nancy Baxter of Guild Press gave us the needed assistance and critique necessary to move the project into its final stages, and is due our gratitude for her enthusiastic participation.

We urge all history students to make use of their local libraries; their horizons and information sources expand as technology changes. We would be neglectful if we failed to mention our favorite librarian, Ray Dickinson of the Cocoa Beach Public Library here in Florida who has supported our efforts in a number of ways. Glenda McWhirter Todd of Winchester, Tennessee, has been a great source of knowledge on a principal regimental player, the 1st Alabama Cavalry (US), and, in her own words "eats, drinks and sleeps the 1st Alabama." Her web site is a testimony to her devotion. Melinda Mason and Steve Loomis are equally as dedicated to the preservation of the history of the 80th Illinois Volunteer Infantry Regiment. My sincere gratitude goes to them both for their help.

My special thanks, too, to Ed Longacre for his foreword and for his early suggestions. He is one of the experts on Civil War raids. The maps are the work of Richard Day, and add a great deal to the tale.

The most important contributor in time, interest and usually constructive criticism was my wife, Donna, who suffered almost daily confrontation with this effort. Her patience and her assistance made this finished work possible. To her I owe much.

Note: Original unpublished accounts and on-the-spot newpaper accounts are in italics.

INTRODUCTION

Colonel Abel D. Streight was agitated and upset. He was a restless, impatient man, and had been brooding while recuperating from a condition described by doctors as "congestion of the cerebellum," which had caused him to be sent home in January 1863.[4] He considered himself well, fully recovered, but he had little interest in rejoining his 51st Indiana Volunteer Infantry Regiment in Murfreesboro, Tennessee. There he would be relegated to just sitting in camp, waiting for something to come his way, as he had for the past three months, after the Stones River battle. He wanted action and the share of glory that war afforded those men willing to risk everything. While in Indianapolis he stewed over his next move, and gradually a plan began to form in his mind. On March 5, 1863, he sent a message to his friend and superior, Brigadier General James A. Garfield, newly appointed chief of staff of the Union's Army of the Cumberland:

> *I hope you will continue to favor me with your influence to induce the General [Rosecrans] to give me a suitable command for the purpose of penetrating the interior of the South. I am more and more satisfied as I study the matter more carefully that I could do them more harm and our cause more good in a three month campaign than I can, situated as I have been during this last year, in a whole lifetime.*
> *Please consider this correspondence highly confidential and if you think it best for me to return at any time, telegraph me at my expense.*
> *I remain most truly your friend*
> *A.D. Streight.*[5]

This was the first step in the movement that would forever be known as Streight's Raid.

It was the spring of 1863 and the war was just half over. Of course no one could know there would be two more years of fighting, and the combatants, both North and South, were already tired of the endless tragedy of battle. In April 1863 it appeared that the South had the advantage. The pitched battles in the East had been won overwhelmingly by the Rebels, and in the West there had been little to cheer about for Northerners.

Most recently the Union's Army of the Potomac, Mr. Lincoln's Army, had been bested by General Lee's Army of Northern Virginia in a bloody December battle in Fredericksburg, Virginia, and the North had changed commanding generals once again. Major General Joseph Hooker was now in charge of the Army of the Potomac and had taken some very positive steps to make his troopers' lives easier: furloughs, new equipment, insignias for the units, and a revision of the organization of his army.

In the West, Union Major General William S. Rosecrans was still regrouping his Army of the Cumberland in Murfreesboro, Tennessee. In December he had fought to a draw against Confederate General Braxton Bragg in the Battle of Stones River, but Bragg had withdrawn from Murfreesboro, making it look very much like a Union win, although both sides had suffered heavy losses. Farther west, Major General Ulysses S. Grant's Army of the Tennessee had been thwarted in his overland drive through Mississippi to Vicksburg when the Confederate Cavalry under Major General Earl Van Dorn raided his base in Holly Springs, Mississippi, in December 1862. Grant had been forced into a series of engineering efforts on the west side of the Mississippi River; in April 1863 he was still frustrated and far from his goal: Vicksburg.

Since December there had been little military activity of note anywhere. There were cavalry skirmishes, reconnaissances, patrols and the like, but no major battles. By April the weather had warmed enough to clear the roads and allow for some more adventuresome movement. Now, in April, cavalry was coming out of its cocoon in all sectors. During the month several major cavalry excursions would begin, most lasting into May. General Hooker's reorganized cavalry, now a single corps, started a raid around Lee's army, beginning the first phase of the Battle of Chancellorsville. Weather delayed his movement, and little was accomplished. Confederate brigadier generals John D. Imboden and William E. Jones had better luck as they set out to disrupt the Baltimore & Ohio Railroad in West Virginia and a corner of Maryland. They were successful to a point, but weather hampered their efforts as well. Farther west, Confederates under Brigadier General John S. Marmaduke took off on a raid into Missouri from their Arkansas headquarters. They gathered some new recruits and horses plus forage, but gained little else.

The most successful of the April raids was one led by Colonel Benjamin Grierson, an Illinois music teacher turned cavalryman who took 1,700 Union cavalry from LaGrange, Tennessee, through Mississippi to Baton Rouge with almost no loss. His real accomplishment was in distracting attention from Grant's southward movement on the west bank of the Mississippi River. It was a significant boost to Northern morale and was featured in all the papers, North and South.

But the strangest of these Union raids was technically not a cavalry raid at all, although history has deemed it as such. It was not a cavalry raid since it involved four Midwestern infantry regiments and only two companies of Alabama/Tennessee cavalry.

The raid was led by an Indiana publisher, thirty-three-year-old Colonel

Abel D. Streight. And the aftermath, the events following the raid itself, adds even more fascination.

A factor that should be explained for that time and location was the practice of parole and exchange. In the early days of the war, since neither side had made provisions for housing, feeding and caring for the huge numbers of captives that were appearing, a fairly cumbersome but effective method was devised that seemed fair to both sides. The captured men were taken to a central point, their names inscribed, and then they were asked to give their word of honor that they would not take up arms against their enemies until the next step was taken, the exchange. The men would then be sent back through their lines for reassignment. The names of these prisoners would be taken to division, army or department headquarters, and matched with a like number of the opposing army, similar in rank. Both groups would then be declared "exchanged" and the men could rejoin their units.

It was a loose arrangement with little control, but until prison systems could be put in place, it was a workable solution. However, it could be enforced, and there is at least one case where a Union officer was hanged in Richmond for violation of his parole.[6] By April 1863 this process was already decreasing in main battles, but was still the rule in the border conflicts of smaller units. This raid would test many of the processes of the system and even impact its future, because cavalry raiders often worked behind enemy lines and could be captured.

An unusual situation, but one which would involve future participants in the raid, had developed in the area close to General Dodge's headquarters in Corinth, Mississippi. The Battle of Corinth, October 3, had followed the September 19, 1862, Battle of Iuka. After these battles, the Union was in control of the two towns. However, in Iuka a cartel was arranged to keep a Confederate hospital in the town; it was staffed by Confederate surgeons, but supplied by Union forces. Many of the wounded from the two battles were too badly injured to travel, so it was agreed that the Confederate hospital should remain. It proved to be a blessing to the wounded but a trial for the Federals, whose troops were thin in that area. In a letter directed from Union Captain James C. Cameron, then Provost Marshal General, District of Corinth located in Iuka, to Confederate Lieutenant General Joseph Pemberton in Vicksburg on December 7, 1862, Cameron conveyed a complaint that the hospital had been searched by unauthorized Rebel troops; and Dr. A. B. Stewart, the Federal surgeon in charge, reported his wife had been mistreated as she lay in her sick bed. Captain Cameron concluded:

General, permit me to say that such conduct must be punished or this hospital located here by the special request of your surgeons will be closed, although many of the wounded of your command are pronounced by the surgeons in charge not in a condition to be safely moved. It has been our pleasure to treat with the most circumspect deference the wounded who have fallen into our hands and the Confederate surgeons in charge of them, and we look for an honorable and speedy redress of those outrages.[7]

On March 19, 1863, an additional complaint was made to Confederate Colonel Hannon, then commanding Southern troops in Tuscumbia. In a letter from Iuka, Dr. Stewart protested the burning of two bridges, a circumstance which interrupted travel to Corinth from Iuka. He suggested that he would abandon the hospital, take all his supplies and withdraw Union forces to Corinth if the bridges were not rebuilt He referred to the original cartel that structured the hospital in Union territory:

For any particulars regarding the cartel and how far the Federals have carried it out on their part I respectfully refer you to any C.S. Army surgeon who has been on duty at this hospital, especially, Surgs. D.C. Roberts, J.C. Roberts and Felton.

Hoping that our official and personal relations may be as pleasant as your worthy predecessor, Colonel Roddey.[8]

Cameron and Roddey squared off over this matter of the hospital. Both Cameron and Roddey would be heard from again as the raid progressed.

THE RAID
UNION

On the Union side, the raid involved two western armies: the Army of the Cumberland and the Army of the Tennessee. The command structure was as follows:

Major General William S. Rosecrans—Commanding Army of the Cumberland; Murfreesboro, Tennessee

Brigadier General James A. Garfield—Chief of Staff of the Army of the Cumberland; Murfreesboro, Tennessee

Brigadier General Thomas J. Wood—Commanding XXI Corps; Murfreesboro, Tennessee

Colonel Abel D. Streight—Independent Provisional Brigade; Murfreesboro, Tennessee

*3d Ohio Infantry—Lieutenant Colonel Robert Lawson
*51st Indiana Infantry—Lieutenant Colonel James W. Sheets (Streight's regiment)
*73d Indiana Infantry—Colonel Gilbert Hathaway
*80th Illinois Infantry—Lieutenant Colonel Andrew F. Rodgers
*2 companies 1st West Tennessee/Alabama Cavalry—Captain David D. Smith

Major General Ulysses S. Grant—Commanding Army of the Tennessee; Millikens, Bend, Louisiana

Major General Stephen A. Hurlbut—Commanding XVI Corps; Memphis, Tennessee

Major General Richard J. Oglesby—Left Wing, XVI Corps; Memphis, Tennessee

Brigadier General Grenville M. Dodge—District of Corinth; Corinth, Mississippi

First Brigade—Brigadier General Thomas W. Sweeney; Corinth, Mississippi
+52d Illinois Infantry—Lieutenant Colonel John S. Wilcox
+66th Indiana Infantry—Colonel DeWitt C. Anthony
+2d Iowa Infantry—Colonel James B. Weaver

Second Brigade—Colonel August Mersey; Corinth, Mississippi
+9th Illinois (Mounted) Infantry—Lieutenant Colonel Jesse J. Phillips
+12th Illinois Infantry—Major James R. Hugunin
+122d Illinois Infantry—Lieutenant Colonel James F. Drish
+81st Ohio Infantry—Lieutenant Colonel Robert N. Adams

Third Brigade—Colonel Moses M. Bane; Corinth, Mississippi
+7th Illinois Infantry—Lieutenant Colonel Richard Rowett
+50th Illinois Infantry—Major Thomas W. Gaines
+57th Illinois Infantry—Lieutenant Colonel Frederick J. Hurlbut
+39th Iowa Infantry—Colonel Henry J. B. Cummings

Fourth Brigade—Colonel John W. Fuller; Corinth, Mississippi
+27th Ohio—Lieutenant Colonel Zeph S. Spaulding
+39th Ohio—Colonel Edward F. Noyes
+63d Ohio—Colonel John W. Sprague
+43d Ohio—Colonel J. L. Kilby Smith

Cavalry Brigade—Colonel Florence M. Cornyn; Corinth, Mississippi
+1st Alabama Cavalry, 1st Battalion—Major Michael F. Fairfield
+7th Kansas Cavalry—Lieutenant Colonel Thomas P. Herrick
+10th Missouri Cavalry—Lieutenant Colonel William D. Bowen
+5th Ohio, 3d Battalion—Major Joseph C. Smith
+15th Illinois Cavalry—Major F. T. Gilbert

The Confederate cavalry opposing Streight was General Nathan Bedford Forrest's Cavalry Division plus Colonel Philip Roddey's independent cavalry command, all in General Braxton Bragg's Army of Tennessee.

CONFEDERATE

General Joseph E. Johnston—Department of the West; Chattanooga, Tennessee

General Braxton Bragg—Army of Tennessee; Tullahoma, Tennessee

Major General Earl Van Dorn—Cavalry Command; Spring Hill, Tennessee

Brigadier General Nathan Bedford Forrest—Forrest's Cavalry Division;
Columbia, Tennessee

Colonel Philip D. Roddey—Roddey's Brigade; Tuscumbia, Alabama
*+4th Alabama Cavalry—Colonel Philip D. Roddey
5th Alabama Cavalry—Colonel Josiah Patterson
*+53d Alabama Cavalry—Colonel M. W. Hannon
*+Julian's Battalion—Major William R. Julian

Forrest's Old Division
*4th Tennessee Cavalry—Lieutenant Colonel W. S. McLemore
*8th (13th) Tennessee Cavalry—Colonel George C. Dibrell
*9th Tennessee Cavalry—Colonel Jacob Biffle
*10th Tennessee Cavalry—Colonel William E. DeMoss
*+11th Tennessee Cavalry—Colonel James H. Edmondson

    * Troops used in and against Streight's Raid
    + Troops used in and against Dodge's Expedition

THE PLAYERS

The leading man in the cast of characters was Colonel Abel D. Streight, the commander of the Union forces making the raid and the instigator of the whole idea. Streight was a successful publisher from Indianapolis. Although his early years on a farm in New York were not easy ones and he had only a common-school education, by age nineteen he had already become a successful contractor. His move to Indiana brought him into his new career in publishing; when the war began he was proprietor of the Railroad City Publishing Company and also ran the New Lumber Yard, both located in the Hoosier capital.[9] He had no military training or military experience but was a prominent citizen of Indianapolis, and that in itself was enough to place him in the forefront of those considered for command in the new regiments formed at Mr. Lincoln's request in 1861. A staunch Republican, Streight was a committed Abolitionist and wrote a pamphlet in 1861 outlining the logic of the forcible return of seceding states.

> We should not compromise in the least if we desire permanent peace, but administer the laws with firmness and justice; and although it may take the force of arms to do so, yet a rivulet of blood, spilt at this time, will prevent rivers of it in the future.[10]

As a journalist he had even been granted an interview with Mr. Lincoln just after Lincoln's election, which further strengthened his admiration for the president.[11]

Streight was a large, erect man with impressive carriage, inclined toward corpulence, who inspired confidence by his very bearing. In 1848 he married Lovina McCarty, who was reported to be a rather direct and assertive person. (Her portrait, not his, hangs in an Indianapolis government office.) He and wife Lovina had one son when Streight was commissioned as colonel of the 51st Indiana Volunteer Infantry Regiment on September 4, 1861. Previously he had been commander of Camp Morton in Indianapolis for several months, but some problems there necessitated a move and he became the commander of the 51st.[12] The 51st had been in reserve at the battle of Shiloh but participated in the siege of Corinth, and was in reserve again at Perrysville. They did participate in the Battle of Stones River in December 1862 and January 1863.

By nature Streight was an aggressive, impatient, restless man who was totally committed to a Northern victory. William Barton McCash, in his University of Georgia Master's Thesis, "Colonel Abel D. Streight's Raid, His Capture and Imprisonment," described him this way:

> The desire for quick, decisive action and hatred of the slower more conservative way of doing things were dominant factors in his personality. Unfortunately Streight's active nature, when uncontrolled, had a tendency toward rashness—an open invitation to disaster. This disposition actually bordered at times on irritable impatience, as exemplified by his exasperation at governmental acquiescence in the face of secession. Nevertheless, qualities of leadership were evident in the Colonel's character, enabling him to command loyalty and instill his men with espirit de corps, an element always having incalculable value in war.[13]

He may have seemed a peculiar choice for a raiding brigade commander, an infantry colonel commanding four infantry regiments in a cavalry-type raid, but Streight's selection was not really that outlandish. As commander of the 51st Indiana, he had been garrisoned in northern Alabama in July 1862. There were reports of mountain men anxious to join Union forces, but they were cut off from the camps by the Confederate Home Guard. Streight, active Unionist that he was, requested permission to go up in the hills to bring these men into his camp. Permission was granted; he came back four days later with forty recruits and a burning desire to go back for more. "Never did people stand in greater need of protection. They have battled manfully against the most unscrupulous foe that civilized warfare has ever witnessed. They have been shut out from all communication with anybody but their enemies for a year and a half, and yet they stand firm and true."[14]

So Streight was no stranger to the territory of northern Alabama, nor to many of its people. His regiment had been with him in Mississippi and shared his desire to aid the Union sympathizers of those northern Alabama counties. Also, the use of mounted infantry was not unusual in Northern military strategy, giving infantry greater mobility.

The other Union player was Brigadier General Grenville Dodge. He was commanding the Department of Corinth (Mississippi). His immediate superior was Major General Stephen A. Hurlbut, who gave Dodge orders to carry out the task of screening the Streight movement. Dodge, a thirty-two-year-old native of Massachusetts and a veteran of a number of minor clashes, had been made a brigadier general early in 1862 after the Battle of Pea Ridge, where he had been wounded. Before the war, he graduated from Norwich University in Vermont and worked as a civil engineer and railroad surveyor in the West. His work in Indian country had given him the name "Level Eye" by the Indians, in honor of his transit survey equipment. He settled in Iowa and was commissioned a colonel of the 4th Iowa Infantry in July 1861. Dodge was both ambitious and out to find his moment of glory, and this raid was a golden opportunity for him to show his talents. Some months earlier he had suggested a raid through the Tennessee Valley, laying waste to the land and making it useless to the Rebels.[15] Streight's raid was a chance for him to put his suggestion into action. He was described by various contemporaries as cautious, hot-tempered, capable and a rather typical Protestant, Republican Yankee. His engineering expertise made him a favorite of Major General U. S. Grant.

The principal opposing characters in this mid-war excursion included the Confederacy's legendary cavalryman, Brigadier General Nathan Bedford Forrest. Forrest led a division under Major General Earl Van Dorn and was operating out of Columbia, Tennessee. Van Dorn, in turn, was a part of the Army of Tennessee led by General Braxton Bragg, headquartered in Tullahoma, Tennessee. Forrest was no military academy graduate, but a successful slave-trader, farmer and businessman from Tennessee. Early in 1861, just before his fortieth birthday, with his fifteen-year-old son and his young brother Jeffrey, he enlisted as a private in Company D of the 7th Tennessee Cavalry. Shortly after his enlistment he was authorized to form a battalion. Although a successful businessman, he had almost no formal education, but had an uncanny intelligence that seemed to rise to any occasion. Physically he was impressive: six feet two, slender and powerful; he was the epitome of a soldier. But he had a problem—a fiery temper which frequently took over his behavior. He served under Major General Joseph Wheeler until a battle at Fort Donelson, Tennessee. Afterwards, as Wheeler was writing his report to his commander General Braxton Bragg, Forrest declared: ". . . there is one thing I do want you to put in that report to General Bragg—tell him that I will be in my coffin before I will fight again under your command!"[16] It was not the last time he would confront one of his commanders.

Forrest's hot temper was matched only by his battlefield bravery. He was totally unaware of personal danger and had no patience with subordinates who were less inclined toward such recklessness. Stories of his abuse toward his staff and his men were common, during and even after this raid. By April 1863 he was a Confederate legend, having a score of triumphs over Union commanders. At Shiloh, one year before, he had been badly wounded, but returned to the saddle and was promoted to brigadier general in July 1862. Most recently he had successfully attacked and captured a Union brigade under Colonel John Coburn near Thompson's Station, Tennessee.

The Forrest family gave a great deal to both the United States and to the Confederacy. John, Nathan's older brother, was severely wounded in the Mexican war and hobbled through the rest of his life on crutches. William, Forrest's younger brother, would be shot in the thigh and badly wounded during Streight's Raid but survived. Another brother, Aaron, died of disease in the Confederate service, brother Jeffrey was killed at the Battle of Okolona, and the last brother, Jesse, was wounded at Athens, Georgia.

Nathan Bedford Forrest was the opponent whom Colonel Streight would confront as they rode across Alabama. Forrest was not the opponent Streight had expected or hoped for.

The second player on the Confederate roster was Colonel Philip Dale Roddey of Alabama. The colonel was born in rural Alabama and had celebrated his thirty-seventh birthday on April 2. He, like General Forrest, came from a poor family with little education, but he was a natural leader and horseman. Before the war he had been a deckhand, a sheriff and a tailor, but when the war began, he organized a cavalry troop and rode off to the war. He lacked the bravado and public recognition of Forrest, but at Shiloh he had proven himself a brave and competent leader. He had been appointed as colonel of the 4th Alabama Cavalry, but that unit was expanded, on paper, to become a brigade and included the 5th Alabama, 53d Alabama and W. R. Julian's battalion. He had recently been appointed commander of the District of Northern Alabama in Bragg's Army of Tennessee, and was headquartered in Tuscumbia, Alabama, just south of the Tennessee River. Most of his experience came as the leader of this independent cavalry force in northern Alabama. He was described as "medium height, model horseman, athletic, calm, resolute, composed."[17]

None of the four principal leaders in Streight's Raid was a West Point graduate. Several of their subordinates had attended or graduated from the Academy, but the strategies used during these weeks of the raid were not those learned in the classroom anyway. These four also are a reminder that war is a young man's game. Forrest, at forty-one, was considerably older than most Civil War officers; many young men in their thirties were given commands with tremendous responsibilities. History books, with their stern portraits of leaders on both sides, fail to emphasize that few of the wartime leaders had reached forty. Stonewall Jackson, for instance, portrayed as an eccentric old man, died at thirty nine. In the spring of 1863, Grant was just over forty, Lee was an elderly fifty-six.

THE RAID—THE MISSION

When General Garfield received Streight's initial message and subsequent detailed plans, he was favorably impressed both with the Indiana colonel and with his plan, so he sent the request to General Rosecrans with his blessing. The Army of the Cumberland had suffered from countless Confederate cavalry raids; any initiative that resulted in an effort to reciprocate was welcome. Rosecrans gave his approval on April 8, 1863, in Special Field Orders #94 issued by Chief of Staff Garfield. Streight was to command an independent provisional brigade, as discussed in verbal instructions already issued by Rosecrans, head to the Tennessee River above Fort Henry, go up the river to "some good steamboat landing," and debark and join a force under Brigadier General Grenville M. Dodge from General Grant's Army of the Tennessee.[18]

Dodge's forces were to provide a screen behind which Streight would take his brigade, cut loose around Tuscumbia, Alabama, and pursue his primary mission, the cutting of the railroad between Chattanooga and Atlanta somewhere in the vicinity of Rome, Georgia. "To accomplish this is the chief object of your expedition and you must not allow collateral or incidental schemes, even though promising great results, to delay you so as to endanger your return."[19] Included in these orders was the instruction, "You will draw your supplies and keep your command well mounted from the country through which you pass. For all property taken for the legitimate use of your command you will make cash payments in full to men of undoubted loyalty; give the usual conditional receipts to men whose loyalty is doubtful, but to Rebels nothing."[20] In this order was the only reference to an escape plan for the brigade, and it was very vague; he was to escape "by way of Northern Alabama or Northern Georgia" if he could. The likelihood of their using an escape route was quite remote; with the raiders creating such a stir, alerting the Confederate troops as they marched through Alabama, there was not much chance of their being able to safely return by that route.

This was not the first attempt at cutting Bragg's railroad line. Just a year earlier, on April 12, 1862, a small band of Union volunteers commandeered a Southern locomotive near Big Shanty, Georgia, with the hope of disrupting miles of the railroad. Confederates gave chase in what has been known as "The Great Locomotive Chase" and captured all twenty-two Yankees. They were in civilian clothes, so were tried as spies; seven, including their leader John Andrews, were hanged. The rest eventually escaped or were pardoned and all were given the Medal of Honor, the first ever awarded.[21] The cost of this second effort would be much higher.

The route of the Provisional Brigade was across the rugged but low-level mountains of northern Alabama, then east toward Rome, Georgia. Part of the reasoning for selecting this route was that the northern portion of Alabama had some strong Union sentiment, a fact made known to Streight a year earlier when he was based near Corinth, Mississippi. Two companies of the 1st Alabama Cavalry (assigned to the 1st Middle Tennessee Cavalry) were comprised of men who had lived in and been recruited from that hilly country, and were the only actual cavalry units to be part of Streight's Provisional Brigade. They would provide the scouting as the brigade moved toward Georgia. The rest of the Alabama regiment was assigned to Dodge and was stationed in Corinth; so it was that part of the regiment which served with the Army of the Cumberland with Streight. The rest served with the Army of the Tennessee under Dodge. It was not a common occurrence to have one regiment split between two armies.

These Alabama mountain people had suffered greatly for their Union loyalty during the first two years of the war, and Streight hoped that they would give aid as he passed through. Some northern Alabama counties had held conventions to state their neutrality; the Union leaders hoped for assistance from these disaffected citizens located in the path of the raid. By this time, however, these people had seen so many raids and foraging troops, both North and South, with the plundering and pillage that was a part of these expeditions, that they were no longer even defending themselves, let alone assisting in any efforts of the combatants.[22] The struggles between the Confederate Alabamians and the "Tories" devoted to the Union were bitter and bloody in northern Alabama, with many atrocities committed by both sides. One resident wrote later, "when Sherman undertook to teach the Georgians that war was hell, the old men, women and children in North Alabama had already graduated in his system."[23]

Streight's brigade was made up of four regiments of infantry: the 3d Ohio, 51st Indiana, 73d Indiana and 80th Illinois. They were accompanied by the two companies of cavalry, I and K from the 1st Alabama Cavalry, which was attached to the 1st Middle Tennessee Cavalry. The 3d Ohio, a veteran unit that had suffered heavy casualties at both Perryville and Stones

River, was commanded by Lieutenant Colonel Robert Lawson. The 80th Illinois was also a veteran unit bloodied at Perryville. The 73d Indiana had fought at Perryville and at Stones River, and its colonel, Gilbert A. Hathaway, had Streight's total confidence. The 51st was Streight's own regiment; he had great faith in the abilities and courage of the men. The two Tennessee/Alabama cavalry companies were to be the guides, the scouts and the protectors of the brigade. Confusion still exists as to the official designation of these two companies, but evidence shows that companies I and K of the 1st Alabama Cavalry was the proper designation at that time.[24] The artillery supporting the brigade consisted of two twelve-pounder mountain howitzers, plus the needed ammunition, scrounged by Lieutenant J. W. Pavey of the 80th Illinois.

Streight's total force when he left Nashville was approximately 1,700 men.[25] He was to leave Nashville on boats, go north, and down the Cumberland River to near Palmyra, Tennessee, where he would take the majority of his brigade by land across to Fort Henry on the Tennessee River, foraging for horses and supplies on the land march. His boats would continue on the river route as the main part of the brigade, mounted on their new animals, moved circuitously across the land; then the boats were to pick up the brigade at Fort Henry. From Fort Henry the boats would take the whole brigade, with their animals, up the Tennessee as far as Florence, Alabama, if possible.

The orders explicitly stated that Streight would not be "trammeled with minute instructions"; general instructions were all he would receive. But one of the closing paragraphs was ominous: "Should you be surrounded by rebel forces and your retreat cut off, defend yourself as long as possible, and make the surrender of your command cost the enemy as many times your number as possible."[26] In the correspondence between Streight and Garfield, Streight suggested his scouts take on the look of the Confederate cavalry and asked, "The Rebels not having regular uniforms, would it be violating the rules of war should I see fit to dress any number of my men, say two companies, after the promiscuous Southern style? Something of this kind might be advantageous, should you not think it an improper course to pursue." Garfield was quick to point out the dangers of that request: "If you dress soldiers in the costume of the enemy, they will be liable to be treated as spies: you should not do this without the consent of the men, after they have been fully advised of the . . . consequences."[27] So, fortunately, Streight kept his men in Federal uniforms. A postscript to Streight's last message was a portent of things to come: "P.S. —This was to be sent by railroad, but orderly missed the train."[28]

Meanwhile, Dodge would lead his three infantry brigades, the First, Second and Third Brigades, plus Colonel Florence Cornyn's cavalry brigade, on a march from Corinth, Mississippi, toward Tuscumbia, Alabama, with the intention of joining Streight in that neighborhood. In order to do this, Rosecrans needed to get cooperation from Grant's Army of the Tennessee, since Dodge was in Grant's army, not Rosecrans'. On April 3, Grant's XVI Corps commander, Stephen A. Hurlbut, telegraphed Dodge in Corinth, "Move as requested by General Rosecrans, with force enough to do it thoroughly."[29]

Thus it was that the main raiding force, the Provisional Brigade, came from General Rosecrans' Army of the Cumberland, while Dodge's screening force was provided by General Grant's Army of the Tennessee. It was not a common occurrence for one army to help out another army in supplying manpower, or anything else. Troops were being requested by almost every commander, and there were only so many available. Therefore most generals hoarded their men and equipment jealously, knowing that they might not be returned if borrowed. In this case, however, there was a distinct advantage in Grant's allowing Dodge to aid Streight. Dodge's commander, General Hurlbut, wired Grant on April 6:

> I enclose copies of messages from Generals Rosecrans and Dodge, which indicate an important movement not only for his corps, but necessarily for this force. If this movement goes on, it will materially aid my contemplated cavalry dash on the railroad below, for it will draw off their cavalry force into Alabama, and leave my field clear. . .
>
> This cavalry dash I desire to time so as to co-operate with what I suppose to be your plan to land below Vicksburg, on south side of Black River, silencing the Grand Gulf batteries.[30]

The Army of the Tennessee was planning its own raid into Mississippi to cut the rail line into Vicksburg and draw attention away from Grant as he sailed south down the Mississippi River, planning to cross into Mississippi and get behind Vicksburg. The raid would be led by Illinois Colonel Benjamin Grierson, who left LaGrange, Tennessee, on April 17. Rosecrans probably knew nothing of this plan.

Dodge reported that he had left Corinth with 3,500 infantry and 1,500 cavalry.[31] Dodge's mission was to engage any Confederate forces that might deter Streight. His plan of operation expanded on that mission: "At the same time I am to strike and take Tuscumbia, and, if practicable, push my cavalry to Decatur, destroy the saltpeter works and the Tuscumbia and Decatur Railroad, which they have just finished, and take all the horses and mules in that country, to prevent them from raising any large crops."[32]

Brigadier General James A. Garfield

CHAPTER 1

FRIDAY APRIL 10 TO SATURDAY APRIL 18

STREIGHT

The command structure of the brigade began with General Rosecrans, and included the XXI Corps commander Brigadier General Thomas J. Wood. The 51st and 73d had both been in his corps in the 1st Division, 3d Brigade, and Wood was aware of the raid. However there is no indication other division or brigade commanders knew their regiments were being sent off. Certainly the brigade commander of the 3d Ohio, Brigadier General JohnBeatty, had no previous knowledge; he wrote indignantly, and a little sadly, in his journal:

> April 7—The incident of the day, to me at least, is the departure of the Third. It left on the 2 PM train for Nashville. I do not think I have been fairly treated. They should at least have consulted me before detaching my old regiment. I am informed that Colonel Streight, who was in command of the expedition, was permitted to select the regiments, and the matter has been conducted so secretly that before I had any intimation of what was contemplated, it was too late to take any steps to save the Third . . . My best wishes go with them.[33]

The secrecy had been successful, even as the regiments left the huge army encampment in Murfreesboro and rode out to war. On April 6 James Gavin Crawford of the 80th Illinois wrote to his sweetheart, "I got your letter a few minutes ago and as we are going on a secret Expedition and one the Major says is full of danger, I thought that I would drop you a few lines as it may be the last time I may have the opportunity of writing to you." He closed the letter, "If we never see each other on earth again I hope we may meet in a better land where there is no war clang, no loud roar of the cannon, but all is peace and quiet reigns supreme."[34]

It is obvious that the chain of command had to be ignored if any secrecy was to be successful. To keep it low key, there was virtually a one-man provisioning committee, with General Garfield as the sole member. In a letter to his wife on April 10, 1863, Garfield wrote "Crete," "I have had the entire burden of getting up and fitting out the expedition of Colonel Streight."[35] General Wood had little input in the matter, simply informing Garfield he hoped that there would be no Rosecrans move until the Streight raid had been completed. He was concerned that any movement by the army would cut off Streight and doom his mission to failure.[36] And that seemed, from the Official Records, to be his only contribution to his brigade's excursion.

There were vague hints of other Rosecrans forces moving toward Tuscumbia or Florence across Tennessee, but no tangible results from the rumors. It was to be Streight's show with Dodge as a supporting character.

Streight's first act in forming his provisional brigade was to choose his staff, which he did while gathering supplies and equipment in Nashville. His choices were:

Acting Assistant Adjutant General—Captain D. L. Wright, 51st Indiana
Brigade Surgeon—Major W. L. Peck, 3d Ohio
Acting Assistant Quartermaster—Lieutenant J. G. Doughty, 51st Indiana
Acting Assistant Inspector General—Captain Edward Driscoll, 3d Ohio
Ordnance Officer—Lieutenant J. W. Pavey, 80th Illinois
Aide-de-camp—Lieutenant A. C. Roach, 51st Indiana[37]

Lieutenant Doughty was issued more than $3,000 in Yankee greenbacks for purchasing animals and supplies on the raid. That money would become a problem to Streight later on.

The timetable which was telegraphed to Dodge by Hurlbut on April 7 suggested that Streight would leave on the ninth: "Expedition preparing rapidly. Will probably start Thursday [ninth]. Ought to arrive at Pittsburg Landing or Eastport by Thursday week at latest [sixteenth]."[38] So Dodge set his expedition in motion to meet that schedule. Trying to coordinate timing of the two forces would prove difficult.

Streight's staff was kept busy trying to provision the 1,700-man raiding group, but one thing was clear: in all areas there was a reported shortage of horses. The Official Records record a rather acrimonious exchange of telegrams among General Rosecrans, Major General Henry Halleck, General in Chief in Washington, and Brigadier General Montgomery Meigs, Quartermaster General, also in the capitol.[39] Generals Meigs and Halleck reviewed the large number of animals which had been provided to Rosecrans in the preceding months and were critical of the loss of so many animals. Meigs telegraphed Rosecrans:

You report to General Halleck that you have received, since December 1 [1862], 18,450 horses and 14,607 mules—33,057 animals; nearly 7,000 animals per month. Is not this a large supply? Except in the first outbreak of war and enlargement of armies, has anything like it ever been done before? The animals cost, by the time they reach you, nearly $4,060,000. You had on hand March 23, 19,164 horses and

23,859 mules—43,023 animals in all, or if I am rightly informed by General Halleck as to your strength, about one horse or mule to every two men in your army. You have broken down and sent off as unserviceable, in addition to these, over 9,000 horses, and report that one-fourth or one-third of the horses on hand are worn out. Now, all this it seems to me, shows that the horses are not well treated.[40]

In retrospect, General Meigs did have a point. The March 1863 tally of Rosecrans' troops showed slightly over 80,000 men. Meigs' figures showed that there were 43,023 animals, horses and mules, on hand March 23, so there were, indeed, mounts for one out of two soldiers, infantry, cavalry and artillery in the Rosecrans army.[41]

Despite Meigs' protest, Rosecrans ordered another 12,000 animals, preferably horses. But in the days just before the raid, the decision was made to mount Streight's infantry brigade not on horses, but on mules. The part of Alabama the raiders would cross was fairly rugged, with the Sand Mountains stretched directly across their path. The reasoning was that mules were more sure-footed, given the mountainous terrain that would be traversed, and that they were tougher and would hold up longer for the two-hundred-mile route. Unfortunately, there was no mention made of the disadvantages of mules. This was indeed a significant omission.

Overall the mule choice was a very unfortunate decision. Not only would the vast majority of animals furnished be the cranky mule, but only about half of the men would have animals of any sort. It was the plan of the high command that the rest of the brigade find mounts as they passed through the areas of the expedition, supposing that the friendly hill people would provide animals in profusion. Since Streight was expecting little opposition, it was assumed speed would not be essential and mules would be perfectly acceptable.[42] That logic proved faulty on all counts.

There is no record of Streight's reaction to the mule decision, but it is possible that to an infantryman, even riding a mule would be better than walking. It should be noted that part of the blame for this switch lay with Brigadier General Garfield, the future president, since, by his own admission, he was solely responsible for outfitting the brigade. Even with this substitution, Streight had high hopes that it would all turn out well. The raid began, therefore, with infantry soldiers, unaccustomed to animals of any kind, mounted on the only animal available, the sturdy jackass.

There is also a possibility that the risk involved in the venture dictated that sound animals not be used, in case they should fall into Confederate hands, a pragmatic but pessimistic consideration.

All four Streight regiments were based in Murfreesboro. They took "the cars" up to Nashville on April 6 and 7, bivouacked three miles south of town, and began making preparations for the expedition. On April 9 a diary entry of Henry Briedenthal, a 3d Ohio sergeant, noted, "We have been busy preparing for a raid somewhere. Details have been made to assist in shipping our animals, saddles, etc."[43] On April 10 the Nashville papers reported that Streight had arrived in Nashville from Murfreesboro, complete with mules. The reporters were unaware that there were only eight-hundred animals for the 1,700 troopers, who had been ordered to supply their own mounts on their way to Georgia.[44]

The first legs of the trip would be through friendly territory, via riverboat; it was hoped the raiders could get as far as Eastport, Mississippi, on their boats. Eastport was about ninety miles south of Nashville; however, since the Confederates still controlled most of the acreage south of Nashville, a ride straight south to the Tennessee River would not be prudent. Streight was to load his brigade, complete with livestock, saddles, clothing, tents, ammunition and his two mountain howitzers, on eight transports, and head northwest down the Cumberland River to Palmyra, Tennessee. There they would unload and march west to Fort Henry on the Tennessee River, a distance of about fifty miles. This would give Streight a chance to scour the countryside for more horses and mules. After dropping the brigade, the boats would then cover 150 winding miles by water to rejoin Streight at Fort Henry. The brigade would then reboard the boats and go as far as possible on the Tennessee. This was an enormous detour for the boats, covering almost 350 river miles to reach a destination that was only ninety miles away.

One more obstacle occurred in the attempt to find gunboats to provide a convoy escort for the troop transports. Garfield had requested boats from Captain A. M. Pennock, who commanded the navy ships in Cairo, Illinois, but the general was told on March 29 that there were no boats available.[45] In response to other requests, a few gunboats did show up in Nashville, but the water in the Cumberland was dropping off enough to be of concern to the boat crews, so they abruptly departed at 3:00 AM on April 7, in spite of orders to remain.[46] Just three days before his departure, Streight had no gunboats to protect his transports as they sailed along banks often populated by Confederate cavalry and horsedrawn artillery.

But the colonel was anxious to get the raid under way, so on Saturday April 11, with half the needed mounts, minus one regimental commander, and without his hoped-for gunboats, he loaded up and set sail.

The missing regimental commander, Colonel Gilbert Hathaway, commanding the 73d Indiana Infantry, had been back in Indiana recruiting and trying to pick up any stragglers he could find; on his return he was embarrassed to learn that his regiment was underway on a new and "secret" mission.

There were other command problems as well. Streight's own regiment, the 51st, was short two key officers, having vacancies for lieutenant colonel and major. Since Indiana's Governor Morton was the only one who could approve promotions of officers in Indiana regiments, Streight repeatedly telegraphed his requests to the governor. Just before he left Nashville he wired, "It is highly important that my field officers be at once announced. I am commanding a brigade and under marching orders for tomorrow and there is a dispute as to who is the ranking officer of the regiment."[47] Two weeks later, in a message to Governor Morton, Colonel Hathaway of the 73d Indiana wrote:

> There is a vacancy of Lieut. Colonel in my regiment and my desire is that Major Walker be promoted to that place and that Lieutenant Edward Bacon be made Major. There is a petition on file before the Gov. to appoint A B Wade, the present adjutant—major and in accordance with the petition I recommend him to his excellency—On reflection I am satisfied that while Lieutenant Wade is an excellent adjutant Lieutenant Ed Bacon, the present quartermaster, will make the best major."[48]

The choice was academic, since Lieutenant Bacon became ill before the raid began and was finally discharged in September. Wade was appointed major on April 25, while the brigade was on the move.[49]

In the 80th Illinois, their newly promoted colonel commanding the regiment, Andrew F. Rodgers, had replaced the regiment's organizer, Colonel Thomas G. Allen, during the raid. The roster shows that he was appointed colonel on April 21, as the regiment marched with Dodge.[50] The 3d Ohio had previously been commanded by Colonel John Beatty, but he was promoted to brigadier late in December, and the regiment was now commanded by Lieutenant Colonel Robert Lawson.

So the four regiments, without a complete complement of officers but with their newly acquired mounts, were off on their adventure. After the regiments had placed all their personal belongings in a Nashville warehouse, they marched to the docks. As the men boarded the transports, they had their first indication of what lay in store for their new relationship with the animals. Trooper Briedenthal of the 3d Ohio wrote, "We [3d Ohio] were placed on board of the steamers *Nashville*, *Hazel Bell* and *Aurora*. We found the lower deck crowded with mules—the odor of which was not agreeable to our 'oil-factories' as old Mother Partington would say; but as we were much fatigued we made our beds side-by-side with our long eared friends and soon we were in the realm of Morpheus . . ."[51]

An officer from the 51st Indiana, Alva C. Roach, was more poetic:

> . . . and on the morning of the 11th, from the decks of the transports as they sped irresistibly along before the mighty force of the

river's current and power of the steam engine, we took a farewell view of the Capital of "Old Tennessee," and soon the church spires and cupolas, reflecting the beams of the morning sun, were lost to the eye, and the rugged banks of the Cumberland, and the spiral columns of white steam ascending from the exhaust pipes of the numerous boats composing our fleet, and forming behind us, over vale and hill, a milky track of the circuitous course of the Cumberland, were the only objects to divert the mind or attract the attention, until we arrived at the place which, in the palmy days of peace, was pointed out to the traveler on the now classic waters of the Cumberland, as the village of Palmyra, but now only a heap of black and charred ruins; representing one of the many scenes of devastation that will tell in years to come, that our country was once convulsed with one of the most unnatural and gigantic wars of any age—a war inaugurated by a people whose sole aim and object was to rear an autocratic government on the ruins of constitutional liberty and human freedom. [52]

McCash gave a portrayal of the raid's beginning: "The fleet, with great stacks belching clouds of black smoke, paddle wheels churning, wallowed down the Cumberland leaving long trails of swirling white bubbles in its wake."[53] After a brief stop in Clarksville in the morning, they managed to land in Palmyra in a cold, driving rain that drenched the men and equipment, as well as the mules. Other memories of the troopers on the boats included sights of wrecked steamers, destroyed by Confederate forces, but there also was considerable comment on the devastation in Palmyra.[54] Palmyra was in ruins after a navy bombardment that shelled the town for hours only a week before on April 5. Had it not been for the pouring rain, the city might still have been smoldering.

They set up camp for the night after they left the boat and sent out shivering pickets supplied by the 73d Indiana. The next morning there was activity enough for everyone. Sergeant Briedenthal summarized the unloading: "The scene of getting the mules off the boat was ineffably ludicrous, beggaring all description and will have to be imagined."[55] Slippery boats, inexperienced mule-handlers, loudly protesting animals, sodden troopers, all presented a drama of the absurd.

Not all of Streight's men were involved in that fracas; some remained on the eight boats for the 150-mile trip downriver to Smithland, Tennessee, the junction point of the Cumberland and Ohio Rivers, then to the Tennessee River and up the river to Fort Henry. The boats were under the command of Lieutenant Colonel Lawson of the 3d Ohio, and carried all the brigade equipment, with three companies of the 3d Ohio and three of the 51st as guards. The boats were critical to the mission, bearing all the ammunition and equipment on board and sailing into hostile waters, so the guards were considered necessary. At Smithland they were to pick up 125,000 rations and forage for General Dodge's troops, then continue up the Tennessee River and rejoin the brigade at Fort Henry. The boats left Palmyra on the twelfth and in the evening passed by Fort Donelson, scene of Grant's victory in February 1862. "We fired a volley as we passed in honor of the braves who slumber sweetly in the graves of patriots . . ."[56]

The primary reason for the disembarkation at Palmyra was to procure more animals on the march to Fort Henry and offer a short training period for the infantry to become cavalry, if that was possible. The majority of the brigade taking the land route was to concentrate on mules: confiscating, breaking, training, catching, riding and feeding the braying, bucking, un-cooperative beasts. Some of the men stayed in Palmyra to work with the animals they had brought; others were sent out in the countryside to round up any mules, or horses if possible, which had eluded other roving bands from both North and South. The mules furnished to the brigade in Nash-ville turned out to be less than had been hoped for. One regimental histo-rian, Theodore Scribner, complained the mules were "nine hundred broken down mules, which had previously been condemned and pronounced un-fit for service."[57] Colonel Streight himself reported later:

> I then for the first time discovered that the mules were nothing but poor, wild, and unbroken colts, many of them but two years old, and that a large number of them had the horse distemper, some 40 or 50 of the lot were too near dead to travel, and had to be left at the land-ing; 10 or 12 died before we started and such of them as could be rode at all were so wild and unmanageable that it took us all that day and a part of the next to catch and break them before we could move out across the country . . .[58]

It was enough of a problem getting the poor, frightened, skittish jack-asses off the boats in the miserable rain the night of April 11, but daylight brought new misery to the dismounted troopers. The sight of these infan-try soldiers being paired with their noisy mounts gave considerable amuse-ment to the infantrymen who either had some riding experience or were not involved in the training program. A. C. Roach wrote of the experience:

> We remained at Palmyra one day and a half, during which every member of the command was actively employed—those to whom the animals were issued that were furnished us at Nashville, "breaking their mules," the remainder scouring the country through in every direction, in quest of animals to put through the same interesting ceremony, during the performance of which the long-eared and stub-

The Movements of Abel Streight, April 7 - 17, 1863

born quadruped before mentioned would tax his ingenuity and muscular power to the utmost, to divest himself of his unwelcome rider. And as our boys were "foot soldiers," they were at first very easily dismounted, frequently in a most undignified and unceremonious manner.[59]

A regimental history of the 73d Indiana reported, "The animals on hand were mostly unbroken and had to be tamed down before they could be of any service on the march. There was much fun and danger experienced in this taming, as most of the mules when mounted would buck, jump stiff-legged, with head down and heels up, and over the rider would go. Fortunately, no one was seriously hurt."[60] Theodore Scribner remembered, "The animals, though lean and scraggy, so soon as saddled, went off on what the men called a 'sheep gallop'. Running about a hundred yards, some planted their fore feet firmly in the loose soil, and kicking up their hind feet, sent their riders flying into the air as if shot from a bow."[61] The search for and training of these inadequate creatures would consume the brigade for days to come. But the comical sights and sounds of the struggle between man and beast could not compensate for the concern of those in charge as they thought of the miles to be covered on these nasty animals.

Sergeant William P. McClure of Co. H, 51st Indiana, reminisced later:

. . . drew a most obstreperous mule that had an ugly habit of 'tilt-ing up behind,' and by a simultaneous and dextrous movement to the right or left, would land his luckless rider on his head. Nobody there-fore would risk his neck on the beast; so, to utilize him, half a dozen camp kettles were strapped to the saddle, and he was turned loose. He made the grand rounds of the camp at lightning speed; then, thrust-ing his head into a brush-heap, he laid down and brayed in a most mournful way. The kettles were taken off, and two boxes of cartridges (1,000 rounds in each) were substituted. With these he started off on the march all right; but it rained that day, and the mule slipped off the road, and was precipitated to the bottom of a deep gulley, where he died in a short time.[62]

It seemed that not all mules were as sure-footed as the senior officers supposed.

Streight decided that it was time to move his brigade toward Fort Henry to find his boats and press on, so on April 13 he led the struggling troopers out of Palmyra toward the Tennessee River. Here, again, the mules rejected their new role, and a number of the veterans compared the "Mule Brigade" to a circus. According to a diary kept by Staunton Brumfield of the 73d Indiana, ". . . it was better than a circus show to see us galloping over the country nearly all on mules (a whole brigade). Some of the mules would get contrary and wouldn't go and then there would be a fuss & some horses would throw the rider or lay down with him very often in the middle of the creek. Some of the boys would get mad and swear they would rather walk but I had rather ride if it is on a mule . . ."[63]

Another dismounted Irish infantryman from the 51st Indiana, Mike O'Conner, remembered his experience converting to "mounted" infantry: "be jabers, mi mule kicked mi hat af mi head and the very buttons af mi coat, and threw me forty fut above its head, and then, divil that he is, he shot at me with his heels while I was in the air!"[64]

One of the dismounted infantry of the 80th Illinois kept a brief journal of that march: "We were to scour the country for horses to mount our men. [April] 13-marched 13 miles through the country, 14th-Marched 20 miles through the heaviest rain I ever saw fall [and] camped at Bell's Old Iron Works on the Cumberland River. We were just completely give out."[65] That day the 73d covered only fifteen miles, and camped on Yellow Creek, reporting that they had little luck in rounding up any new mounts; "the people had got warning of our movements, and the stock was mostly run off."[66] They departed Yellow Creek early on Tuesday the 14th and headed for Fort Henry. The regimental history of the 73d stated:

> This was the first day's march as Mounted Infantry, though as yet only about one-third of the men were mounted—a discouraging start for a most hazardous enterprise, and had it not been for the enthusiasm of the soldiers, who up to this time had known nothing but success in their military career, would have had a most depressing influence. But the lovely spring weather, the bright flowers and foliage, and above all the novelty and excitement of the duty they were on, made them see the best side of the undertaking and the prospect of failure never entered their minds; but the fortunes of war are of all things the most variable.[67]

The animal count may have been understated, since Streight reported that although one hundred Nashville mules had given out between Palmyra and Fort Henry, the "mount count" had risen to 1,250 by the time they reached the Tennessee River on April 15.[68] The mules that had been "confiscated" in the foraging turned out to be healthy, in marked contrast to those animals issued in Nashville. After the rain, the roads across the narrow peninsula between Palmyra and Fort Henry were muddy, being churned up by the Union task force, and progress was slow, but the men seemed to fare well. Job Barnard of the 73d wrote, "Tuesday night we camped at the Cumberland Iron Works in the vacated houses of the town

[Dover, Tennessee]. We lived on the choicest hams during this march, and what so e'er we wished, we made our own, by right of 'foraging.' The roads were extremely muddy and the march was no very pleasant task."[69]

When they arrived at Fort Henry on the 15th, the brigade expected the boats to be there, ready to take them further south. However, that was not the case. The steam-boats had not arrived yet, but were still on their winding way coming up the Tennessee River, finally reaching the Fort midnight on the 15th, Wednesday. While on the boat trip, Captain David A. McHolland was asked by Streight to try, once again, to contact Governor Morton in regard to the vacancies in the regiments. He wired Morton on the 14th, "Has the field officers for 51st been made if so who are they?"[70] While no telegraphic response was found, service records and rosters indicate Captain James W. Sheets was promoted to lieutenant colonel and Captain David A. McHolland was promoted to major on April 25, 1863.[71]

When the boats finally arrived, they were led by Brigadier General Alfred Ellet and his Marine Brigade, which had five transports, two gunboats and a ram-type boat.[72] Ellet's brigade had infantry and cavalry forces that were to be used to support any naval effort to be mounted against land forces. They had yet to have their first test in battle. Ellet's brigade was to guard the Streight fleet to Eastport, Mississippi. Although an army officer himself, Ellet was at that time in some disfavor with army officers, since he considered himself responsible only to Washington, not to any local commanders. On April 14, General Hurlbut reported to Grant that Dodge was waiting for news of Streight and Ellet's boats: "If Ellet has gone up the Tennessee, as directed, he will be in time to co-operate. If not, he should be cashiered for running by me without reporting."[73] There had been some communications lapses among the various forces—Rosecrans', Streight's, Hurlbut's and Ellet's—partially because of Admiral David Porter's involvement. Porter commanded the inland Mississippi River Squadron and assumed the Marine Brigade was a naval force under his command, a fact which Ellet disputed. In any event, Ellet lay docked in Paducah waiting for Streight, while Streight camped at Fort Henry waiting for Ellet and his ships.[74]

After arriving in Fort Henry about midnight the night of the 15th, the ships rested until early the next morning, when the impressive task of loading the brigade and their new animals commenced. The river pilot announced that water levels would keep the boats at Fort Henry until the next day, in spite of Streight's urgent pleas. But the night of the 16th found the 73d Indiana, under Major Ivan Walker (Hathaway was still missing) on board the *Baldwin* and the *Aurora*, with the rest of the brigade on the transports *Hazel Bell* and *Nashville* as well as four other ships. Colonel Steight established headquarters on the *Hazel Bell*.

On the 17th, about 5:00 AM, on a bright and sunny day, the fleet of about eighteen boats finally headed up-river to their appointments with destiny. To the transports and Ellet's ships had been added two gunboats commanded by Lieutenant Leroy Fitch, and two more of Fitch's ships joined just past the mouth of the Duck River. [75] On the night of the 17th, the boats tied up at Thompson's Landing and deployed some troops, including the 80th Illinois, who were sent out to scour the countryside for bushwhackers. Back on the river the next two days, the trip was interrupted occasionally by snipers. James Brown's journal notes, "We were frequently fired upon from the shore, but no one was hurt that I heard of."[76] On the river, some of the troopers noticed refugees lining the banks, heading north, away from the Confederacy. Sergeant Henry Briedenthal was moved by their plight, and their patriotism; he wrote in his diary:

>   As we made a bend in the river we came in sight of some two hundred Union refugees, consisting of men, women and children with their scanty effects piled upon the bank and awaiting some friendly boat to transport them to the promised land of freedom. As we drew near they assembled together in groups, and as we passed they sent up a shout for our old flag and the Union. Ah, I tell you, it stirred the blood, swelled the heart and moistened every eye and drew a yell from us of hearty response, that echoed along the valley and over the hilltops—an occurrence very seldom with the boys now, as they have long since ceased to manifest enthusiasm for every rag that is waved at them.[77]

These refugees were the victims of a Confederate raid that had burned and destroyed their homes, outbuildings and crops, and had taken livestock and animals. They were Union loyalists, Tennesseans and Alabamians who once again had been visited by the Confederate Home Guard. One of Ellet's men wrote, "They seemed delighted at the appearance of the fleet, and greeted it with waving of handkerchiefs, and with heartiest cheers for the Union. The sight was pathetic, and deeply touched the hearts of all who beheld it."[78] To help out these beleaguered refugees, Ellet landed a portion of his Marine cavalry force, which caused the Rebel cavalry to "precipitately retire." On their way to rendezvous with the fleet, this Marine cavalry burned and pillaged the countryside itself, causing even more devastation. This was a prime example of the treatment, by both sides, accorded those in the disputed areas.[79]

As the troopers moved farther south, in the quiet hours they had on the boats, many began to think about the dangers ahead. One of them, Joel Barnard of the 73d Indiana, expressed his apprehension in a poem:

Up the Tennessee River
Whose banks are all bordered with green
On board of the steamer 'Baldwin'
We glide at a rate serene.
Farther from home and from dear ones,
Farther away we come;
Each round of the ponderous water-wheel
Carries us farther from home.

In my mind there dwelleth a query–
Though the sun gleams bright today.
Will he be out tomorrow.
To gladden us on our way?
Shall those whose glee is the loudest,
Whose cheeks with health-roses bloom,
Again go down the river,
When the tints of Autumn come?

No; in the soil of Alabama,
Me thinks will moulder the clay,
Of many brave souls that are gliding.
With us up the river to day.
Oh yes on board of the 'Baldwin'
Full many who gleefully come,
Will never go down the river,
To join the loved ones at home.

Still farther from home and dear ones,
Farther away we come
Each round of the ponderous water-wheel,
Carries us farther from home.[80]

On the night of the 18th, Saturday, the fleet anchored, or tied up, on a fair and pleasant night, in the little river town of Savannah, Tennessee.

CHAPTER 2

FRIDAY APRIL 10 TO SATURDAY APRIL 18

FORREST AND RODDEY

While the Midwesterners were coping with animal training on their circuitous route toward the South, the Confederates who would be involved in their chase were facing other Union forces. General Braxton Bragg, commander of the Confederate Army of Tennessee (not to be confused with Grant's Union Army of *the* Tennessee), was headquartered in Tullahoma, Tennessee. However, he had kept his cavalry forces under Major General Van Dorn in Spring Hill, closer to the Union Army of the Cumberland, Bragg's principal foe. Spring Hill was just south of the town of Franklin, which was one of the three main points of concentration of the Union army, occupied since January by Union troops.[81]

Probably completely unaware of Streight's move, Brigadier General Nathan Bedford Forrest had returned to Spring Hill, Tennessee, the night of April 10, 1863, after a near disaster. Major General Earl Van Dorn, mistakenly informed that the city had been abandoned by the Federals, had ordered an attack on Franklin on April 10. Based on his information, he had ordered a reconnaissance by Forrest's division and that of Brigadier General William Jackson. They were to approach Franklin from two main roads: Jackson up the direct road, the Cumberland Pike, and Forrest to the east on the Lewisburg Pike, roughly following the Harpeth River. Forrest had been a little too casual in his approach, with his horsemen spread out, rifles unloaded, not expecting any opposition. Jackson, as he neared town, spotted pickets and mounted a charge.

Union infantry on picket in the town stopped Jackson's attack causing heavy Confederate losses, particularly to the 28th Mississippi Cavalry. Forrest, on the other road, was totally surprised by a cavalry charge led by Union Major General David S. Stanley. Forrest's men were scattered up and down the Pike, but directly in front of Stanley was Freeman's Battery, the main artillery force under Forrest. Captain Sam Freeman and some thirty of his men plus his four guns were captured, but quick reaction on Forrest's part brought rescue troops to Freeman's aid. The guns and some of the men were rescued. In the confusion, though, Freeman was shot and killed by a 4th U.S. Cavalry trooper under circumstances that were called murder by the Confederates. In the melee it was hard to know the exact details of his death, but his body lay by his guns as the Federals retreated into what was to become Fort Granger, and the Confederates counted their losses and prepared to go home to Spring Hill.

Forrest was deeply shaken by the loss of this artilleryman who had been with him almost from the beginning of the war and had Forrest's full confidence and friendship. Freeman was a lawyer from Franklin who felt compelled to become part of the fight for Southern independence. As Forrest came up to the body of his captain after the fighting had died down, with tears in his eyes he whispered "Brave man; none braver!"[82] Freeman's funeral was on April 12, Sunday, and was attended by most of the officers and the men. The *Atlanta Southern Confederacy* reported on April 22:

> *His burial took place yesterday at Spring Hill, and was attended by both military and civilians. I noticed General Forrest and Colonel Starnes among others in the assembly. Deep sorrow was visible in every face. Even Gen. Forrest—that bronzed warrior, who has gazed unmoved upon the desolation of so many battlefields, became a child again, weeping tears of unfeigned grief to see his faithful companion-in-arms, his tower of strength in time of need, fallen so low. Captain Freeman was a model soldier, an excellent gentleman and a true Christian.[83]*

Conducting Freeman's funeral was a Forrest private, Rev. A. A. Whitsitt, who was impressed by Forrest's grief. "The next day was Sunday and I officiated at Freeman's funeral," he wrote. "General Forrest stood at the side of the grave, his tall form bent and swayed by his grief. It was a sight to remember always, the sternest soldier of the army bathed in tears and trembling like an aspen leaf in his pain."[84] General Forrest was a tiger in a fight, often barely in control of himself, but at times such as this he displayed a side that seemed to astonish those around him.

Although Streight's purpose had not yet been discovered by the Confederates, he was under observation by some Confederate forces under Colonel Thomas G. Woodward, 2d Kentucky Cavalry. Woodward was responsible for creating as much trouble as he could in the primarily Union territory in western Tennessee and Kentucky. Streight had mentioned in his report that Woodward led a force large enough to keep the Union horsemen from venturing out to find even more animals, and Woodward was keeping a close eye on the scavenging Midwesterners. He reported Streight's presence at Palmyra to Van Dorn; in turn, Van Dorn reported to Bragg's Chief of Staff on April 17:

> A spy on the Cumberland, in the neighborhood of Nashville, reports that all the gunboats on the Cumberland River have been ordered to the Tennessee [River] . . .

By a dispatch sent to you yesterday from Colonel Woodward, you will learn that transports have landed troops in the vicinity of Palmyra, to operate against him. Last night I learned that a force from Nashville had marched out as far as the iron bridge, with a view, I presume, of intercepting Colonel Woodward when he falls back. The colonel is, however, aware of all their movements, and will not be caught. I have ordered him in.[85]

It appeared that Van Dorn believed Streight's goal was to intercept Woodward, and that, at least for the moment, was an aid to Streight, who had Rome, Georgia, as his target instead.

During this same time period, Forrest had a major blow-up with his superior, Van Dorn. In March Van Dorn's cavalry had participated in a clash with Federal cavalry near Brentwood, just below Nashville. Most of the action had been by Forrest's regiments, and his prizes were very impressive: three ambulances, nine six-horse wagons, two two-horse wagons, sixty extra mules and six horses in addition to 896 prisoners.[86] The newspapers gave Forrest most of the credit, even though the raid was commanded technically by Van Dorn. This did not sit well with the commanding general, and the feud festered for some time.

In addition, Forrest had equipped his own men with captured rifles and clothing after the Brentwood affair, and the Division Quartermaster had taken exception to that liberty. According to him, army regulations dictated that captured material of any kind was to become quartermaster property, not property of the captors. Forrest thought that the men who had fought for the equipment had a right to use it, and this added to the friction. Van Dorn was a West Pointer, very conscious of the proper military method of doing things, and sided with his quartermaster. Rumors had come back to Van Dorn that Forrest, or one of his staff, had been planting stories in the press, praising Forrest and neglecting to mention Van Dorn's role in the Brentwood matter.

Finally, Van Dorn confronted him, accusing members of Forrest's staff of writing articles that praised Forrest. According to the only witness, a member of Van Dorn's staff, the rage that sat just under Forrest's surface took over, and Forrest and Van Dorn, both brave and courageous Confederate officers, were on the verge of attacking each other. Forrest wanted to know the source of the information, Van Dorn produced no satisfactory response, and the antagonism built to a climax. But before it could explode, Forrest regained his composure and quietly said, "General Van Dorn and I have enough to do fighting the enemies of our country without fighting each other!"[87] With these words the two cavalrymen parted; they would never see each other again.

The other Southern force that would face Streight's raiders was located in Tuscumbia, Alabama, well south of Forrest in Spring Hill. It was the reduced brigade of Colonel Philip D. Roddey, consisting at that time of his own regiment, the 4th Alabama Cavalry, the 53d Alabama Cavalry and a group of others loosely labeled Julian's Battalion. Altogether they numbered about 1,200. Roddey had begun his military career with a company and had progressed to command both the District of Northern Alabama and a brigade. His original company, raised early in 1861, had included fifteen steamboat captains.[88] (The significance of this fact seems to have been lost, but it seems worthy of note.) This was the only brigade directly in the path of Dodge's much larger Union expedition. Dodge had roughly 5,000 men and was planning to take Tuscumbia, Alabama, as a means of screening the principal Union player, Abel Streight.

As Dodge was beginning his slow move toward Tuscumbia from Corinth, Mississippi, he sent a scouting party toward Tuscumbia to estimate the enemy force that he would face. Leader of the scouts was Captain George E. Spencer, one of Dodge's favorites, a scout who had repeatedly been able to enter and leave Rebel camps and cities, bringing back information on which General Dodge placed great weight. It was Spencer who, in April, rode toward Tuscumbia, carrying a white flag of truce, ostensibly to discuss exchanges of prisoners. Halted in midstream as he neared Southern territory, Spencer told the Confederate captain he was carrying dispatches relating to the exchange of prisoners. The Southerner, who had a friend in Corinth whom he desired released, was elated. Ignoring the rule that those carrying flags of truce were to be detained at the edge of enemy territory, he agreed to take the Federals to Roddey, the man to see about such things. Spencer was at the outskirts of Tuscumbia before a Confederate lieutenant stopped him.

When the commander of the town learned the Northerners were close, he grew furious at Spencer's presence and sent him out of town; Spencer was forced to spend the night seven miles from Tuscumbia. The next morning he heard from Roddey about the proposed exchange and returned to Corinth.[89] Roddey's reply was,

> Captain Spencer, Commanding Flag of Truce
>
> Captain: I am directed by the general commanding district to inform you that all prisoners of war held by him were paroled on the 7th instant and sent to the Federal lines.
>
> P. D. Roddey, Colonel Commanding Cavalry.[90]

While it may have seemed that Spencer's foray gave him some inside analysis of the troops in Tuscumbia, it actually worked against the Union.

Dodge reported Spencer's exaggerated findings to General Hurlbut:

> My assistant adjutant general has just returned from Tuscumbia. Two brigades and one battery have been added to their command since last Sunday a week ago. Under general reconnaissance it appears that they expected a move by way of the Tennessee River by Major-General Rosecrans. They have now there [Tuscumbia] 6,000 men and eleven pieces of artillery. This is certain. I sent full report to General Oglesby, with request for him to send to you.[91]

Spencer's highly detailed report pinpointed the various regiments, most of which were nowhere near Tuscumbia. Confederate sources maintained that only Roddey's brigade was in that area. One of the members of Roddey's command wrote:

> Brigadier General G. M. Dodge at Corinth sent George E. Spencer Assistant Adjutant General over to Tuscumbia in the capacity of spy to get information of the Confederate forces at that point capable of interfering with Streight as he might pass there on his expedition. This was April 17, 1863. Spencer carried back a full report ostensibly obtained by personal examination of the Confederate camp. He said Roddey was at Tuscumbia with a brigade of cavalry among various other troops. Captain Spencer Adjutant General saw much as Falstaff saw.[92]

Spencer would see Roddey many times again.

The civilian population was deeply affected by the military movements, and many times families were evacuated from areas as reports, or even rumors, reached them of the approach of opposing forces. After two years of war, those in border states realized the devastation caused by battles, even if they were not fought close-by. The foraging and bivouacs of large bodies of troops as they approached each other denuded towns and plantations of both food and animals needed for work or for transportation. During the Dodge movement toward Tuscumbia, a young girl from Courtland, Alabama, Ellen Virginia Saunders, kept a diary, recounting recent events:

> April 19—General Roddey was ordered a week ago to Tuscumbia, and on the 17th the Yankees advanced from Corinth to Big Bear Creek. Their force was not known, but variously estimated from 15,000 to 20,000, while General Roddey has only 1,200 men. He has captured a cannon. It is the general opinion that the Federals will immediately enter our valley, since our force is not strong enough to

prevent. Captain Sloss's company was in the fight.

April 26—And I am in Huntsville and a refugee! How strange! My sisters and Lawrie and I came here on the 22nd when the Yankees were within five miles of our home. Father will take mother and Lizzie to a safe place also. We are with our aunt, Mrs. S. W. Harris.

May 2—We see much company, but sister says mother would not approve of my having beaux, so I do not have as nice a time as I might otherwise. I hear the Federal soldiers have reached Courtland and have burnt our house. A mistake. Lawrie has gone to Decatur to meet mother and bring her and the servants to Huntsville.[93]

She reported on May 7 that after the Yankees returned to Corinth, her parents had returned home to an undamaged house.

Roddey's Brigade contained approximately 1,200 men. Although Forrest sent part of his division to reinforce Roddey, those regiments did not arrive until April 24. These few troops of Roddey's, not the 6,000 reported by Spencer, were the only Confederates available to harry Dodge as he began his eastward march.

Library of Congress Collection
Brigadier General Grenville M. Dodge

CHAPTER 3

FRIDAY APRIL 10 TO SATURDAY APRIL 18
UNION MOVEMENTS

DODGE

In Corinth, Mississippi, the weather had finally turned decent. In a letter to the *Jewish Messenger*, J. C. Cohen of the 27th Ohio, who was the war correspondent in Corinth, describes the change he found when he came back from a recent furlough: "April 10, 1863—In my absence, Spring had made its debut. The trees are budding, wild flowers are opening, and the grass has grown green again. The weather is delightful, which, after as much rain as has fallen here, is highly appreciated."[94] General Dodge was happy to see the change in weather.

In Dodge's camp few knew of the coming mission, but rumors had been flying as more dispatches and camp activity showed the involvement of the general and his staff. Private George P. Stratton of the 66th Indiana was not unaware of the rumors and speculation when he wrote home on April 10:

> *There is not much of anything going on here now though there are some prospects of us having to go on a march in a short time. Some think to be gone several weeks. Our Quartermaster has received orders to have all of the mules shod and the wagons all covered. And the word is that we have orders to have three days rations cooked. It is reported that there are ten thousand Rebels building a bridge across the Tenn river near mussle shoals and that is their passing place between Vicksburg and their army in front of Rosecrans and we have got to go out there to destroy that bridge but you know how to take camp rumors it may be so and it may not.*[95]

But General Grenville Dodge had a mission to perform; he was about to begin a rather ponderous move east as part of his role as Streight's protector. It is very possible that he moved as cautiously as he did because of his reliance on Spencer's report. Thinking there were 6,000 troops in front of him made his approach more conservative than if Spencer's report had been accurate.

Prior to Dodge's movement, one of his newly assigned cavalry regiments was enroute toward Corinth from their duty station in Germantown, Tennessee. They started at daybreak on the 14th, supplied with two hundred fresh horses, a present from General Hurlbut, still complaining bitterly about being "horribly crippled for want of horses."[96] This unit was the 7th Kansas Cavalry, the "Jayhawkers," a rough and tumble group from the West.

One of its troopers later prophetically observed, "We think mounted infantry, with a cumbersome pack train, is a poor outfit for a raid. It is our opinion our best cavalry should have been sent."[97]

As the march progressed, the first casualty of the expedition was incurred on April 15. On that day two privates of Company D of the 7th had straggled, riding considerably behind the regiment. As they approached Saulsbury, Tennessee, a Rebel, home on furlough, fired twice, killing Private Oscar G. Porter, and sending Private Perry Allen galloping toward the regiment's rear guard. The Jayhawkers did arrive in Corinth on April 17 with no further losses.[98]

The Dodge movement had already begun. His cavalry brigade under Colonel Florence Cornyn had left Corinth April 15 with two regiments, the 10th Missouri Cavalry and the 15th Illinois Cavalry, to chase some Rebel cavalry toward Glendale, Mississippi. During their pursuit, they were joined by the 9th Illinois Infantry (Mounted); when they arrived at Burnsville they added several companies of the 1st Alabama Cavalry. The Rebels raced back toward Tuscumbia, with most of the Union command in pursuit until dark, when Cornyn went into camp about four miles west of Iuka. Colonel Cornyn reported that the roads were miserable; that delayed his cavalry and let the Rebels escape.[99] There they stayed until the rest of Dodge's expedition arrived on the afternoon of the 16th. The reports that night were that Roddey's troops were on the east side of Great Bear Creek, just inside the Alabama line. Dodge made ready to cross the creek early the next day.

Early the morning of Friday the 17th the cavalry brigade led the way across the creek, preceded by a small artillery barrage, and met no opposition. "In a few minutes Col. Cornyne [sic] at the head of the 10th Mo. Cav. made a dash for the ford and plunged into the stream, telling the 10th Mo. to follow him, the cowardly rascals."[100] The rest of the brigade followed: 1st Alabama Cavalry, 7th Illinois Infantry (now mounted), 9th Illinois Mounted Infantry and the 15th Illinois Cavalry. They were so excited with their success that they continued toward Tuscumbia, leaving the infantry crossing some distance in their rear.

Roddey saw his opportunity; he moved his Confederate troops between the Union cavalry and the infantry, capturing Lieutenant Edward Krebs of the 9th Illinois, two artillery pieces and forty-two men who were guarding the weapons. The 9th Illinois history detailed the loss:

> As soon as all the mounted force was over, and one section of Tamrath's Battery, [1st Missouri Light Artillery] we moved forward on the Tuscumbia Road . . . The weather being intensely hot, the horses in the section of battery with us became too much exhausted to move further. Their ammunition also was about exhausted. The two

guns were consequently left at this place [Buzzard Roost or Cherokee Bluffs] to await the arrival of the main force. Lieutenant Krebs
with Co. D, was left to support the guns in case of attack. . . . This
body of the enemy, 250 strong, came upon the two guns of Tamrath's
Battery that we had left at Cherokee Bluffs, and before the guns could
get to us, they, and all of Co. D, except three men, and the seven men
of Co. I, were captured. We moved rapidly back and succeeded in re-
capturing one of the guns in "Lundy's Lane."[101]

In this skirmish at Buzzards Roost, several Yankees were wounded, including Lieutenant N. B. Klaine and Lieutenant John Hazard of the 10th
Missouri, and several Confederates. One of Roddey's men, whose leg had
been shattered by artillery fire, was left behind as Roddey withdrew, and,
shortly after his capture, died. [102]

When Cornyn discovered the loss of the guns in his rear, he reined in,
reversed his direction and ordered a charge by the 1st Alabama, 10th Missouri and the 9th Illinois, hoping to recover his lost artillery. The Official
Records report two versions of the charge. Dodge's report praised the 1st
Alabama: "The charge of the Alabamians with muskets only, and those not
loaded, is creditable, especially as they are all new recruits and poorly drilled.
In this charge Captain Cameron, the commanding officer of the Alabama
cavalry, a deserving and much lamented officer, was killed."[103] This was the
same Captain Cameron who had complained about the Confederate hospital in Iuka in December 1862. But Cornyn's report was less complimentary:

> . . . I ordered a charge by the First Alabama Cavalry, which, I am
> sorry to say, was not obeyed with the alacrity it should have been. After
> charging to within short-musket range of the enemy, they halted for
> some cause I cannot account for, and the enemy escaped to the woods
> with one of the pieces and limber of the other, it having been previ-
> ously thrown down the railroad excavation. Here Captain Cameron
> was killed, and a private of the 10th Missouri and one of the First
> Alabama . . .[104]

These were some of the first battle fatalities of the expedition; there
would be many more to come. A reason for the Alabamian's halt may be explained by another report. Private P. D. Hall had a slightly different version
of Cameron's death:

> . . . the Rebels advanced near our lines, some with blue coats on, and
> we took them for our fellows and were firing a few random shots as
> they advanced; their leader waved his hat and our Major [Cameron]
> ordered us not to fire, as they were our own men we were firing at. Our

firing ceased and the Rebels advanced to within easy range and poured a galling fire into the ranks of the 1st Ala. killing our Major, Cameron, and we made a hasty retreat for about a half a mile. Then we rallied, charged in turn, and drove them to a final stand.[105]

Nineteen-year-old Private Hall then modestly explained his part in the charge,

> My horse being a hard-mouthed iron gray and my curb-chain be-ing broken, he got the reins from me and when the Johnnies made their stand and checked our dash he ran on too near their lines to be comfortable, which threw me considerably in advance of our column. The Rebels perhaps thought the boy on the iron-gray horse the brav-est in our command, but had they known my feelings at that time they would have thought differently.[106]

Captain James C. Cameron was a recent addition to the 1st Alabama. A native of Ottawa, Illinois, he had been a captain in the 64th Illinois Infantry, stationed in northern Alabama and Mississippi, until he was authorized to raise a regiment of cavalry, the 2d Alabama Cavalry. The captain was seek-ing Union recruits from the loyal citizens of northern Alabama.[107]

As the Union cavalry galloped toward Tuscumbia, the Union infantry troops were preparing to cross the Great Bear Creek, approximately forty yards wide and very deep at Steminine's Ford. The 3d Brigade under Colo-nel Bane led the crossing, with the 50th Illinois Infantry in advance. They found a few Rebels on the opposite bank, and brought up their artillery, ". . . after firing a few shells the enemy take to their heels and our front is cleared," wrote Charles F. Hubert.[108] There was almost a "friendly fire" incident, as the shelling continued even as the cavalry was crossing. Al-though several shells fell among the 9th Illinois, fortunately no one was hurt.[109] Just down the river the 7th Illinois and 57th Illinois were ordered to strip and cross. Private George P. Stratton of the 50th wrote home:

> The stream was very swift and about 7 rods wide, and no bridge across it. Ropes were stretched across it for the men to hold to, and then the men were ordered to strip off and prepare to wade the stream and in a short time the men had all of their things tied up in their gum blankets and on their shoulders marching across the creek. When we got across and got our clothes on we felt a great deal better. Our brigade was the first to cross the creek of the infantry, the cavalry crossed before us.[110]

Streight's raid through Alabama, April 11 - May 3, 1863.

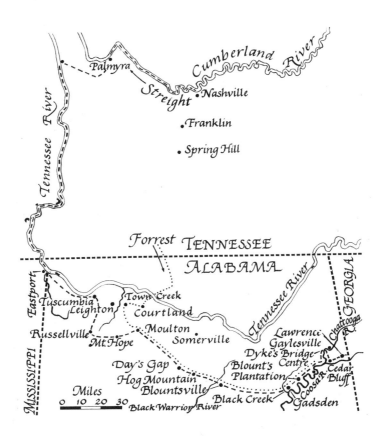

Private John J. McKee, of the 2nd Iowa, noted in his diary:

> *April 17—Started at 6 AM, crossed the Big Bar Creek at noon. We had to strip off our clothes and hold up our cartridge boxes and wade across by rope. The water came up nearly to my armpits. Started at sundown and marched past Dixon and nearly to Cherokee and stopped for the night and tried to sleep till morning. Weather dry. Cavalry fought today. Lost one piece of artillery on our way to Cherokee when we had to wade the big creek.*[111]

A history of the 7th Illinois recounted the eagerness of the regiment: "But the Seventh being impatient and eager to dash upon the enemy, they buckle their cartridge boxes around their necks and plunging into the river they wade across; and without waiting to wring out their clothes, push forward, and are soon engaged in a brisk skirmish . . ."[112]

After the cavalry charge-counter-charge, the infantry had come up and, according to Dodge, was placed in ambush alongside the road to wait for Roddey's Cavalry to come at them. Roddey charged after the Union cavalry, who were the bait for the ambush, intending to bring Roddey to the Yankee infantry. That infantry, Colonel Moses Bane's Third Brigade, according to Dodge's report, ". . . opened a heavy and destructive fire, which caused the Rebels to fall back in confusion, utterly routed."[113]

That brief skirmish involved the 50th and 7th Illinois Infantry with the 57th Illinois in reserve. After their first volley, the Confederates pulled back, and that was the end of the day's fight.

In the beginning, the Confederates had been pushed back thirteen miles toward Tuscumbia, but Dodge still believed Roddey had 4,000 to 6,000 men in front of him, so at the end of the day he was content to retreat those thirteen miles and camp along the east bank of Great Bear Creek, virtually where he had started the day. It would appear that Roddey had only his own regiment on that date; Forrest's 11th Tennessee did not arrive until later. Dodge's report on April 19 stated,

> I crossed Bear Creek Friday morning; commenced fighting and drove the Rebels 13 miles, to Crane [probably Caney] Creek. This morning I advanced again, but did not pursue, as I received no news from Rosecrans, nothing from Marine Brigade, and because infantry force in my front is larger than mine, and the cavalry force 4,000 strong. I have lost about 100 men, and one piece of artillery disabled . . . I desire Fuller's brigade, with one battery and 800 extra rounds of artillery ammunition, to join me.[114]

Again, he was convinced the enemy was in great strength.

It might seem odd that although Dodge had moved fairly easily toward his objective, Tuscumbia, at the end of the day's fighting he reversed his course and moved back to the banks of Great Bear Creek. The key seemed to be his lack of knowledge of Streight's whereabouts. In the early communications between Rosecrans and Hurlbut, the Streight and Dodge expeditions were to start together, and, not having heard from Streight, Dodge may have been concerned about holding his positions close to Tuscumbia. His notation in his report was simply, "This day's work brought us 13 miles in advance of our main force. Colonel Streight not arriving, I fell back with the advance to Great Bear Creek, where the rest of the command was posted, to await his coming."[115] On April 18 Oglesby had sent Hurlbut a message: "Another scout from Booneville brings rumors of 16,000 Rebels, and adds that Forrest, Morgan and Roddey, with part of Van Dorn's force, are also between us and Tuscumbia."[116] The scouting parties "saw" Confederates who weren't there. Forrest, Morgan and Van Dorn were all still in Spring Hill, Tennessee.

The day's engagements had cost the Union forces three killed, ten wounded and seventy-five captured. The 9th Illinois historian reported, "The loss of the enemy was according to their own statement 17 killed, 50 wounded and 23 taken prisoner. The 9th Illinois lost 5 wounded and 59 captured (Co. D)."[117] In various reports, the several actions on April 17 were called Bear Creek, Cherokee Bluffs, Barton's Station and Lundy Creek, depending on the units and the area involved.

It was his scout's misinformation that caused Dodge to hold up on the Bear Creek, waiting for Streight to support him in an effort to take Tuscumbia. He reported on April 19 to Hurlbut: "It will be impossible for Rosecrans' cavalry, in my opinion, to pass Tuscumbia except I take it and hold it, while they are gone, in connection with gunboats." He closed with a plaintive question, "Where is the Marine Brigade?"

The next day, April 18, all of the troops in Dodge's command rested in camps near the Big Bear Creek, waiting for word from Colonel Streight and his "lightning mule brigade," already two days overdue.

CHAPTER 4

SUNDAY APRIL 19 TO WEDNESDAY APRIL 22

DODGE AND RODDEY

It is safe to say that on April 19, after the Great Bear Creek encounter, Confederate Colonel Roddey knew that the Union's General Dodge was on the move; but up north in Columbia, Tennessee, General Forrest probably knew little of the Union activity south of him.

In a report sent from Dodge to General Hurlbut on April 13, Dodge expressed concern that the Confederates had heard about the raid, and it was one reason he believed the exaggerated troop strength in Tuscumbia.[118] That was not the case, though; Streight's early movements seemed to the Southerners to have little connection to a raid toward Georgia. One thing had become reasonably clear to the Rebels: Dodge was moving in considerable strength toward Tuscumbia. At the time, all that stood in his way was Roddey and his 1,200 men. But Roddey's unknown ally was the phantom 6,000 men that Dodge believed Roddey had.

Colonel Roddey had had mixed success during the spring of 1863. For almost two years he had been performing scouting duties in northern Mississippi and Alabama for various Confederate commands. For this work, he was eminently suited, and repeatedly praised and commended. Then, in early 1863, General Joseph Johnston had reassigned him to Van Dorn in Spring Hill, Tennessee. Van Dorn sent him scouting for Lieutenant General Leonidas Polk. In March, Polk chastised Roddey severely for failure to keep him fully informed of Union movements near Chapel Hill, Tennessee.[119] Roddey took this to heart, and for the next two weeks he made reports virtually every six hours, mostly reporting "no activity."

On March 31 General Bragg released Roddey from Van Dorn and sent him, with his regiment, to command the District of Northern Alabama in Tuscumbia. On April 2 General Bragg reported his inspector general had given a highly complimentary review of Roddey and Colonel Josiah Patterson's 5th Alabama Cavalry. So, after the events of April 17, Roddey must have felt pleased with his accomplishments, holding back four brigades of Union infantry and cavalry with his small force.

As night fell on April 17, Roddey camped some one and a half miles from the forward Union units. The expected Yankee move did not come the next day; as a matter of fact, the next move by Dodge with any enthusiasm would not be until April 23. A small group of the Union scouts clashed with Roddey's pickets on the 18th, but withdrew. The next several days would see exchanges of gunfire between the two camps, but no casualties. Roddey was content to keep his scouts out and fire occasional shots at the Union skirmishers and patrols.

Sometime during the days after the Great Bear Creek fight, the 53d Alabama Cavalry joined Roddey to add strength to Roddey's brigade. One of the Confederates wrote in his journal of the part played by the 53d: "We met him near the Mississippi line, we contested every inch of ground. . ."[120] Roddey had a few captives of his own as a result of the battle, mostly men of Co. D, 9th Illinois Infantry, along with the two artillery pieces. Regimental records of the 9th show that almost all of those captured on the April 17 had been paroled, exchanged and returned to the regiment within three weeks.[121] It was the practice in most border areas to release those captured as soon as possible, accepting their oath that they would not fight again until properly exchanged, then releasing them. Prison space was limited by April 1863 and, in most cases, a long distance away.

Meantime, after Great Bear Creek, Dodge sat quietly in his various camps, waiting for some word of the whereabouts of Colonel Streight. On April 19 he wired again to Hurlbut: "Where is the Marine Brigade?"[122] Since he had understood that his move was to begin at the same time as Streight's move toward Georgia, he was uncertain about whether to move forward, into the supposedly well-fortified Tuscumbia, and be required to hold the town until Streight's arrival, or to sit at Great Bear Creek and wait. He chose the latter, believing he would need both Streight and the gunboats to take Tuscumbia. His departure from Corinth had been somewhat hurried, and his men were issued, depending on their unit, anywhere from two to five days rations for the expedition. In almost all cases, those rations were gone by the 19th, and the time in camp gave the soldiers a chance to "forage" for their subsistence, a procedure they knew well.

George P. Stratton of the 66th Indiana wrote,

> . . . we had no bacon with us only two days rashions that we took in our haversacks. General Dodge said he expected the men to forage their meat and there were plenty of hogs and cattle all through the country for they would not kill them as they had no salt to keep them and the hogs were all in fine order for the part of Alabama that we traveled through. It is the finest country I most ever seen in my life.[123]

(A brief item in the history book of the 52nd Illinois shows that Thomas Sweeney, commander of the First Brigade, was promoted to brigadier general on April 20. He was in the field with the brigade, so when he was formally notified is not known. He was an old line regular; he lost his right arm in the Mexican War and was wounded severely at Wilson's Creek in August 1861, but overcame both disabilities to be given his first star.)[124]

On April 18 foraging was the order of the day, and the 7th Illinois took full advantage of the fertile Alabama provisioning. Their regimental historian Daniel Leib Ambrose recounted, "As soon as our arms are stacked, Colonel Dick Rowett rides along the regiment and calls for five brave men from each company, for, he says, I am going to do something that will call for that kind of metal. Following him they dash into the mountains, and in about one hour he returns with about thirty sheep and a quantity of bacon, found hid away on the mountains by the rebel citizens. The Seventh live like kings to-night."[125] Charles Hubert, with a sister regiment, the 50th Illinois, said with a little less enthusiasm, "In the evening Colonel Rowett of the 7th Illinois with five men from each company went on a foraging expedition and soon returned with a lot of sheep as prisoners. The 50th did not go to so much trouble, nor did they pursue so military a way to replenish their larder, but they had mutton and plenty of other substantials, taken from a rebellious and stiff-necked people."[126] And William Cluett of the 57th Illinois said, "The foraging was good and the boys lived high."[127] It was fortunate that the troops were well fed that day, because during the night of the 18th there was heavy wind and a torrential rain, "giving everyone a general wetting."[128]

Two days later, amidst the soggy troops at Great Bear Creek, reinforcements arrived to bolster Dodge's already adequate numbers. The 7th Kansas Cavalry had come from Germantown, Tennessee to Corinth, then traveled to Great Bear Creek. The 7th was selected by Dodge for his foray, but in Germantown they had suffered from lack of horse as had everyone else. In addition, Colonel John W. Fuller had heard the call from Dodge and arrived at Bear Creek with three regiments of the 4th (Ohio) Brigade. Fuller was convinced that masses of Confederates lay in his path.[129] So he requested another regiment, the 43d Ohio Infantry, to join him as he moved to find Dodge. Permission was granted and the 43d caught up with Fuller's 4th Brigade outside Great Bear Creek.[130] This brought the Dodge expedition to about 7,500 men—it was about to be joined by Streight's 1,700. Fuller's departure from Corinth had left that city considerably under strength, so General Oglesby ordered the garrisons from Jackson and Bolivar to Corinth, to shore up its defenses.[131]

Finally word came from Streight, suggesting that he would be in Eastport, Mississippi, on the Alabama-Mississippi border on April 19. On the 18th Colonel Streight messaged his wife from the boat:

Steamer *Hazel Bell* Tennessee Fleet, 40 miles above Pittsburg Landing.—I am in command of a fleet of some 20 boats, including several gunboats, also a large force of infantry, cavalry and artillery . . . I am entering into a most difficult and dangerous service.

My command is curious to know where we are going. The general has trusted to my hands a very important command. I hope I will not disappoint him.[132]

He then wired Dodge from Savannah, Tennessee:

Yours of the 14th is before me. I will move up the river at daylight to-morrow morning. We have 130,000 rations on board for you. Will halt at Hamburg for messenger from you, and if I do not hear from you there, I will proceed to Eastport, where I shall endeavor to open communication with you. Ellet's Marine Brigade and four gunboats are with us.[133]

And so it was that Streight and his Provisional Brigade came to Mississippi on their way to Alabama on a very pleasant Sunday afternoon, April 19, while generals Dodge and Roddey kept their wary vigil in separate Great Bear Creek camps. The mule brigade was already three days late and, judging from the situation with their animals, there would be additional delays. After landing at Eastport, the Indiana colonel set out immediately that afternoon to see Dodge, twelve miles away at Great Bear Creek, and to prepare for the raid. While he was away he missed one of the wildest scenes of the whole foray.

Lieutenant Colonel Lawson was left in command at Eastport to disembark the troops, equipment and the fractious animals. Sergeant Briedenthal described the village of Eastport: "The village which is half a mile back on a bluff, is in terribly dilapidated condition which we rendered more so, if possible, by burning the greater part of it for some depredations the inhabitants had done—shooting at one of our soldiers, I understand."[134] As the restless animals left their "arks" after nine days of water travel, their pent-up delight at getting off was heard for miles. The Confederates heard it, too:

While he [Streight] was absent, in conference with General Dodge until midnight, the great cargo of mules had been put ashore, and with clarion tones these noisy animals were celebrating their deliverance from their natural dread of a watery grave. . . . The braying of mules was not an unusual sound to Roddey's cavalry, who were hovering around the Federal encampment, with the true instincts of the Confederate cavalrymen, seeking what they might devour.[135]

It didn't take long for the Confederates to strike. After the war, the Pruitt brothers, who were in Roddey's command, reminisced gleefully about the Great Mule Stampede.

General Roddey, knowing that the Pruitts had a way with cats, sent Tommy and Clay into the woods to catch as many as they could. They caught two. The Howells did better, bringing in two huge hornets nests in sacks; Clay also had another jug of yellow jackets.

In the dead of night this crew, along with several others, slipped past the guards with their assortment of deadly weapons. Then with rebel yells and the firing of pistols, they let the cats out of their bags and threw their hornets nests. The mules were stampeded into ice cold Tuscumbia Spring, and those that were not drowned or died of insect stings took to the countryside.

John Howell was a little smarter than the others. Instead of delivering his hornets' nest in person, he pulled over a sapling and catapulted it in. Such was the great mule stampede at the Tuscumbia Spring.[136]

Dodge was not impressed with the Provisional Brigade and said so in his later report:

> Sunday afternoon, Colonel Streight commenced landing his force at Eastport, but came poorly prepared for his contemplated movement. He had 2,000 infantry and about 1,000 mules. At least 400 of them were unserviceable, and in unloading them, through the carelessness of one of his officers, 200 strayed away. He was under the impression he would find plenty of stock in the valley to mount the rest and replace those broken down.[137]

While the stampede provoked much laughter from those involved, it was a severe blow to the success of the raid. Between three hundred and four hundred of the best animals had been lost, animals Streight needed desperately to set out toward Georgia. He sent his mounted men off in every direction, trying to find the beasts. In spite of the best efforts of the searchers, fewer than two hundred of the mules were recovered, and two more days were lost in the recovery process. Streight's official report stressed the importance of this loss:

> Daylight next morning revealed to me the fact that nearly four hundred of our best animals were gone. All of that day and part of the next were spent in scouring the country to recover them, but only about two hundred of the lost number were recovered. The remainder fell into the hands of the enemy. The loss of these animals was a heavy blow to my command, for besides detaining us nearly two days at Eastport, and running down our stock in searching the country to

recover them, it caused still further delay at Tuscumbia to supply their places.[138]

Another result of the mules' presence was the announcement to the Confederates that a substantial Union force was now at Eastport, and while the great stampede and chase were taking place, the Confederate senior officers were given a chance to react. Roddey's scouts had reported the landings on April 19, and word was forwarded to General Johnston, then in Tullahoma, that a large force was being added to Dodge's troopers. There is no evidence that the senior Confederates had any prior concern for the Alabama area, except for Dodge's move toward Tuscumbia. However, Streight's many delays gave them additional time to consider strategies to cope with the increasing activity in northern Alabama.

Streight finally accepted the loss of his mules, mounted the men he could, and set out to join Dodge in his Great Bear Creek camps on the afternoon of April 21, in a heavy rain. Sergeant Briedenthal wrote in his journal:

> As there was not a sufficient number of animals to mount the whole command, the greater number of our regiment [Third Ohio] and part of the Eightieth Regiment were compelled to march on foot. So about five PM we took up our line of march, toward General Dodge, through bogs and fields, over hills, etc. the latter being pretty windy. When we had got six or eight miles the guide lost his way, and we were obliged to make the best of our way through rain, water, muck and mud, knee deep, and in inky darkness until past midnight; having come fourteen miles and being much fatigued, we halted in the woods for the night. I made me a shelter by leaning a few rails against the fence and spreading a tent over and my oil cloth under me, lay down, wet as I was and slept, the rain making music on my tent.[139]

The morning report of Co. G, 73d Indiana, stated tersely, "April 21—March to M&C RR [Memphis & Charleston Railroad] very disagreeable weather and tiresome march."[140]

The following morning, the two Union forces met near Buzzard's Roost, some thirty miles west of Tuscumbia. That same day the missing Colonel Hathaway appeared and assumed command of the 73d Indiana. Hathaway also brought about fifteen men and Lieutenant L. P. Williams to add to his roster.[141] It would be a fateful assignment for Colonel Hathaway.

Colonel Hathaway was not a young man, but his fifty years were compensated for by a youthful face and firm, steady eyes, coupled with a mature and quiet confidence. His arrival cheered the men of his regiment, who had an almost worshipful attitude toward their commander. He was a popular and respected officer, and Streight had chosen the 73d in large measure because he trusted Hathaway's calm and reassuring presence. Hathaway looked even younger than Streight, his brigade commander, although he was sixteen years older than Streight.

Now that the two Union forces were united and Streight's command structure was in place, the eagerly anticipated, much-delayed, problem-plagued Streight Raid would begin.

CHAPTER 5

THURSDAY APRIL 23 TO SATURDAY APRIL 26

DODGE FEINTS

With Dodge's and Streight's commands finally together, there were nearly 9,500 Union personnel involved in the movement against Roddey's Confederate cavalry, estimated to be fewer than 2,000. But Confederate reinforcements were not far away.

Early on April 23 Dodge began his movement toward Tuscumbia. He sent the 52d Illinois out in advance as skirmishers, with the rest of the 1st Brigade right behind. They crossed Caney Creek on the Memphis & Charleston Railroad bridge, and fired occasionally at Roddey's men, who harassed them periodically as the Yankees moved gradually toward Tuscumbia. At 1:30 PM they rested for an hour, then moved toward Little Bear Creek, expecting to find resistance from Roddey there. Roddey had pulled back from Little Bear by the time Dodge's advance guard arrived, so Dodge made camp about six miles from Tuscumbia and waited for all his men to come up.

An historian of the 7th Illinois recounted that day:

> This morning the command 'forward' is given to the impatient men, and they march briskly, their steps are firm. Today we witness war's desolating scourge on the plantations. The devouring elements of fire are doing their work. The Alabama Union cavalry and the Kansas Jayhawkers are on the war-path; their day has come—their day of retribution.[142]

While Dodge's people were moving, Streight's regiments fell in behind, trying to be inconspicuous, not taking part in any of the skirmishing.

Briedenthal detailed the march of the 3d Ohio, witnessing the devastation of the countryside and the continuing problem with the mules:

> General Dodge's command passed us early this morning for Tuscumbia. We followed at nine AM, marching twenty miles, through some better country. In places we saw evidences of severe skirmishing, dead horses, defaced and burned houses, etc. We saw corn six inches high, and it looked healthy, but wheat and rye looked very bad, and very, very, scattering. We have pitched our "pup" tents a day's march nearer (not home—heaven bless the hallowed spot and the dear

ones there) Tuscumbia which is nine miles distant . . . The weather to-day has been truly delightful, and the only draw-back experienced by us rear-guards was caused by some of our carrier mules giving out under their packs, thereby detaining us considerably.[143]

Much of the destruction that was described was caused by the cavalry, as the 57th Illinois history acknowledged: "Some plantations have been set on fire by the Kansas Jayhawkers and Alabama Union Cavalry, the smoke could be seen curling above the tree tops for quite a long distance. Go it Jayhawkers."[144] The Alabamians were making up for abuses the loyal mountain people suffered under Confederate Home Guards. The Jayhawkers were just efficient marauders, taking forage and destroying what they couldn't carry.

By the evening of April 23, all the Federal troops of both commands were camped outside Tuscumbia, wondering what resistance they would find as they finally attacked the town. At dawn Dodge ordered his men forward, creeping toward the city expecting fire at any minute. But aside from a few scattered rounds fired by Roddey's rear guard, the move attracted little hostile fire, and the town was considered secure by noon. "This is a beautiful town in northern Alabama, noted for its beautiful springs of water that leap from the rocks like gushing and swelling fountains. How well do the weary soldiers love to kneel down by these flowing streams after their hard day's march, and drink of their refreshing waters," was the happy memory of Private Daniel Ambrose.[145] His regiment, the 7th Illinois, had little time to enjoy the water in Tuscumbia: they were ordered, with the 9th Illinois, to go north, up the road to South Florence to capture that city.

George P. Stratton described the ease in taking Tuscumbia:

> We staid on this hill until Thursday morning of the 23d when we started on the march again and crossed Little Bear creek and marched in shelling distance of Tuscumbia and planted the batteries on a hill. We did not know whether there were any force in town or not. A flag of truce was sent in [on the 24th] to ascertain the condition of things, but they had all left the night before only their pickets and they fled at the sight of our flag when they seen it two miles from town so the citizens in town told us. Our brigade [First] was the first to enter the town.[146]

This was the heavily defended fortress feared so much by Dodge, virtually abandoned by the Confederates; its capture should have been embarrassing to Dodge. But the peaceful town was a welcome sight to the troops, after having witnessed the desolation at Palmyra, Fort Donelson, Pittsburg Landing and Eastport. John J. McKee was also impressed by the beauty of the area:

Started at 9 AM. Crossed the Little Bair on a RR bridge. Stopped within 1/2 mile of Tuscumbia at 11:30 AM. Crossed Spring Creek on RR bridge and marched through the city and camped on the east side of it. General Swaney has command of our brigade and all the cavalry in the division and we have to march in the advance all the time. Tuscumbia is situated in a beautiful country. The land around the city is nearly all under cultivation. There are a great many natural curiosities here. There is a cave about 75 feet underground and a large creek running through it. There are some very large springs, one of them is 10 feet deep and a short distance down where the water comes out is a basin where the water is cold and crystal clear. . . . The trees are in full leaf and the flower gardens in full bloom. Everything looks so lovely. Flowers of all kinds.[147]

There was little action on the 24th, so the men started their normal foraging activity. The short rations provided by General Dodge had insured that his men would need to scrounge what they could, and Tuscumbia appeared to be ripe. "Foraging is good and the boys are happy," one Illinois trooper, William Cluett, expressed it.[148] And Streight's men were as eager to look for food as Dodge's troopers were, and just as adept at it. The 3d Ohio was out on a scout, looking for horses, mules, food or anything else, but not without some discomfort. They had drawn new animals and set forth from Tuscumbia on Friday morning, April 24. Briedenthal's memory of their morning was vivid: "This morning early we received our outfits for our animals—the most noticeable article was the thing we had to ride on, it being nothing but a No. 1 pack saddle, which required a half dozen blankets to preserve the mules' backs and another bundle to guard or protect us in the rear. . . The ride was very severe on us as we were not accustomed to the 'saddle'."[149] The scout resulted in little of value, probably because the Ohioans were more concerned about staying mounted than finding any forage. In addition, Briedenthal reported, "This is a good country, but foraging parties have drained it of almost all of its products. The weather remains delightful. We have collected some forage together for our stock."[150]

Before leaving camp the morning of the 23d, the colonel for the first time told his men the object and the destination of the raid: The 73d Indiana regimental history recorded that Streight . . .

explained the perilous undertaking upon which we had started. That we would have to penetrate hundreds of miles into the enemy's country, would be surrounded by a wily foe: for weeks, if successful, we would have to subsist entirely upon the country for rations that might be hard to obtain.

The information seemed only to quicken the spirits of the men,

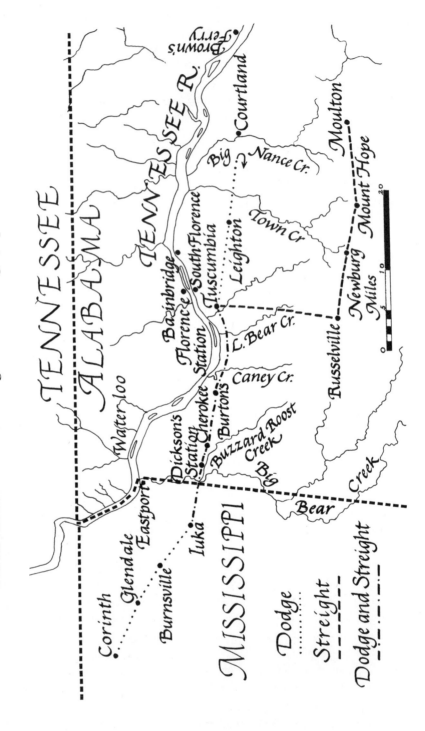

The movements of Grenville Dodge and Abel Streight, April 15 - 29, 1863

nerve them for the hardships of the march and brace them for the fighting which they now saw would have to come."[151]

As the infantry took their places in Tuscumbia, Dodge ordered some infantry and cavalry to go up the road and see what resistance was ahead in Florence. Under command of Lieutenant Colonel Jesse J. Phillips, the 7th Illinois, together with companies A and B of the 9th Illinois and part of the 15th Illinois Cavalry, proceeded north toward Florence. The historian of the 9th Illinois described the taking of Florence:

> Arriving on the bank of the river, opposite the town, and observing a small force of cavalry in Florence, he called to them to send him over a boat, as he desired to send over a flag of truce. They replied, telling him to go to that place, where I suppose but few, if any, desire to go. The Colonel did not feel disposed, at least to obey their orders, and thinking he had that with which he could enforce obedience to his, he placed his two rifled guns in position, and made a second demand for a boat. To this he received the same reply as before. Immediately he opened upon them with his two guns, throwing shell into the town. The cavalry on the other side broke and run. As they passed up the street, a shell was thrown among them, killing one horse. In a very short time white flags were hung out all over the town. In the meantime a small raft had been constructed, on which a flag of truce was sent over, and the Mayor of the town made a formal surrender.[152]

Florence was then in Union hands, but it wouldn't be for long. Since it had been determined that there was little resistance, therefore few troops, in Florence, the Union troops returned to the main body in Tuscumbia, leaving only a small force in South Florence.

Another move made by Dodge was sending Cornyn's cavalry to pursue the Confederates as they retreated from Tuscumbia. Dodge had planned to secure both Tuscumbia and Florence with infantry, but had the hardest work, chasing the Rebels, assigned to Cornyn's cavalry. They had been sent on the southern route on the Frankfort-Tuscumbia road to protect the flank and arrived in Tuscumbia later than the infantry forces. Cornyn's report explained, "Owing to the difficult nature of the road and the greater distance traveled, my command did not reach Tuscumbia until after the infantry and the main body of our force."[153]

The infantry was first to arrive in the city, but most sat quietly after they arrived. Then, part of Cornyn's troops moved through the city and went galloping off to the east in hot pursuit of Roddey's Rebels. Cornyn had about eight hundred men, most of the 7th Kansas and 10th Missouri cavalry regiments; they moved along the railroad tracks, finding Roddey's trail just outside town. "Moving on rapidly in pursuit, following the trail across several plantations until about 4 miles east of Tuscumbia, we struck the enemy himself. He rapidly retired, we pursuing," was part of Cornyn's description in his voluminous report.[154] Roddey retired to the edge of a woods, near Leighton, where he placed an artillery piece which opened fire as soon as the Union troopers came into range. Both sides then began a series of advances, retreats and semi-charges, apparently with little effect. In the next hours, the 7th Kansas, mounted on their horses, were ordered to charge Roddey, but found their move stymied by a deep drainage ditch. Using the ditch for cover, they commenced firing at the Confederates, easily within range. Captain Levi Utt was in charge of the charging Kansans, still in the ditch.

The fight was tersely described by Private Fletcher Pomeroy, 7th Kansas:

> *Friday, 24th—We continued our march. The infantry kept the main road along the valley, the cavalry moved on a parallel road on the right flank near the mountains, and came into the main road near Tuscumbia. There were about 200 rebel cavalry men in town who fell back as we approached. Our cavalry was sent in pursuit. Four miles out we came upon a much larger force. A fight immediately followed, during which we drove the enemy six miles. Our force was about 850, while the enemy were supposed to number 2,500 [more likely 1,200]. General Forrest in command [he was not there]. Our loss is one killed, three wounded; loss of the enemy not known. We are camped to night one mile east of Leaton and ten miles east of Tuscumbia. The enemy is in line one mile in front of us.*[155]

The regimental history of the 7th Kansas recounted this episode:

> John Smith of Highland, an excitable Irishman, boldly mounted to the top of the fence in front where he could have a better chance to hurl epithets at the enemy. In his excitement he let his horse go. Utt ordered the man down and caught his horse, but at this moment a shrapnel shell landed in the earth directly under Utt's feet, where it exploded, blowing him up in the air some distance and tearing off his left leg at the ankle. The hind leg of the horse was torn off also. The poor creature in its agony hobbled up to its master and whinnied for relief.[156]

There were several more movements toward Roddey and exchanges of artillery fire, but little was accomplished; by sunset Roddey's 1,200 men had been driven to a camp some four miles east of Leighton. Both sides went into camp on the field; although Cornyn had been ordered to return to Tuscumbia that night, he chose to stay put.

Casualties for the Union cavalry at Leighton were one killed, and fourteen wounded.[157]

On the night of April 24, the Yankee cavalry lay in camp just east of Leighton; the troops of the Florence expedition set up their tents on the south bank of the Tennessee, and the rest of the brigade rested quietly in Tuscumbia.

CONFEDERATE FORCES—FORREST

Meanwhile, at General Bragg's headquarters in Tennessee, some sense of concern was being felt by the Confederates as reports were received of skirmishes involving Roddey, who was fighting a considerably larger force in northern Mississippi. Between April 11, when Streight left Nashville, and April 23, Forrest kept his men busy operating out of Columbia and Spring Hill in Tennessee, recovering from his Franklin losses and replacing some of his mounts. On April 19 Roddey had reported gunboats landing troops at Eastport; the addition of more Federal troops in that part of Alabama/Mississippi seemed to spark concern. Finally, late in the evening on April 23, Bragg ordered Forrest to take his division south to come to the aid of Roddey's units.

The secrecy that was so important to the Streight raid was still intact, but the delays that Streight had experienced were threatening to cancel the advantage gained through secrecy. There was still, on April 23, no evidence that the Confederate commanders knew of Streight's intention to break away from Dodge, so Forrest was ordered to simply join Roddey and take command.[158] Forrest's first order was to send Colonel James H. Edmonson's 11th Tennessee Cavalry to Bainbridge, Alabama, a few miles east of Florence, Alabama, to cross the Tennessee River and give aid to Roddey. Edmondson left immediately, riding out of Columbia about midnight on the 23d. Earlier that day Corporal E. Thomas Allen, Company G, 11th Tennessee Cavalry, had been killed by an accidental gun shot. This made for a somber beginning.[159]

The rest of the old Forrest brigade followed early the next morning, headed for Decatur, Alabama, by way of Bainbridge on the Tennessee River. The brigade, now formally a division, was made up of some of the Confederate's finest cavalry, Tennessee regiments seasoned in battle many times, and led by veteran commanders: the 4th Tennessee under the temporary command of Lieutenant Colonel W. S. McLemore (Colonel James W. Starnes, the usual commander, was recovering from illness and did not go with Forrest); the 8th Tennessee (sometimes known as the 13th) under Colonel George C. Dibrell; the 9th Tennessee under Colonel Jacob Biffle;

the 10th Tennessee under Lieutenant Colonel De Moss (the usual commander, Colonel Thomas J. Cox, was being held in a Federal prison); and the 11th under Edmondson. Some records indicate that the 10th did not play a significant role in the pursuit, while others maintained it was with the 8th at Florence.[160]

There was an eight-gun battery of artillery, too, under Captain John Morton, who had replaced the fallen Freeman. With Forrest himself was a company of scouts, led by his brother William, and Forrest's Escort, a company of talented and accomplished raiders. At that time the division numbered roughly 1,600.[161]

The march for these regiments began early on Friday April 24, and they covered ninety miles in their first thirty-six hours, getting to Brown's Ferry on the Tennessee River and crossing on the evening of April 26.[162] Before crossing his men in two leaky ferries, the general ordered Colonel Dibrell to take the 8th and 10th regiments, with one section from Morton's artillery under Captain Mullins, along the north bank of the Tennessee River toward Florence, to hold or retake Florence. Then Dibrell was to begin a noisy bombardment of South Florence to make it appear that a large force was getting between Dodge and his home base in Corinth. Forrest boarded the ferry at Brown's Ferry, with the 4th and 9th regiments and the rest of his artillery, to cross the river and join forces with Roddey, who was then near Courtland.[163]

One of the young Confederate horsemen who left Columbia on the April 24 was seventeen-year-old John Preston Watts Brown, who had recently escaped from a Federal prison. On April 23 he and friend Player Martin were celebrating their first day as members of Company G, 9th Tennessee Cavalry:

> *Most of the men were from 14 to 25 years old and fine high strung young men who loved adventure. We joined our company the night before they started on their march for Alabama in pursuit of Strait. My first night in camp was quite an event to me though nothing transpired beyond the ordinary routine of camp life. I made acquaintance rapidly with the company and when we camped the next night at Richland Creek near Reynolds Station, Giles County, Tennessee "I was one of them" and knew them all well.[164]*

Early on Monday April 27, the 9th moved toward Courtland, planning to join Roddey early on the 28th.

Back in the Federal camp there was a certain lack of concern—operations moved at a leisurely pace on April 25 and 26. The cavalry which had camped near Leighton the night of April 24 was ordered to retreat to the main force in Tuscumbia, again giving up ground fought over and won. Dodge's cavalry brigade occupied itself on Sunday by going north to the Tennessee River at Bainbridge to destroy any boats that might have been available for the Southerners to utilize in crossing. Finding no craft of any kind, the 7th Kansas and 10th Missouri turned their tired mounts to the south and went back into camp.

Colonel Streight had followed the Dodge move from Bear Creek, and all the while had his men scouring the countryside for mounts. He was not too successful; many men still had no mounts, and many more had animals unsuited for the task that lay ahead. General Dodge then ordered six hundred animals to be taken from the 9th Illinois (Mounted) Infantry and placed in the hands of the Indiana unmounted infantry.[165] Streight, however, in his August 22, 1864 report put the number at two hundred, not six hundred. "We arrived at Tuscumbia about 5 PM on April 24. Here General Dodge furnished me some 200 mules and 6 wagons to haul ammunition and rations," was Streight's later report.[166] (In an earlier report on April 26, 1863, Streight told Garfield he had received four hundred animals.)[167] The colonel was still agitated at the poor quality of his mounts furnished by Garfield at the raid's beginning and the problems he had encountered since leaving Nashville:

> I am at last supplied with animals sufficient to mount all but 200 of my command. I have met with a great drawback on account of the mules drawn at Nashville being such poor ones . . . General Dodge has let me have nearly 400 animals, and has done everything in his power to aid me, but the people in the country here run off most of their horses and mules. This, with the worthlessness of those brought from Nashville, together with what Colonel Lawson lost in the stampede in my absence, as referred to in my last, has put me to my trumps; nevertheless, I am very hopeful and confident of success.[168]

There also appeared to be ample time to have the Provisional Brigade examined by Dr. William Peck and the regimental surgeons, weeding out those men who had sickened in the more than two weeks of travel since they left Nashville. For two days the brigade sat in Tuscumbia, searching for animals and sending some two hundred troopers marked as unfit for the "arduous duties before us" back to Corinth or Nashville on the boats.[169] After the doctors finished their examinations and eliminated the unfit, there still were some two hundred Streight troopers on foot, and brigade strength was down to an estimated 1,600.[170]

It was obvious that the brigade was in no hurry even then. Possibly an explanation was that the officers and men were all infantry, used to the slow and ponderous movement of the ground troops. They had little concept of the mobility of a veteran Confederate cavalry unit and the speed with which it could move. It was hard to anticipate a Forrest cavalry, led by the Confederate hero in an exhausting, persistent and determined pursuit.

Sergeant Briedenthal's diary entry on the 26th suggested some homesickness:

> We have been foraging for corn, fodder, animals, etc. I gathered some sweet flowers and sent them home. Oh! I would love to see Linna and our sweet little flower, Willie. I trust they are all enjoying good health, and all the blessings possible for them in their present circumstances. If they feel as I do they are very lonely. By this I mean that the heart feels a solitariness at times, when separated from home, akin to sorrow; and although one may be surrounded by busy thousands, yet the aspiration of the yearning soul is for the dear ones-home's treasures. Under the influence of such elevated feeling, how true, and sweet are the lines of Payne:
> No matter where we roam,
> There's no place like home.
> The weather has changed as it is now (9 PM) coming down storming furiously, the rain coming down in a flood. We leave here at midnight.[171]

Colonel Streight, just before his brigade left on its mission, wrote his wife:

> Leave here to-morrow morning at 1 o'clock for parts unknown. My whole command is now mounted excepting about 200 men which I am hoping to mount to-morrow. I am confident of success, but may fail, in which case I may be taken prisoner; but I trust all will come out right. If I succeed it will aid our cause more than everything that has heretofore been done by our entire army.[172]

It seemed obvious that the brigade's progress was not what had been expected, but the Indiana colonel seemed to be unconcerned about his schedule and the lost time. The delay waiting for the boats at Ft. Henry, the two-day delay in Eastport, the two-day delay in Tuscumbia, plus the slow progress of Dodge's move to Tuscumbia, made him at least nine days behind his original schedule as he prepared to leave Dodge and get on with his mission. The large Dodge/Streight force had been shadowed and harassed by Roddey since April 15, so it was obvious the Confederates were aware of the Federal movement, if not of the raid itself. Had it not been for Bragg's failure to send Forrest south on April 19 when he first knew of the Streight troops' arrival, Forrest could have been in position to attack the raiders with equal numbers as they left Dodge. Once he got his orders, Forrest wasted no time getting to Alabama, taking only three days to get to Courtland, outside Tuscumbia, compared to Streight's fourteen-day trek to Tuscumbia. Finally, at 11:00 PM on the night of the 26th, Streight took his 1,600 men, in a driving rain, and headed south to Russellville, Alabama, and then on to Moulton, forty miles away. The raid had begun.

CHAPTER 6

MONDAY APRIL 27 TO WEDNESDAY APRIL 29

THE BATTLE OF TOWN CREEK

Before Streight's Provisional Brigade headed south, leaving Dodge in Tuscumbia, the two Yankee commanders had agreed that Dodge would press the Confederates toward Courtland. If the Southerners were to move toward Moulton, Dodge would send his cavalry to delay them. Before Streight left, it had become obvious to Dodge that General Forrest had arrived, had crossed the Tennessee River and could now be expected to be in Courtland. He shared that unhappy news with Streight, but both seemed to be confident that Dodge would put enough pressure on the combined Roddey/Forrest cavalry that any pursuit of Streight would be delayed enough to let the Provisional Brigade complete its mission. So the morning after Streight's late night departure, Dodge prepared to move toward Town Creek, cross it and do battle.

Dodge spent April 27 moving his division from Tuscumbia east to Town Creek, with some minor skirmishing and artillery fire on the way. The 50th Illinois was in the lead as the division approached Town Creek and came under fire briefly from Forrest's guns. "The first brigade being in advance to-day we made fifteen miles, arriving at Town creek, where resistance came in the shape of a three-gun battery, which opened fire upon our advancing lines. Night coming on the brigade went into camp behind a thickly grown hedge fence. . . ."[173]

The 7th Illinois Infantry veterans remembered that night: "The Rebels falling back across Town Creek we go into camp for the night about one mile from the creek. The soldiers, weary and warm, fall down upon the damp ground and are soon sleeping."[174] But a letter from cavalryman John J. Wunderlich said the day was not quite finished: "It was about 4 o'clock in the evening when thair artillery opened fire on us but we didnt run and all at once fireing was sieced [ceased]. Then we was going to camp along the Creek and just as we had our beds fixed along in the fence corners they opened fire on us again and commenced shelling us out but then you ought to see us skidaddle up the hill where they could not reach us no more . . ."[175]

Fletcher Pomeroy noted in his diary on the 27th:

We moved on from there five miles which brought us to Town Creek. There we met rebel pickets who we drove across the creek emptying two saddles. We were forming in line on the west bank of the creek. The enemy was strongly posted in the edge of the wood a half mile east of the creek. After standing in line about a half hour we were ordered to fall back about 100 yards and feed our horses from a large corn crib which stood nearby. Just as we had gotten our horses to eating the Rebels opened on us with artillery. As the shells came a little closer than was agreeable we respectfully withdrew under cover of a hill. A shower of rain came up at the same time.[176]

On the same day, Forrest was still heading toward Roddey near Courtland, just east of Town Creek. He arrived early the next morning, just in time to beef up the outnumbered brigade of Roddey, which had been so successful in keeping Dodge's progress at a snail's pace. But by nightfall on the 27th, Dodge had moved his entire division over the slick, muddy road into a line of battle. What Dodge faced the next day would be different: the 1,600 veteran cavalry and artillery of General Nathan Bedford Forrest would be in place.

Just before battle, troops tend to become introspective, not knowing what the future might hold for each individual soldier. One 7th Illinois trooper, Private Ambrose, set down his thoughts:

Tuesday, 28th—To day we expect to meet the foe, who threaten to dispute our passage across Town Creek. The morning is beautiful, nature is smiling, and the sun is far up, moving on its path of blue. The soldiers are ordered to rest themselves as much as possible, for the indications are that much will be demanded of them ere the sun sinks to rest. Looking beneath a tall pine our eyes rest upon a soldier leaning against its base, with his musket on his arm. His head is bowed and his eyes are closed. We imagine he is dreaming,—that shadows of light are flitting through his spirit's chamber. He now arises, and we discover it is our poet soldier, Sergeant S. F. Flint. Our eyes follow him as he is now seated with pencil and paper. His genius is now at work, and soon after the artillery commences to send forth its harsh echoes over the hills and through the vales of Alabama, he produces the following:

The Soldier's Wayside Dream

The word was "rest", the dusty road was rocky, worn and
    steep,
And many a sun-browned soldier's face sank on his breast to
    sleep.
Afar the Alabama hills swept round in billowy lines,
The soft green of their bowery slopes was dotted dark with
    pines,
And from their tops a gentle breeze, born in the cloudless sky,
Stole through the valley where a stream was warbling by;
And as it passed it brought a cloud of odor in its plumes,
Of violets and columbines, and milk-white plum tree blooms,
The coolness and the perfume o'er my weary senses crept.
And with my musket on my arm I bowed my head and slept;
No more the Alabama hills, no more the waving pines,
But still the scent of violets and red wild columbines,
I drew my breath in ecstasy, my feet were shod with joy,
I dreamed I trod the prairie sod in my beautiful Illinois,
The lark sung welcome in the grass the well known path
    along,
And the pulsations of my heart seemed echoes of his song.
I thought the sunlight never shone so gloriously before,
But sweeter were the smiles of love that met me at the door,
Oh hold my hand while yet you may, love of my earlier years,
And wet my face, my mother, with thy proud and happy tears,
And bless me again, my father, bless me again, I pray,
I hear the bugle, I hear the drum, I have but one hour to stay.
Alas! my dreaming words were true, I woke and knew it all,
I heard the clamor of the drum, I heard the captain's call,
And over all another voice I oft had heard before—
A sound that stirs the dullest heart—the cannon's muffled
    roar.
No longer "rest" but "forward"; for e'er the day is done
It will tell of the fearful glory of a battle lost and won,
And ere the breath of its blackened lips has time to lift away,
My hand must be red and warm with blood, or white and cold
    as clay.
O! pray for me in thy gentle heart, love of my earlier years,
And mother, only weep for me those proud and happy tears,
And bless again, my father, bless me while yet you may,
My dream words may be doubly true, I may have but an hour
    to stay.[177]

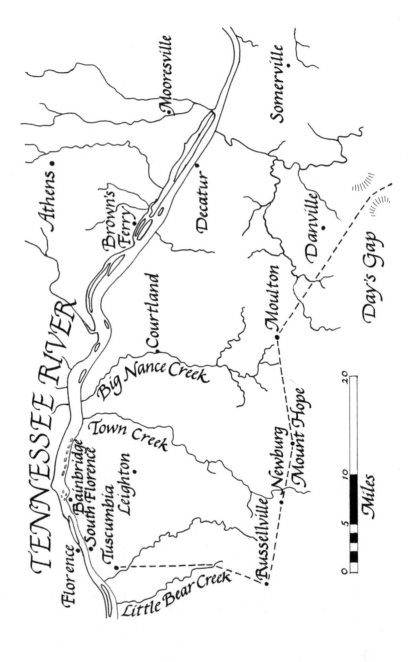

Streight's Route from Tuscumbia to Day's Gap—April 26 - 30, 1863

According to the Confederates, the firing began early on the 28th:

> Happily, much swollen by recent heavy rains, the stream was nearly unfordable. The rising sun was gilding the distant mountain-ridge to the south. All was quiet in the encampment opposite, as the Confederate commander ordered Captain Morton to throw a shell from one of his [captured] steel guns through the Federal headquarters. The aim was skillful; in another instant the inmates of the building in question swarmed forth, and armed men rose from the earth all along the Federal lines—literally like the those of the Grecian fable, born of the dragons' teeth sown by an enemy.[178]

Those opening salvos were also described by a Yankee of the 50th Illinois, Charles F. Hubert:

> On the 28th the ball was opened by the enemy firing a rifled shell at General Dodge and staff who were on a knoll to our front and right. The sight of these officers, evidently reconnoitering, drew numbers of the command to the same spot, out of curiosity. Over the creek to our front could plainly be seen the rebel cavalry, and an officer on a white horse riding up and down its lines. We were told by prisoners already captured that General Forrest was mounted on a white horse, and such proved to be the fact, for during this day this horse was wounded by the 7th Illinois, word to this effect being later received through prisoners.[179]

Thus began an artillery confrontation which kept the infantry, and the cavalry, pinned to the ground as shell after shell crashed into opposite sides of the creek. The Federal forces had the advantage, having eighteen pieces compared to only eight Confederate guns, but the advantage meant little until the infantry and artillery could cross.[180] Hubert remembered one incident:

> As we covered the knoll we saw a puff of smoke and then a shell coming toward us, end over end, finally burying itself in the ground in our midst. At a depth of two feet it was found, and upon examination Captain Richardson of the 1st Missouri artillery, found its fuse set for four thousand yards. Calling up one of his guns, the Lady Richardson, and training her upon the rebel battery, he presented his compliments with a returning shell, which striking a brass gun exploded and turned it completely topsy turvy . . . Everybody was on the alert, and each arm of the service reacted differently. The artillerymen dismounted, the cavalry skedaddled to a safe place in the rear; while the infantry spread themselves flat on the ground.[181]

Another event that was well remembered was the mail that came to these men as they lay under the fire of Confederate cannon. There had been little mail since they left Corinth, so, in spite of the racket of incoming shell-fire, the Federals devoured the news from home. This welcome respite was described by Daniel Ambrose:

> While thus drawn up in line of battle, the mail messenger brings us a mail, and there, unmindful of shot and shell flying around us, we read the little love freighted missives; some almost forget that the dogs of war are barking as they peruse the lines from home circle, for no doubt they may be thinking that perhaps these may be the last lines they will ever receive from mother or sister, for ere 'tis night they may lay themselves down to take the soldier's last sleep.[182]

Hubert remembered that mail, too:

> During the day our hearts are gladdened by the unexpected arrival of the mail from home. What a joyous treat it is to receive the tender and loving messages from the dear ones whose hearts are in constant trouble because of our danger, and whose prayers to God for our preservation comes from souls wrestling in the Gesthemane's of the land, pleading that the bitter cup may be passed by untasted. And yet every letter bears, not only its message of love, but of loyalty, and from its reading strong men rise up with tear-washed eyes, it is true, but with hearts firmly resolved on duty, whether for weal or woe.[183]

Amos Kibbee, a trooper from the 15th Illinois Cavalry, wrote his cousin,

> *I received a letter from you forwarded to me in the field, literally in the field of battle for I sit on my horse within sight of the long line of the enemy who were drawn up in line of battle to dispute the passage of a ford while the artillery upon each side throwing shell and solid shot were making everything howl and tremble . . . More than one of the enemy's shells bursted overhead during its perusal.*[184]

The job of preparing a bridge for the troops to cross was given to Company B, 50th Illinois. "The Fiftieth was ordered into line and Company B detailed to prepare a crossing over the creek which was speedily accomplished by felling trees from bank to bank."[185]

In spite of the preparations, the raging river proved enough of an obstacle to Dodge that the long-prepared-for battle of Town Creek turned out to be primarily an artillery duel, with neither side inflicting much damage. The high cresting of the river was another piece of bad luck for the raiders, preventing Dodge from crossing and holding Forrest's attention, leaving Forrest free to start after Streight. Had Dodge moved across the river with any vigor, Forrest would have been required to stay around to confront him. But that did not occur. One of the 57th Illinois, William W. Cluett, explained:

> For an hour a fierce artillery duel is kept up by the contending forces, with little harm done to our side. The division is drawn up in line of battle with the intention of crossing the creek. The artillery fire now ceases, and the division crosses to the other side and forms a line of battle. The skirmishers move forward followed closely by the division, which moves slowly and in order, presenting a grand and imposing scene; but it all ended in a slight skirmish. The cunning Roddey would not stand, but retreated into the mountains, leaving General Dodge in undisputed possession of the Tuscumbia Valley. The division re-crossed Town Creek and went into camp for the night.[186]

The entry in the morning report of Company E, 81st Ohio, read, "4/27—Marched 15 miles camp near Town Creek. rain all day. 4/28—Enemy opened artillery fire on us from opposite side the stream for 2 hours have heavy cannonading from both sides—our infantry across and drive the enemy until dark—81st Ohio crossed first!"[187]

When Forrest placed his regiments in line, waiting for the Federal advance, he put the 11th Tennessee on the right flank, north of the Memphis & Charleston Railroad. The railroad bridge seemed to be a logical place for the Union infantry to cross the raging creek, so he had Colonel Edmonson's 11th Tennessee placed in the woods to cover the east end of the bridge. His orders to Edmondson were explicit: no firing until the Yanks tried to cross.[188] As the Tennesseeans lay in the woods, part of the Union 1st Brigade filed out of their hedges and occupied a stockade west of the railroad bridge. Although Forrest had ordered the 11th to hold fire unless the Yankees started to cross, they became over-excited and started blazing away. This caught the attention of a number of Federal artillerymen, and they commenced a heavy fire into the woods, causing some casualties among Edmonson's men.[189]

Confederate losses at Town Creek reported by Bragg were only one killed and three wounded.[190] The only record of Dodge's losses was the brief notation by the historian of the 81st Ohio that there were "several wounded" in the clash.[191] A curious footnote to the casualty figure is in the pension record of D. W. Smith, Co. E, 11th Tennessee Cavalry. Private Smith was shot in the left thigh; in his pension application he indicates on the date of the wounding that the company only had one officer, Lieutenant R. J. Anderson, because "other officers were under arrest."[192]

New recruit John Preston Watts Brown was getting his first taste of the fighting. He wrote later, "We overtook the Yankees at Courtlands, Alabama where we had a slight skirmish. The first time I was ever face to face with the enemy. I cannot describe my feelings, though they were not pleasant, . . ."[193]

Although this is considered the major battle of the Dodge expedition, Dodge downplayed it in his report dated May 5th:

> I moved forward Monday [April 27] morning, and drove the enemy across Town Creek that night, and ascertained that they were in force, under Forrest, on the opposite bank. That night I communicated with Colonel Streight, at Mount Hope, and ascertained he was all right.
>
> Tuesday morning, the creek rose 10 feet, and the current was so swift that neither horse nor man could cross. I immediately made disposition to cross at three points, to cover the railroad bridge and throw across foot bridges.
>
> The resistance of the enemy was very strong, and their sharpshooters very annoying. The artillery duel was very fine, part of Welker's, Tannrath's, Richardson's and Robinson's batteries taking part in it. The practice on both sides was excellent. The Parrott guns [Union] drove the enemy away from their pieces, disabling and keeping them away for two hours, but the fact of my being unable to cross infantry prevented our securing them.
>
> About noon I crossed the Eighty-first Ohio and Ninth Illinois Infantry, and soon after crossed the rest of my force, except the artillery, on foot bridges and drove the enemy within 3 miles of Courtland, when they, hearing of the force in Moulton, [Streight] fled to Decatur. I followed up, and then returned to camp at Town Creek that night, being unable to cross any of my artillery . . .
>
> Having accomplished fully the object of the expedition, and drove the enemy, which was 5,500 strong, to Decatur, and having been on half rations for a week, I fell back to Tuscumbia . . .[194]

Whether or not he really had "accomplished fully" his mission was debatable. He had kept the Alabama forces away from General Grant's Army of the Tennessee, complementing Colonel Grierson's Mississippi Raid, but had he done everything possible to protect Streight, from a different army, the Army of the Cumberland? He also touted the Confederate force at 5,500, which was an exaggerated figure; they were probably closer to 2,500. Had Dodge continued to press Forrest back to Courtland, he could have bought some valuable time for Streight, but for some reason Dodge believed Forrest was retreating toward Decatur and that Dodge's usefulness to

Streight was at an end. This was another example of the disastrous results of poor scouting.

While the battle was underway, one of Roddey's scouts, James Mhoon, came in from a scout south of Town Creek, reporting that a large mounted force had broken away from Dodge and was headed eastward toward Mount Hope and Moulton.[195] Forrest at first paid little attention to the report, being much more concerned with the Yankees in his front.

Various historians have different interpretations of what happened next. Some cite Forrest's immediate grasp of Streight's purpose, others were more inclined to allow him time to digest this news and plan accordingly. In either case, Forrest and Roddey did not engage Dodge as he crossed Town Creek, but pulled back to analyze the events. The result was that by nightfall on the 28th, Dodge had pulled back, re-crossed the creek, except for the 7th Illinois and 2nd Iowa, and was camping for the night. This could have triggered the Confederates to consider Streight the main threat, not Dodge, and react accordingly. As Forrest pondered his next move, on the night of the 28th he wired General Johnston in Tullahoma, and Johnston telegraphed Richmond, "General Forrest, at Courtland, near Decatur, reports enemy 10,000 strong in his front, with a heavy column threatening his left and pressing him back."[196] At that point, in Courtland, Forrest had not made his final analysis.

CHAPTER 7

WEDNESDAY APRIL 29 TO SATURDAY MAY 2

DODGE RETREATS

Dodge had made his decision: he was heading back to Corinth. He considered that he had acquitted himself well and had fulfilled his mission. He needed additional ammunition and rations and wanted to check with his gunboats.[197] His reasoning was partially justified the next day as he arrived back in Tuscumbia. He was told that word had come from the small force he had left in South Florence that a large force under General Earl Van Dorn had arrived from Spring Hill and had begun a heavy bombardment at 4:00 PM, shelling from the north side of the Tennessee River. The Dodge gunboats and transports had already left by the time he got to Tuscumbia on the 29th, and there was a fever of activity as the Federals learned of Van Dorn's reported arrival.

The truth was that General Van Dorn was nowhere near the Tennessee River, but was still in Spring Hill, Tennessee, observing the Yankees in and around Murfreesboro. Colonel Dibrell and the 8th and 10th Tennessee regiments were still in and around Florence, and, in a shrewd move, passed the word to Confederate sympathizers in Florence that Van Dorn had arrived and was preparing to cross the Tennessee River to cut Dodge's supply line. This probably was easy for Dibrell to do, since he was well known in the Florence area, having been assigned there all through the month of March, and had returned to Spring Hill, Tennessee, only recently, on April 10. The Rebel citizens of Florence were reluctant to see him go, and passed a city resolution thanking him for his fine service in the Florence area.[198]

Resolved: That for their marked propriety of conduct, their uniform good order, and gentlemanly bearing while stationed in our town, the members of said regiment [8th Tennessee Cavalry] are fairly entitled to, and we tender them, the special and grateful thanks of this community; and we beg to assure both the officers and men of the regiment that we shall see them leave our town with sincerest regret, and that whatever the fortunes of war may carry them hereafter they will always be kindly remembered by this community, and our best wishes for their health, safety and success will always accompany them.[199]

Some of the more ardent Southerners, who had heard Dibrell's information about Van Dorn, forded the river and managed to convince a number of the citizens on the south side of the river that Van Dorn was coming. The word spread like wildfire. At the same time, Dibrell opened up with his artillery, firing at the Yankees still in South Florence on the southern shore, and that was the all the confirmation they needed. Dodge's report on May 5th said:

On arriving there, I received information that the gunboats had gone down the river, taking the transports with them, a part of Van Dorn's force having made their appearance on the north side of the Tennessee River, and shelled South Florence that day at 4 PM. They also planted a battery at Savannah and Duck River; but my precaution in destroying all means of crossing the river on my advance, preventing him getting in my rear, and the gunboats, to save the transports, left the day before, having a short engagement at Savannah and Duck River. Van Dorn's force then moved toward Decatur. That was the last we heard of them.[200]

The reason they heard no more from Van Dorn was that he was never there. This was not the last time that a ruse would baffle Streight's excursion.

In a report from General Hurlbut to General Rosecrans on May 1, the myth was continued: "On the 28th Van Dorn appeared at Florence in heavy force, with fifteen pieces of artillery . . . Van Dorn is at Brush Creek, near Eastport. Roddey fell back to Decatur, and is not following Dodge."[201] Indeed, Roddey was not following Dodge, but he was about to take up the chase after Streight, the very action Dodge was supposed to prevent.

The 8th Tennessee regimental history tells the story:

General Forrest ordered Colonel Dibrell with the 8th Tennessee, and Major Forrest [Jeffrey, the General's brother] with the Tenth Tennessee cavalry and one section of Captain Huggins Battery, to move immediately and rapidly down the Tennessee on the north side to Florence, and to make such demonstration to cross and move on Corinth, the base of Gen. Dodge's supplies, as would induce him, with his large infantry force, to return to Corinth, and give Gen. Forrest, with the rest of his force, a chance to enter the chase after Streight and his command. The two regiments moved rapidly to Florence, arriving there about three o'clock PM. Upon entering the town the writer was met by a former merchant of Tuscumbia (Mr. Warren) who had just crossed over from that town in a skiff, without the knowledge of the small garrison left at Tuscumbia, who inquired as to our strength and intention. He was informed that this was the advance of Gen. Van Dorn's cavalry, and that our destination was Corinth, in order to destroy Gen. Dodge's supplies in his absence. Mr. Warren was urged to recross the river immediately and bear the intelligence to the officers in command at Tuscumbia. Details from the two regiments were put to work at Bainbridge, Florence and Garner's Ferry, as if to raise the sunken boats at each of these crossings. Huggin's artillery was brought upon the hill, and kept up a cannonade across the river into South Florence, occasionally throwing a shell where there was no danger, and then firing blank charges. The citizens of the place were greatly alarmed. They hung out table-clothes, white sheets, etc., and yelled across to us that there were no Federals there; but we continued the firing until night, and kept the details at the ferries, making as much noise as possible. Early next morning we were notified our demonstration was a perfect success—that the advance of Gen. Dodge's army was rapidly passing Tuscumbia and pressing on hard to beat us to Corinth, while we were resting and watching the destruction by fire of many buildings by Dodge's army. We saw the flames plainly that were destroying La Grange College, and many other buildings in their line of march.[202]

Whether Dodge received word about Van Dorn in time to have it affect his decision to return instead of pushing toward Courtland, as he had promised Streight, is not known. In all likelihood his decision to go home was made simply because he considered he had done enough. As early as April 27 General Sweeney issued his orders for the coming day:

Brigade commanders are hereby notified, in obedience to instructions from the general commanding, that at daylight to-morrow morning a movement will be made on the enemy in front, if he is found to be in force; the passage of the creek will be in force, otherwise the movement will result in throwing a strong cavalry force over to destroy corn-cribs, bridges, &c. as far as possible, after which the troops will take up the line of march in return.

As part of his tactic, he practiced a little deception of his own.

All inquiries of the inhabitants will be answered with the idea the column is falling back on Tuscumbia for re-enforcements, and great pains taken to impress them with that idea, the object being to mislead them as to our intentions.[203]

Thus it would appear that by the 27th Dodge had already decided to go back.

The division's march back to Corinth was marked by the devastation of the countryside. Northern strategy toward property destruction in the South was changing. Previously, the North had been fairly circumspect in its treatment of Southern territory, most often limiting their damage to search for forage, fodder and wood. While in some areas the effects of even that practice were severe, the newer concept put forth by Grant was more brutal; it included destruction of all property which could have value to the enemy.

The historian of the 50th Illinois confirmed the devastation:

> April 29th.—We are now placed on half rations, and in the early hours orders are received, and at 5 o'clock AM are in full march for Tuscumbia. It is a disappointment that we could not reach the enemy; a difficult thing for infantry to do with cavalry for an opponent. . . . By 3 o'clock PM we have reached and passed through Tuscumbia, and for the night camp on Little Bear Creek, three miles beyond. There is all around us a picture of "war's wide desolation" which we shall never forget. Between Tuscumbia and Town Creek we pass by thirty-eight houses in ruins. We here learned the object of our expedition. We have been holding Forrest until Colonel Streight can get well on the way to Rome, Georgia, there to destroy a foundry and supply depot.[204]

Confederate historians were appalled at the wanton destruction as Dodge moved west. Jordan and Pryor's *The Campaigns of Lieut. Gen. N. B. Forrest and His Cavalry* was particularly critical of the new policy and its effect on the Tennessee Valley:

> And accordingly General Dodge began a hurried retrograde movement, the impress and memory of which will be hard to efface from the beautiful valley of the Tennessee. From mountain to the river-marge, from Town Creek to Tuscumbia, that night it was lurid with the flames of burning fences, granaries, meat-houses, stables and of mansions that for years had been the scenes of a boundless hospitality and domestic comfort, but of which, the next morning, there remained little, save heaps of smoldering ashes and ruined, blackened walls.[205]

A footnote to that paragraph cited Cornyn as the architect of the destruction: "Prominent in this and other ruthless, inexcusable works of desolation was the notorious ruffian Colonel F. N. Cornyn, who assumed for his band the designation of the 'Avenging Angels.' Among the edifices burned were those of LaGrange College, an old and well-founded seat of learning, with numerous buildings for many students, all of which were reduced to a mass of ruins."

Even some of the Yankees were upset by the ruthless treatment of Rebel property. The correspondent for the *Jewish Messenger*, Private J. C. Cohen of the 27th Ohio Infantry, wrote in his paper on May 6:

> *Attached to the expedition were the 7th Kansas Cavalry and [1st Alabama Cavalry], the latter composed of refugees from the Northern and Eastern part of Alabama. Most of these men had been driven from their homes by the rebel conscription, and their houses and other property had either been destroyed or confiscated, consequently when they found themselves around the scenes of their sufferings and persecution, they began to wreak vengeance on all that came within their reach. Aided by the "Jayhawkers," whose desire for plunder only equaled their deviltry they commenced a series of atrocities, the equal of which this army has never before been disgraced with.—Some of the finest mansions in the state were ruthlessly entered, their inmates abused and maltreated, property destroyed or pillaged, and then the buildings laid in a heap of smoldering ruins.*
>
> *In fact, during the whole march from Town Creek to Iuka, these men destroyed everything they came to, burning houses, fences, outhouses, etc., without any consideration or judgment whatever, never asking whether the owner was a loyal man or not. That question was useless with them. As long as they could satisfy their spirit of destruction they were content. The whole route of General Dodge is marked by desolated plantations and the ruins of buildings so wantonly destroyed by our soldiery. After it was all over, General Dodge ordered that any man thus plundering or burning should be instantly shot. The orders came, however, too late, as many a citizen of the Tuscumbia Valley can bear witness to.*[206]

A 7th Kansas Cavalry trooper, Wesley Moses, said, "[We] burned all the corn and most of the houses. We found the country beyond Tuscumbia about the best and richest I ever saw and left it nothing but a wilderness with nothing scarcely but the chimneys left to show where once had been the habitations of man."[207] In a book about the Kansas Jayhawkers, this observation was made: "Whatever the Seventh may have done in disobedience of orders—and Wesley Moses' letter makes it evident that its derelictions were far greater than General Dodge was aware of—the regiment had earned the general's good opinion for its behavior in the brief campaign."[208]

John J. McKee, a private in Company E, 2nd Iowa, wrote matter-of-factly in his diary: "Our brigade [1st] is in the rear going back as we are always near the enemy. We burned all of the plantation houses between Mauketter Creek and Tuscumbra [Tuscumbia] except one or two, burned

La Grange college. One of the plantations had 30 or 40 houses together with probably $30,000 worth of fine furniture and we burned 3000 carriages and there was none less than 105 houses burned."[209]

In Streight's early orders from General Garfield, his instructions on this point by Rosecrans was clear: "You are particularly commanded to restrain your command from pillage and marauding. You will destroy all depots of supplies of the rebel army, all manufactories of guns, ammunition, equipment and clothing for their use, which you can without delaying you so as to endanger your return."[210] But Dodge's orders had no such limitation. Streight did expand on his instruction in a letter to Garfield: "Every cotton mill, tannery, or other manufacturing establishment, and all quantities of corn, bacon, salt, or other supplies necessary for the use or subsistence of an army within rebel lines is indirectly, if not directly, supporting the enemy."[211] Streight was expanding his definition of possible damage to be inflicted, but he would be kept too busy to attend to such tasks.

The majority of Dodge's infantry troops were probably too exhausted to go out of their way to destroy anything, as they struggled back to Corinth. William Cluett of the 57th Illinois remembered, "April 29th—This morning we take up the march back toward Corinth. Our supplies are running short and we are on half rations. The roads are hilly and the weather is warm . . . This evening we passed through Tuscumbia and went into camp three miles beyond. The men are considerably fatigued and go to rest very soon."[212]

By April 30 the men were in even worse shape, but had a chance to rest, eat and feed at Great Bear Creek, site of their earlier combat. "On the 30th we take an early start and arrive at Bear Creek, eighteen miles, by noon, where we go into camp, the afternoon being spent foraging in the midst of plenty. The rapid march to the front and the return this far has worn us out; we are weary and foot-sore, if not hungry, so everything in the way of a pack animal is brought into service to lighten our load," the 50th Illinois history recounts.[213]

Daniel Ambrose of the 7th Illinois wrote eloquently of the troops' return to Corinth April 30 to May 2:

[April] 29th—The weather is now very warm, and the roads being rocky and rough, the marching is severe, and we are compelled to denominate our regiment "the footsore Seventh." A great many of the men's shoes are about worn out; some are barefooted, and in consequence many are limping; and as the continental army could have been tracked by the blood at Valley Forge, so can this army be tracked by the blood that makes crimson the rocks on the road leading down the Tuscumbia Valley: but on they move and no murmur is heard. . . . War is now making a most terrible sweep down the valley to the right and left: the direful element of fire is doing its devouring work, innocent ones are suffering, suffering because their brothers leaped from the cradle of freedom and struck the mother that gave them birth. Mad, mad men![214]

On May Day the march continued. When the men reached the banks of the Great Bear, the river was too high to cross, and the bridges they had destroyed on their eastward march required some repair or replacement before the weary troops could cover the last miles to Corinth. The 50th Illinois didn't let the creek stop them, according to Trooper Hubert:

> May 1—Five o'clock in the morning and we are marching, our brigade [3d] in advance. The bridge we cut away in our advance has floated down the stream a mile and a half and lodged against the abutment of the railroad bridge, so we march down, and after some work cross safely over, and by eight o'clock are on our way to Iuka, ten miles distant, where we arrive at noon and dine, then away we go and near the setting sun reach Burnsville and camp. The driver of the headquarters wagon, a company B man, is not forgetful of his company comrades, so having during the day captured a sixty pound porker, it is quietly put in possession of that company. There are plenty of hogs running wild and the Blind Half Hundred [50th Illinois] go agunning for some of them, for which our Major is put in arrest. We are ravenously hungry and at first mad that our Major should be arrested, but all is changed when at nine o'clock a train arrives from Corinth, bringing plenty of food and bearing back our sick and disabled comrades, who, with the Major, reach Corinth at daylight. As for us fellows who are well, we roll ourselves up in our blankets, and possessed of full stomachs once more, sleep with "the stars of heaven shining kindly down," only to be aroused at early hour and soon march to Corinth, our home. At five o'clock we march into camp amid the cheers and salutations, happy to be back once more and find those we left behind all right, and well. The Major also being relieved from arrest.[215]

Thus the twenty day, two-hundred-plus-mile Dodge expedition came to a weary end in Corinth on May 2, 1863, about 5:00 PM.

Hurlbut, in Memphis, sent an initial report to Grant on May 5 which gave high praise to Dodge's expedition:

> I inclose herewith a short statement from Major-General Oglesby of the results of Dodge's expedition. You will perceive that it has been thoroughly a success, so far as this command is concerned. There is

more doubt of the expedition from Rosecrans. . . . The movement on Tuscumbia, on the one side, drew attention and gathered their cavalry in that direction; while the movement on Coldwater and Panola drew Chalmers [Confederate Brigadier General James R. Chalmers] and his band in the other. Thus our gallant soldier, Grierson, proceeded with his command unheeded, and has splendidly performed the duty he was sent upon.[216]

Dodge's commander, Major General Oglesby, touted the Dodge accomplishments in a report to Hurlbut on May 3:

> The expedition left Corinth April 14, 4,000 infantry, 1,500 cavalry and mounted infantry, with two light batteries, and was re-enforced on the 21st by Fuller's brigade (about 2,000), the Seventh Cavalry, and one battery. His forces were engaged four times—Bear Creek, Little Bear, Leighton and Town Creek; captured 40 prisoners, 900 head of horses and mules, 60 bales of cotton, and a large amount of provisions; destroyed 1,500,000 bushels of corn and a large amount of bacon, three tan-yards, and five mills; took the towns of Tuscumbia and Florence and destroyed 60 flat-boats on the Tennessee River, breaking up every ferry from Eastport to Courtland. Cattle, sheep and hogs were captured and used by the thousands. Nothing was left in the valley that would in the least aid the enemy.
>
> General Dodge turned over to Colonel Streight 500 animals, 12 mule teams and wagons complete, and all his hard bread. A large number of refugees and negroes joined him on his return. His loss, all told, does not exceed 100; 3 only were killed, some 40 taken prisoners and the residue—most of them—slightly wounded. The enemy's loss was heavy at Bear Creek, Leighton, and Town Creek. They report a loss of 300.[217]

From the standpoint of the Army of the Tennessee, Dodge had been successful in his mission, the protection of Grant's movements. To them his mission to protect Streight had been of secondary importance.

It is not clear where the Confederate loss figures came from; no official reports were ever made for the Dodge engagements. Best estimates from other sources put their losses at about eleven killed, twenty-three wounded, and unknown numbers captured, paroled and released.

Hurlbut sent his report to Rosecrans in Murfreesboro on May 6: "Dodge's movement has been a brilliant success, and Grierson's magnificent."[218]

However, there was unofficial report filed, this one by reporter J. C. Cohen; it was published in the *Jewish Messenger*:

This was the plan. Strategy that would do justice to old Mars himself. Worthy of the fertile brain of Ulysses. Our forces moved forward. Suddenly they find themselves in the presence of the rag-tags of the Confederacy. But General Dodge recollects the terrible warning of his superior, and "moves on" the enemy, as they don't happen to have any "works." A short but decisive skirmish ensues; our forces are forced to retire. In a short time our columns are massed and again move forward. This time the enemy retire, and they do not stop retiring until they have traversed some thirty miles, when at Town Creek, about eighteen miles southeast of Tuscumbia, Ala., they make a stand. General Dodge has no orders to proceed further, as he expected to find his game at Tuscumbia, so he halts. Colonel Streight makes a detour, gains the flank of Rodd[e]y, and content with escaping observation, shoots for the mountains, leaving General Dodge to deal with the wary foe, while he seeks to accomplish the object of his expedition. What the precise nature of that is, and how he will succeed I must leave the Telegraph to inform you, as at present the information is contraband.

Gen. Dodge, finding that Rodd[e]y had out-generaled and dodged him (though by what means has not yet been discovered), determined on returning within his fortifications at Corinth; on the 28th the "about face" was ordered, and on the 2nd inst. the column arrived here.[219]

Another result of Dodge's excursion was noted in a Dodge biography:

To Dodge's surprise, Negroes from all parts of the Tennessee Valley followed him back to Corinth. Forming a column several miles long, these freedmen employed every conceivable method of transportation, from wheelbarrows to expensive carriages. Hundreds walked, their household goods packed on a cow, ox, horse or mule. At night their camp covered a large region, and, Dodge observed, their fires were "surrounded by the most motley and most poorly-dressed crowd I ever saw." Reaching Corinth, Dodge without authorization, armed and equipped two companies of Negroes, who then guarded those freedmen put to work on nearby plantations.[220]

As Dodge's troops rested, recovering from their extended march, there was little rest for Streight and his Provisional Brigade, in the rugged lands of northern Alabama.

EPILOGUE

For those of Dodge's troops who were left behind in Corinth, there were also problems. Sickness took its toll while the division was gone: Private Warren Middlesmart of the 39th Iowa died in the Corinth hospital on April 18; Private Christopher Leatherman, 66th Indiana, died of pneumonia contracted on Dodge's march on April 20; Sergeant John McLewis died on April 23; and Private William Shafer of the 1st Alabama Cavalry died in Nashville of pneumonia. Back in Corinth on the 27th, Private William Galich passed on; and on the 26th, Private G. W. Webster was shot accidentally on the march and brought back to Corinth. On May 6 Quartermaster Gustave Korn, 9th Illinois, died from exposure on the march to Tuscumbia.

For those who were left behind from Streight's original brigade, both in Nashville and in Eastport, danger still lay ahead. One of the 73d Indiana reported being sent back on the steamer La Cross *on April 21: "We went on down the river, stopping some days and running but slowly others, until on the evening of the 28th we reached Fort Henry. The Rebels fired into the marine boats sending some five or six-pound balls through the* Autocrat *and some through the* Diana. *On the* Autocrat, *the flag boat, two men were killed, and others wounded. We remained on board the boat at Fort Henry for a day or two, during which time we buried two men, making six that had passed from the Old La Porte to narrow soldier's graves since we left Eastport."*[221]

Colonel Florence Cornyn was killed in a duel with his second-in-command, Lieutenant Colonel W. D. Bowen, on August 10, 1863, at Corinth, Mississippi. "Killed by pistol in the hands of Lieutenant Colonel W. D. Bowen."[222] *Colonel Bowen was never tried but resigned in October 1863.*

Brigadier General Sweeney had a fistfight with Brigadier General Dodge in Corinth in October 1863. Dodge preferred charges; Sweeney was never convicted, but his career waned.

General Dodge received his second star in June 1864 and his second wound at Atlanta in August of the same year. He resigned the service in 1866, went on to become a Republican Congressman, and died at eighty-five.

Lieutenant Hazard remained hospitalized for months and finally transferred to the Invalid Corps August 29, 1863.

Captain Utt lost his leg, but returned with a wooden leg to lead his company, finally mustering out at the end of the war.

Of the men in Lieutenant Krebs' captured command, all returned to duty, the last one returning in September. Sergeant Amos Smith returned September 17, not as a sergeant but as a private. No explanation was given. Lieutenant Krebs had been captured once before in September 1862. He stayed with his company until he ended his tour of duty in August 1864.[223]

The scout George Spencer was appointed Colonel of the 1st Alabama Cavalry in late 1863 and remained with that unit until the war ended.

CHAPTER 8

THURSDAY APRIL 29 TO FRIDAY APRIL 30

PRELUDE TO BATTLE

As General Dodge moved back across Town Creek on the night of April 28, he left Forrest encamped in Courtland, Alabama, puzzling over the news from Mhoon. The news that a Yankee force had cut loose and was heading south toward Moulton was a surprise to Forrest. As a second scout came in with similar information about the Federal movement, and Dodge showed no signs of pressing Forrest, Forrest became convinced that this unknown force heading south might be the most important prey. As he pondered, he called his officers together and passed out his orders to his waiting cavalry regiments. The 8th and 10th Tennessee were already in place and doing their job in Florence, but since Forrest still was not certain about Dodge's plan, he sent Roddey's 4th Alabama Cavalry plus the 11th Tennessee and one of Roddey's battalions, Julian's battalion, to be a buffer between Dodge and Streight. This would prevent either Yankee column from helping the other. Then he sent a section of artillery under Captain John Morton to fortify Decatur on the south bank of the river east of Courtland. The other regiments, the 4th and 9th, with the rest of the artillery and the Georgia battery, commanded by Captain C. B. Ferrell, were to take up the pursuit, with Forrest himself commanding.

Just to make sure that Dodge didn't come back, Forrest sent the 53d Alabama and Baxter's battalion, with another section of Morton's artillery to guard Town Creek. He also sent word to Colonel Dibrell at Florence to increase his activity, which Dibrell was doing already, bombarding Florence and patching up scuttled craft to make it appear that he was planning a crossing.[224] Then, with his usual efficiency, Forrest saw to the preparations for what he assumed would be a long and difficult march. His men had then been on the march or in battle for five days, with little chance to rest or relax.

In Courtland, preparations were underway by evening of the 28th. Forrest was everywhere, supervising the double-teaming of his artillery, seeing that three days' rations were issued to all troops and shelled corn was available for the horses, and cautioning all his men to "keep their powder dry" under all circumstances. Horses were examined carefully and reshod if necessary. Even though Confederate cavalry was expert at traveling lightly, all kinds of equipment were examined to make sure that the chase would not break down when the two forces became engaged.[225]

All night long these soldiers who for five days had marched and fought almost continually worked to get ready for the test ahead. The portable forges of the farriers were fired up, and anvils rang as horses were shod. Ammunition was checked and inspected, the best animals were selected for the artillery and guns and caissons were double teamed. Rations were cooked, two days' feed of shelled corn to be carried on the saddle was issued, supplies and gear of every sort were gone over, with Forrest himself planning, directing, overseeing the whole of the preparations. He did not know just who Streight was nor what he was up to but he did know that a formidable column was loose and headed into the South, where there were no Confederate forces, and that it had a long head start.[226]

Finally, late the night of the 28th or early on the 29th, satisfied that everything that could be done had been done, the regiments moved out to their respective positions and began the pursuit. Not long after they left Courtland, heading for Moulton, they met Roddey and Edmondson, moving back to the division.[227] Roddey and Edmondson had verified that Dodge's division was moving back toward Tuscumbia before they left their post, and assured Forrest that he was after the real threat. It was here in Moulton that Forrest learned, probably for the first time, that this was Colonel Streight's brigade, and he guessed that Streight was headed for Georgia.

The bad luck that had dogged Streight since Nashville continued as he splashed out of Tuscumbia, while Dodge was waiting to stall Forrest at Town Creek. In the middle of the night of April 26, Streight's brigade mounted their animals and headed south down the Russellville road in a drenching, dismal rainstorm. With some two-hundred-plus infantry still walking, progress would have been slow even in the best of conditions, and on this Monday night, conditions were abominable. Starting at one AM, according to Briedenthal, the brigade made only five miles by daylight "on account of the poor condition of the roads and the depth of the streams."[228] It was Streight's hope to reach Moulton, about forty miles from Tuscumbia, by nightfall on the 27th, but the driving rains caused the brigade to slip and slide, slowing the pace and making that time of arrival impossible. They covered almost thirty-four miles over mountainous and treacherous roads before making camp in little Mount Hope. Then they spent almost twelve hours waiting for the last of the Union troops to straggle in, soaked, exhausted and famished.

There had been minor Confederate appearances along the road, one reported by Briedenthal: ". . . our advance-guard (Company F, Third Ohio) was ambushed by a company of bushwhackers, but fortunately we received no injury, we all dismounted, and leaving every fourth man to hold the stock we started and deployed out to flank them, but they 'lit out' as soon as they delivered two rounds. We then scouted each side of the road for two miles but did not succeed in capturing any of them."[229]

In Mount Hope, Streight himself had quarters in the home of a "wealthy old rebel" who fortunately had a daughter who was loyal to the Union.[230] William Hartpence of the 51st Indiana witnessed the scene and wrote about it: "[She] professed to sympathize with us and our cause, and did everything in her power for our comfort. In fact her actions went so far to prove her professions of loyalty that Colonel S. ordered the quartermaster to pay her for a beautiful riding pony taken by one of our tired and sore-footed 'boys'"[231]—it being General Rosecrans' orders to pay all loyal citizens for whatever property taken for the benefit of the command. The men, however, spent their night in their pup tents, trying unsuccessfully to keep warm and dry as the rain continued.

There was both good news and bad news for Streight as a courier arrived from Dodge. The good news was that Dodge reported he had pushed the Confederates back almost to Courtland. The bad news was that Dodge was going back to Corinth, having decided that he had fulfilled his mission. Further bad news was the report that it was Forrest who had fought with Roddey at Town Creek and was now in the area. Dodge gave Streight the word that he had "driven the enemy, and that I should push on."[232] There was little Streight could do the night of the 27th except wait for his bedraggled troops to straggle into the Mount Hope camp. Another delay.

While the men waited, Colonel Hathaway sent out a foraging expedition from Mount Hope:

> By order of Colonel Hathaway, Adjutant Wade, with Company G, went on a foraging tour to the plantation of Dr. Napier, who was in the rebel army. Large quantities of well cured meat and an abundance of corn was found and taken, against the indignant protest of three handsome young ladies on the premises. The adjutant, though a tender-hearted bachelor, did not listen to their entreaties, as he knew there were many hungry men in camp waiting for his return to appease their appetites.[233]

As the rain continued to soak the column, at least both the men and their animals had a chance to rest. The men also had found a number of fresh horses and mules as their slow march allowed for a search for beasts of any kind. The 51st Indiana reported one example:

> Captain W. W. Scearce, learning that citizens in that vicinity [Russellville] were running off their stock, and that two heavy trains

were only a few miles distant on the Franklin road, reported the facts to Colonel Streight. "Go for them," said the Colonel in his usual blunt way. Captain Scearce, with his company [Company K], dashed off upon the Franklin road, and reaching Sand mountain, captured one wagon and fifteen horses. Taking five picked men—including Mike O'Conner—the captain proceeded along a by-road, in pursuit of a train reported in that direction, and dispatched the rest of the company, under the orderly sergeant, further along the Russellville road to make other captures. After galloping a few miles, a train was discovered. Captain Scearce, accompanied by Mike O'Conner, rode up and demanded its surrender. The man in charge was armed with a shotgun, and drawing his piece to his shoulder, peremptorily declined the order, whereupon Mike, with lightning speed, cocked his gun, and bringing the muzzle within a few inches of the rebel's breast, shouted, "Deliver it up in a jiffey, or its meself will let sunshine through ye mighty quick." The gun and train were at once surrendered.[234]

With this kind of effort, the brigade created some luck of its own, this time good luck; when the troops moved out of Mount Hope shortly before noon, virtually all the men were mounted, although not all on the finest mounts. The rains continued and the conditions of the roads became even worse, so it was well past dark when the lead elements of the brigade, believing the Rebels held the town, charged into Moulton, one full day behind the schedule set in Tuscumbia.

The charge was led by Captain David D. Smith's Alabama scouts. The unit was then referred to as the 1st Middle Tennessee Cavalry. They were men from this very part of northern Alabama, and they knew both the land and its people. "The jail at Moulton was found to be crowded with natives of Alabama who had been arrested and imprisoned because of their loyalty to their country and who had refused to be driven into the Rebel army. Many of these men were friends and acquaintances of Captain Smith or his men, and a majority of them were natives of the county. On Captain Smith's request they were released from the prison, in which they had been held for months. . . ."[235]

The brigade arrived in the town about dark and camped; one 3d Ohio trooper, John A. Duncan of Company I, recalled later:

Before leaving Nashville we drew pup tents. We had put them up for the first time as it looked like rain. About ten o'clock it began to rain, and it just poured down. We would go together in threes; I and Jim Watson and Mike Vincent were in one tent. When it began to pour down the water run under us and we had to crawl out and hunt a dry place to sleep. We were told that all the troops that were mounted were to report to Headquarters about

11 o'clock PM. I and Jim Watson and Mike Vincent got into an old log corn crib.[236]

So there probably was not much sleeping done the night of the 28th.

The Alabama men of Captain Smith's scouts were at the center of a number of confrontations between townspeople and Streight. One of these involved an old Southerner, a Lawrence County judge, who asked for the return of some of his confiscated property. Sergeant Briedenthal reported:

He then appealed to our sympathies, saying that it was hard, very hard, for him in his old years to be deprived of his all and turned adrift in the world; that he had done nothing to merit this misfortune; that he had always been a law-abiding citizen, was always a Douglas man. "You know" said he appealing to the [1st Alabama] guide to corroborate his statement. "Yes" said the guide, "I believe you were once a Douglas Democrat, but that is no reason or apology now why you should, in your old age, prove recreant to those principles, and lend all your influence and devote all your time and means to the interest of secession and the traitor Jeff Davis" . . . "What could I, an old man, do? I was elected a delegate to the convention that met at Montgomery, with instructions to go with the State; and although I was in favor of remaining in the Union, . . . when the State went out I went with her. Now, would you not have done what I did?" "No" was the emphatic answer. "Yes, but you are a young man and have no wife or family, and home associations to sacrifice, and you could go where you listed [wished]." "You are mistaken" was the quick, cutting retort; "I have a wife and two little children that are as dear to me as yours are to you, and I left them, and now you see me here. It is true you did give notice to the disaffected ones toward your pretended government to leave the State in forty days, yet when they took you at your offer, they were apprehended; and if they refused to enlist in the rebel army, they were thrown into prison, as you have done in the cases of Messrs. _____(here he gave their names, but I have forgotten them) whom you had placed in Moulton jail last spring, and left their families to suffer, and you shall have to answer for it. This is but a small portion of the fearful retribution that will be meted out to you," and the indignant guide strode away.[237]

While the exact wording may be suspect in the sergeant's journal, it illustrates the division of the hill people in that part of Alabama, whose lives were so disrupted by their required choice in the early war years: Union or Secession.

Their pause in Moulton was brief. Streight allowed only enough time for a short rest, a skimpy meal, and feeding of their animals. Then by midnight of the 28th, the brigade was back in the saddle, riding out of Moulton toward Days Gap, a pass through the Sand Mountains, and Blountsville on beyond. As they moved toward Days Gap, the trail started up, reaching an elevation of 1,000 feet at the Sand Mountain Plateau.[238] Near Days Gap, the terrain turned increasingly rocky and steep, as the brigade followed the old Indian trail.

April 29 turned out to be probably the best day of the expedition. By dawn the weather had cleared, the roads began to dry, and there was a new feeling of optimism. Even though their original mules and horses were not good enough to keep up with the needs of the brigade, the continual scouting for new mounts seemed to resupply the animals lost on the march. Streight's adjutant, Lieutenant Roach, wrote later of the experience:

> On the following day [29th] we captured a number of wagons, containing a large quantity of bacon, guns, ammunition, &c. Such of these prizes as were necessary for the complete equipment of our command, were issued to the men and the balance destroyed. We also picked up during the day's march a number of animals, which were indeed very much needed, as those drawn at Nashville were failing very fast from excessive fatigue; also from distemper, before referred to. In fact, from ten o'clock in the morning our line of march was literally strewn with exhausted horses and mules, many of them dead and dying, and it was only by extraordinary labor and exertion that their places were supplied as fast as they gave out.[239]

Streight may have become optimistic about the success of his mission as the brigade moved toward Sand Mountain. His men were finally mounted on reasonably sturdy mounts, the weather was turning favorable, and they were in partially friendly country. In his later report, Streight said, "We were now in the midst of devoted Union people. Many of Captain Smith's men (Alabamians) were recruited near this place, and many were the happy greetings between them and their friends and relations. I could learn nothing of the enemy in the country, with the exception of small squads of scouting parties, who were hunting conscripts."[240] With this happy frame of mind, the column covered thirty-five miles, over mostly ascending roads, and camped about sunset at Days Gap, in the Sand Mountains. Some of the news that came that evening shattered the confidence of the command. Briedenthal's journal related:

> Late this evening some of our scouts brought in ten or twelve wagon-loads of contraband women and children from our front,

whom the Rebels were running off South. . . . As one of our foraging parties was going out, one mile from camp, they came unexpectedly on a squad of ten Rebels, fired into them, scattering and capturing several prisoners, among them a mail-carrier. It appears that the enemy is in pursuit of us. General Dodge, on account of the high waters, it appears was not able to cross the Tuscumbia River [Town Creek] and engage Roddey, in accordance with the programme, which leaves the latter free to follow us, and he is now in hot pursuit of us . . . [241]

Streight may not have realized that Forrest was the pursuer, but he would soon find out. "In the evening, April 29th, we reached the base of Sand Mountain, and went into camp as the command was suffering for want of rest and sleep and the animals were greatly exhausted for want of feed. It was hoped the next day would send us many miles on our road, although we had plenty of evidence that the enemy was rapidly concentrating and closing in on us."[242]

Indiana State Library

Colonel Gilbert Hathaway, 73[d] Indiana Regiment

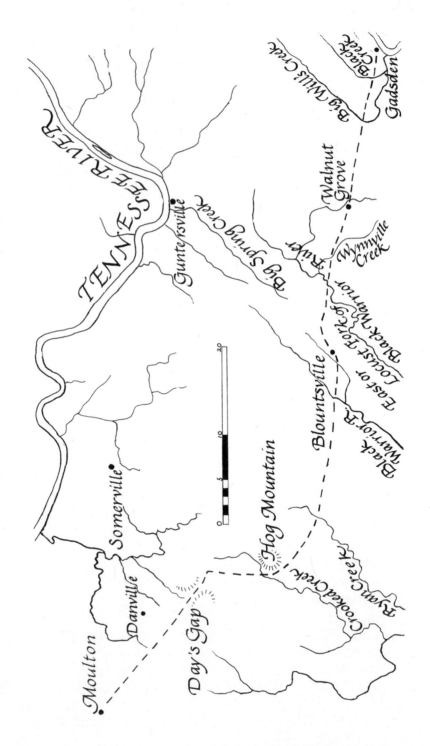

Streight's route east of Moulton, April 29 - May 2, 1863

TENNESSEE RIVER

Guntersville

Big Spring Creek

Somerville

Danville

Moulton

Day's Gap

Hog Mountain

Crooked Creek

Ryan Creek

Blountsville

Black Warrior R.

East or Locust Fork of Black Warrior River

Wynnville Creek

Walnut Grove

Big Wills Creek

Black Creek

Gadsden

0   5   10   20

CHAPTER 9

THURSDAY APRIL 30

BATTLE OF DAYS GAP, ALABAMA

A British general who observed Forrest during the war, Lord Garnet Joseph Wolseley, Commander in Chief of the British Army, later wrote of Forrest and his men:

> They were reckless men, who looked on him as their master, their leader, and over whom he had obtained the most complete control. He possessed that rare tact—unlearnable from books—which enabled him not only effectively to control those fiery, turbulent spirits, but to attach them to him personally "with hooks of steel." In him they recognized not only the daring, able, and successful leader, but also the commanding officer who would not hesitate to punish with severity when he deemed punishment necessary. . . . They possessed as an inheritance all the best and most valuable fighting qualities of the irregulars, accustomed as they were from boyhood to horses and the use of arms, and brought up with all the devil-may-care lawless notions of the frontiersman. But the most volcanic spirit among them felt he must bow before the superior iron will of the determined man who led them. There was something about the dark-gray eye of Forrest which warned his subordinates he was not to be trifled with and would stand no nonsense from either friend or foe. He was essentially a man of action, with a dauntless, fiery soul, and a heart that knew no fear.[243]

Forrest would demonstrate all these traits in the coming days. One of his biographers wrote:

> While the Union troops were sleeping, Forrest's hardy riders were reeling off mile after mile of their heavy task. At Moulton they had stolen another hour of rest, with saddles off to cool the horses' backs while feeding the hungry animals. Just as the bugles sounded to "saddle up" the sunlight broke through a rift in the western sky, and as their chieftain mounted his horse and gave that ever famous command, "Move up, men!" twelve hundred hats were lifted, and the rebel yell that split the air might well have shaken the sparkling pendants of rain from the tender green leaves of that April afternoon. The moment was auspicious. The wild enthusiasm of his men was to him

the harbinger of success. Never was mortal man more in his element than Nathan Bedford Forrest at this hour.[244]

He went on:, "... there began a race and running fight between two bodies of cavalry which, in the brilliant tactics of the retreat and the stubbornness in defense on one side, and the desperate bravery of the attack and relentlessness in pursuit upon the other, has no analogue in military history."[245]

It had been just a week since Forrest had heard from Bragg that he was to move south to protect against the Northern invaders. By the time they bivouacked early in the morning of April 30, Roddey and the 11th Tennessee had joined them, bringing the Confederate force to almost 2,000 men, significantly more than Streight's 1,500. However, in a new move, he sent the 4th and 9th Tennessee regiments off toward the north on roads parallel to Streight's route, in hopes they could get in Streight's front to cut off the Union column.[246] That left about 1,200 Confederate veteran cavalrymen camped in Danville, about to test the saddle-sore Union infantry the next morning.

Forrest was wakened at daylight that Thursday, and Streight was but four miles ahead. April 30 would begin a test of the endurance of men and animal that would cease only when one or the other gave way.

While most of the bone-weary Southerners were getting a brief rest in Danville, Forrest sent scouts to feel out Streight's position and strength. The scout group was led by Captain William Forrest, the general's younger brother, and it was an unusual, company-strength unit. The Forrest Scouts were not Confederate soldiers, but were more like independent contractors. They were not paid, but were given free license to forage and keep what they could find. Nicknamed the Forty Thieves, they were considered experts at the forage trade. They left General Forrest's camp and scouted the edges of Streight's campfires.[247] While the Yankee fires glowed in the distance, the Rebel scouts quietly captured ten Union videttes, mounted scouts patrolling the camp.

But Captain Bill Forrest and his Forty Thieves did not lie down that night. They rode to the outskirts of the camp, captured the vidette, then crawled within sight of the campfires at the foot of the gorge. They reported their findings and, before dawn, lay down to sleep. After a short while the most ungodly noises, echoing and re-echoing, came out of the gorge. They sat up and looked at each other wonderingly. They gave up all idea of sleep and broke into loud guffaws. Hundreds of mules, with continuous and anxious brays, were calling for their breakfast.[248]

Forrest felt that he almost had Streight in a box; with the 4th and the 9th regiments racing to get in front of the Yankees, and Forrest pushing the rear troops, Streight would be trapped in the narrow canyon.

Streight's lightning mule brigade had announced its presence with the mule reveille call. The call came early, as usual, and followed a reasonably good night's rest. The 73d Indiana historian later wrote, ". . . an early start was made and the brigade was on the move. The sun rose through a clear sky and shone out bright and beautiful on a lovely spring day. As we moved out of camp and left the smoldering campfires, the gray mist of the mountain tops sparkled like gems, and the scene was well calculated to inspire and encourage the weary soldiers."[249]

Streight led the brigade as they wound up the old Indian Trail through Days Gap to the crest of Sand Mountain. The brigade was strung out for a mile, with the Alabama scouts bringing up the rear. As the brigade moved, escorted by the jackass chorus, the rear-guard was cooking their breakfast by the fires, apparently in no hurry to move out.

> But Streight was a wily fox, one of the most skillful and stubborn officers in Lincoln's service. He was well under way before daylight, and by sun-up the wagons and head of his brigade had reached the crest of Sand Mountain. It was a mile from the foot to the top, and his men were strung out along the whole distance. The rear guard, under Captain Smith, still loitered over the breakfast kettles, stragglers lazied in the sun.[250]

Captain William Forrest's company of scouts had moved up quietly, almost to the edge of the clearing, and their presence was announced by shells from the guns of Captain Ferrell. Right behind the shells came Forrest's scouts, complete with the Rebel yell. It took only seconds to clear the camp, and it may have been the delightful cooking smells that stopped the charge in its tracks. The Southerners were so hungry, nothing could keep them from those cooking pots and food that was theirs for the taking. Before the officers could get them back in the saddle, they had their fill of the still-steaming Union breakfasts. The surprise element, however, was gone. The shells had hit no one, but Streight, a mile from the action, knew that his heretofore unmolested march was now under some real pressure.

Streight had felt the first burst of optimism on the 29th, but his nagging concern was still the condition of the men and, just as important, the mules they rode. He must have known by then that Garfield's and Rosecrans' decision to use mules was flawed at best. Mules were adequate as pack animals, but long distance riding left both mounted and mounts chafing and miserable. "The mules alone caused him concern. From the beginning they had given him no end of trouble. Morning, noon, and night they kept the entire countryside informed of their presence; and their stubbornness when urged forward, the difficulty in stopping them when in full flight, and their general intractable nature was wearing down the patience of the riders. Nor did the infantry's chaffed and burning crotches tend to ease the dilemma."[251]

In Streight's report he also explained the problem, and its impact on the troopers: "I will here remark that my men had been worked very hard in scouring so much of the country, and unaccustomed as they were to riding, made it still worse; consequently they were illy prepared for the trying ordeal through which they were to pass." He continued, "I had not proceeded more than 2 miles, at the head of the column, before I was informed that the rear-guard had been attacked, and just at that moment I heard the boom of artillery in the rear of the column."[252]

Streight did not record his thoughts at that moment, but the attack must have been a shock, coming with so little warning. However, the Indiana colonel was quick to put a plan into action. At first, he hoped that a battle would not be necessary, since he remembered that his orders clearly stated his mission was to disrupt Bragg's communications, not skirmish with local cavalry. But as he heard the sounds from his rear-guard, he determined to make a stand on the mountain.

The terrain was fairly rugged, with a pass cut through to the mountain top, with several plateaus on the route. The route was flanked by other passes, both higher and lower than the Days Gap, and allowed for easy flank attacks by alert cavalry. Streight reported:

> I soon learned that the enemy had moved through the gaps on my right and left, and were endeavoring to form a junction in my advance; consequently I moved ahead rapidly until we passed the intersecting roads on either flank with the one we occupied. The country was open, sand ridges, very thinly wooded, and afforded fine defensive positions. As soon as we passed the point above designated (about 3 miles from the top of the mountains), we dismounted and formed a line of battle on a ridge circling to our rear. Our right rested on a precipitous ravine and the left was protected by a marshy run that was easily held against the enemy.[253]

Then he took his mules and horses down into the ravine, out of the line of fire, and set his men in position. According to Briedenthal, the line of Union soldiers ran across the gap, behind a slight ridge, with the 73d on the far left, next to the 51st; in the middle were the 3d Ohio, with two mountain howitzers manned by men of Major James C. Vananda's section; and the 80th Illinois was on the far right. Captain Smith, who was still in the rear of the column, would form the rear guard after he arrived. His duty, with his Alabama scouts, was to hold the Confederates for a short time, then allow them to chase him up the slope toward the crest, and lead them to an ambush set up on the ridge, with the troopers dismounted and hid-

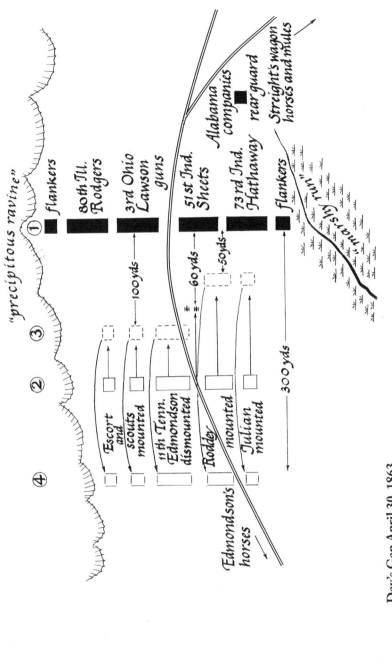

Day's Gap April 30, 1863

1. Streight, with about 1800 dismounted men, lay down, concealed by a ridge.
2. Forrest with less that 1000 men formed for attack.
3. Roddey advanced too fast and broke the line. Streight's men threw Forrest back.
4. Forrest reformed with 200 more men and attacked, but Streight had resumed
   the march.

den from sight. "The lines were left sufficiently open to allow Captain Smith's command to pass through near the center."[254] Roach wrote about the battle:

It was a novel and imposing sight to witness here amid the blue and towering mountains, covered with the verdure of spring, the green sward smiling a welcome to the season of flowers, and the bright sun, unclouded, lending a genial, refreshing warmth, that little band with shining bayonets, equipped for the stern conflict of war. The hour for action has come, and the battle of Day's Gap soon comes.[255]

Before the Union brigade had a chance to get nervous, Smith's Union cavalry came galloping up to the Union line, which opened as planned, then closed to fire the first real volleys of the battle at the approaching Confederates. The unfortunate Confederate who led the charge was Captain Bill Forrest; he was the first casualty, taking a musket ball in the thigh, unhorsing him and throwing him to the ground. His scouts reined abruptly and scampered back toward their main force. General Forrest rode up to assess the situation, and placed his regiments in line to battle Streight. He positioned Roddey and Julian on the right; then he dismounted Edmonson's 11th Tennessee and put them in the center with his scouts and escorts on the left. The movements impressed Roach, who wrote, 'The rebel regiments can be discovered moving into line; the 'stars and bars' can be distinctly seen, but opposite floats proudly and defiantly the old stars and stripes—battle flag of the Union and banner of liberty!"[256]

By that time, General Forrest had fewer than 1,000 men with him, out of the more than 1,200 who had started with him. The rough ride, the exhausted animals and the rugged terrain had caused many to straggle.[257] In addition to the regiments, two of Morton's guns, under Lieutenant Willis Gould, and six of Ferrell's had arrived and commenced shelling the Federals. Their fire was ineffective, with Streight's men concealed and protected by the ridge.[258] As the Confederates fell into line, Forrest immediately ordered a charge. Unhappily for the Southerners, it was delivered piece-meal: Edmonson's men in the center attacked on foot, while the scouts and the escort company were mounted on the left flank, and Roddey and Julian were mounted on the right flank. As soon as they were formed, Forrest gave the order and began a slow sweeping approach in full view of the anxious Yankees. Union cannon were rearmed, muskets reloaded, and bayonets fixed as they waited nervously for the Rebels to come into range.

It became apparent to Streight that the gaps were opening between the mounted units on either flank and the slow-moving center of Edmonson's regiment. In the confusion, Roddey's men mounted an unsupported charge toward the crest, running head-on into murderous fire from the 73d and parts of the 51st. It was on the second Union volley that the Confederates broke, running pell-mell back to their lines, leaving Edmonson's flank open. The smaller scout units on Forrest's left were checked by Yankee skirmishers, and it soon became evident that Edmonson's center was dangerously exposed. Streight saw the situation, and, as the Southerners retreated or wavered, he mounted a charge of his own. In this charge Union Lieutenant Colonel James W. Sheets was mortally wounded, and others fell as well.

According to the history of the 73d Regiment, as the brigade lay behind the ridge waiting for Forrest's attack, the officers debated strategy:

In a short time Colonel Streight rode along the line giving orders and instructions to the regimental commanders. As he approached the Seventy-Third Indiana, Colonel Hathaway saluted and awaited orders.

Colonel Streight said, "Colonel Hathaway, what do you think of charging the enemy when he comes to the top of the hill?" Colonel Hathaway replied, "Colonel, your orders, whatever they are, shall be obeyed." Colonel Streight, not quite satisfied with the reply, said: "But, Colonel Hathaway, I want to know what you think of making such a charge." Colonel Hathaway replied, "I think it would be a good move." "Well, let it be done, then," said Colonel Streight, "and when the charge is made let it be done with a rush and as much noise as you can make."

Colonel Hathaway walked along the line of his regiment and said to his officers, in the plain hearing of the men, "Colonel Streight has ordered a charge to be made when the enemy comes to the top of the hill, and I want you, as soon as I give the order, to rise, take deliberate aim and fire, reload your guns as rapidly as possible, and when the order to charge is given, make a grand rush upon the enemy, firing at the same time, and yell in doing so as never men yelled before."[259]

The Union charge came over the top of the ridge, pushing hard on the retreating Confederates. It was pandemonium; as the two Federal mountain howitzers threw shells at the Rebels, the guns of Forrest's artillery banged away at Streight, but it shortly became a Rebel rout. The 3d Ohio, according to Briedenthal, was the first to make the charge, ". . . at the command every man sprang to his feet and skipped off on a run, gun and hat in one hand, yelling like so many Mohawks, taking their battery of two pieces and one limber, and some horses, without firing a gun, the Rebels taking to their heels and horses and 'lighted out.'"[260] Roach of the 51st said, "The enemy fights well for they are principally General Forrest's trained veterans. A loud and prolonged shout now bursts on the ear. It comes from the Third Ohio and the Eightieth Illinois, who have charged and taken the enemy's battery. The enemy feels the loss of the guns and the line wavers! Cheer after cheer bursts from our brave boys, for the enemy are giving way! . . . But the victory is won by the sacrifice of some of the best and bravest blood in our heroic little brigade."[261]

It was a happy moment for the Provisional Brigade; in its first real test against the legendary Forrest, one of the South's best, they had acquitted themselves well. Most Southern biographers of Forrest gave considerable credit for Streight's skill in the mission; his tactics and control were worthy of a much more experienced commander.

Sometimes the men were a little melodramatic as they later retold the events, so Briedenthal perhaps could be forgiven as he waxed eloquent over the charge:

> . . . let me say here that the movement just ended, lasting one hour, was one of the most brilliant affairs that I have yet witnessed, especially the bayonet-charge upon the enemy, where everyone went in with a vim and those having the strongest legs getting their first and those with the strongest lungs making the most noise.[262]

As the Union attack overran the two Rebel guns, just sixty yards away there was considerable damage done to the traces, and the artillery animals were virtually all killed. "Some of the horses were killed and others hopelessly entangled in chains, harness, and bushes."[263] With this damage, it was easy to take Forrest's two guns.

Confederate Private Thomas D. Duncan acknowledged the extent of the rout:

> Then he [Streight] placed his men in ambush and drew us into a deadly trap. In a rushing movement we were surprised and knocked out of all formation. It was the only time in my entire service of four years with Forrest that I ever saw him purturbed. He tried with all possible boldness to stem the tide; but our men had ridden hard all night, and they simply could not meet the advantage and odds of fresh troops.
>
> After losing a number of men we "stood not upon the order of our going," but recoiled from the front of flame; and on our retreat the enemy pursued us so closely that we lost two of our field pieces. Our retreat so enraged General Forrest that he was ferocious and wild as a lion.[264]

This incident, the loss of Forrest's guns, was to simmer for weeks and finally end in tragedy. Forrest blamed Lieutenant A. Willis Gould of Morton's Battery for the loss of these prize possessions, possibly comparing Gould with Captain Freeman, Forrest's artillery commander killed just three weeks before.

This whole affair brought to light one of the Forrest character traits: a towering, uncontrollable rage. One of his biographers put it this way:

> This firm and rough treatment he had received at the hands of Streight stirred the General's bile. But when he failed to retake his pet guns, two of the four he had taken at Murfreesboro in [18]62, he flew into one of those rages which were the marvels of his commands. They were so fierce and intense they ceased to have any personal quality. They became almost abstract. His men never crossed him at such a time, for he was far more dangerous than any enemy could possibly be.
>
> He dashed up and down the broken line, beating with the flat of his sabre every straggler who looked longingly at the rear. He told every man to hitch his horse to a sapling—one man in four was usually detached as horse-holder—that if they did not get back his guns, they'd have no more use for their critters. He told them he aimed to get back his guns if every man died in the attempt. He told them many more interesting things which they would experience; and as he told them, his lips flashed like a tinder box. It was said long afterwards that whereas he undoubtedly took the Lord's name, he never took it in vain.[265]

Each man reacted differently when he was exposed to Forrest's temper, but one of his officers, Captain Henry Pointer, remarked with some resignation to another staff member, Captain Charles A. Anderson, as he unwrapped a food package: "Captain, we had better eat this now, I reckon, for from the way the old man is preparing to get his guns back it might spile before we get another chance at it."[266]

About this time, two Confederate regiments, McLemore's 4th and Biffle's 9th, came in from their fruitless attempt to get ahead of Streight. They had raced through the gaps paralleling the Indiana colonel, but his move was too fast. They had returned to Forrest too late for the skirmish; however, they were welcome additions to the Forrest division. As they arrived about 3:00 PM on the 30th, Forrest placed them in line: McLemore on the right, Edmondson and the 11th on the left, with Roddey and Biffle in the center. Leaving their horses tied to the trees, as demanded by Forrest, they began a cautious move toward Streight's position, mindful of the morning experience, but found only a handful of skirmishers. Streight had moved on.[267] The Southerners had to retrace their route, back down the hill to get their horses, delaying their pursuit of Streight for about an hour.[268]

That ended the Days Gap battle (sometime called Davis' Gap), but there was more fighting to come.

Years later a Forrest biographer wrote about Streight's performance in his first battle:

> The Federal commander handled his men with decided nerve. Massing them, by a resolute charge he obliged the Confederates to fall back, quite three hundred yards, to another position, which he likewise attacked with equal spirit, but was this time repulsed, with small loss on either side. He [Streight] then drew back to the position in which he had first awaited battle; and Forrest resumed possession of the ridge in his immediate front. From these opposite ridges an animated skirmish was maintained between the sharpshooters of both forces until three PM.[269]

The Southern casualty figures in that clash are not known, but an analysis of regimental records and Union Surgeon William Spencer's list show Union casualties for the April 30 battle as eleven killed, thirty-nine wounded and twenty-four captured. Ten died later of wounds.[270] Several Southern reports indicate that Confederate losses were heavy, since the Union regiments were in well-entrenched positions. Forrest biographer Henry Mathes reported that Forrest admitted to forty prisoners taken and about thirty dead with many wounded, including his brother William.[271] Other records indicated that the 11th Tennessee, 4th Alabama and Julian's battalion suffered severely.[272] It is known that Lieutenant Colonel James W. Sheets, commander of the 51st Indiana, was one of the first to be wounded. He was hit in the hip and severely wounded while leading the Streight charge that captured the Forrest artillery. His wound ended his brief career as a regimental commander. Ironically, Streight had, only a few days previously, succeeded in getting Sheets his appointment as lieutenant colonel.[273]

Other casualty figures differed: the 73d Indiana reported the Provisional Brigade casualties as thirty-one officers and men killed and wounded, and cites Rebel losses at about 150 officers and men, about thirty prisoners captured, and paroled later that the day.[274] Also badly wounded in the head was the brigade ordnance officer, Lieutenant Charles Pavey of the 80th Illinois.[275] Roach reported the same number of Federal casualties, but a slightly higher Confederate number, 180 instead of 150.[276] Streight's report stated, "The enemy, after a short but stubborn resistance, fled in confusion, leaving two pieces of artillery, two caissons, and about 40 prisoners, representing seven regiments, a large number of wounded and about 30 dead on the field. . . . Our loss was about 30 killed and wounded . . ."[277]

A record of the 3d Tennessee Cavalry shows that Private W. F. Forrest, (the General's son), Company D, was detailed to stay with the wounded at Days Gap, probably to be with his uncle Captain William Forrest, badly wounded in the first charge. Young Private Forrest must have requested to join his father's expedition since the 3rd Tennessee Cavalry Regiment was not on the scene at Days Gap.[278]

The wounded were treated as best they could be by the various regimental surgeons. As the Union regiments made their withdrawal from the ridge, they took the wounded and dead with them.

One grim report came from the history of the 73d:

Two of Company K's men, Henry Bird and Shannon Carr, had left the command early in the morning as foragers, and about the time of the engagement were captured by Roddey's men, who turned them over to a squad of guerrillas, calling themselves Home Guards, and by them were taken to a lonely ravine, where they were deliberately murdered. This horrible butchery was seen by one of our cavalrymen, a native of Alabama, who was expecting a similar fate, but by a bold dash succeeded in escaping and more than fifteen months afterwards told the writer about this slaughter.[279]

The morning fight was ended, but the day was far from over.

N. B. Forrest
Lieut. Genl.

CHAPTER 10

THURSDAY APRIL 30 PM.

CROOKED CREEK—HOG MOUNTAIN

As soon as Forrest saw that Streight had taken the bulk of his brigade off the ridge, he made a further deployment of his men. He knew he had Streight cut off from Dodge, but he still thought there might be a move back to the north, so he sent Edmonson's 11th north toward Summerville to make sure that there would be no opportunity to recross the Tennessee River. He also sent Roddey to Decatur with Roddey's 4th Alabama plus Julian's battalion, which totaled a hundred men and two pieces of artillery; some fifty Union captives; and the Confederate wounded able to travel with instructions "to resume command in that quarter."[280] It is possible he was somewhat displeased with Roddey's rout in the morning battle, and since Rod-dey's men were relatively raw and untrained compared to the Forrest cavalry, he may have opted for their banishment.

The situation after Streight's successful withdrawal was described in a narrative of five Tennessee brothers, the Fisher boys, who served with Forrest:

> Streight's purpose, of course, was to continue his eastward march to reach the rail spur of the Western & Atlantic Railroad at Rome, Georgia, *not* to fight battles along the way. His path to Rome was through difficult mountain terrain, lightly populated, but with a fair number of Union sympathizers, many of whom had sons and fathers among Streight's troops.
>
> Streight would have preferred proceeding without the hindrance of Forrest's horsemen who, once they caught up with him on April 29, pressed him continually, causing Streight to pause and improvise rearguard actions to keep them from overrunning his command.
>
> Forrest's tactic was not only to continually press the rear of Streight's command, but to send regiments around the flanks of the Union force and to press home his attacks continually, so as to give Streight, his officers and men no rest, no possibility of resuscitation, no sleep, no opportunity to halt and chow down, no possibility of re-organizing their resources, of feeding or watering horses and mules, of caring for the dead or the wounded or their animals.
>
> On the other hand, Streight, although he complained that his mules, which he had chosen as mounts, because of the difficult moun-

tain terrain, were deficient, diseased and broken-down, had the advantage of a larger force, and an ability to scour the country to secure replacement mounts leaving their broken-down animals in their wake as replacements for Forrest's horses which dropped out of the race. Furthermore, by setting ambushes for their pursuers at natural defensive positions of their own choosing, Streight's forces were able to induce a degree of caution in Forrest's horsemen.[281]

By the afternoon of April 30, Forrest had the 4th and 9th Tennessee Cavalry Regiments, plus about one hundred of his escort and scouts, totaling roughly 1,000 men and six guns, for the actual pursuit of Streight.[282] Streight's 1,500 men were now down to 1,400, with about one hundred captured, dead and wounded. It was difficult to straggle in this barren and, for the most part, unfriendly country. According to one source, "The first blood and the first honors were to Streight, for, after all, his mission was not to fight barren battles on top of remote Sand Mountain, but to make his way to Georgia and cut railroads."[283] This commitment to the mission was what pushed Streight to break off contact with Forrest and head on east. The part played by the Union Alabama Cavalry had been significant, and continued to be so in the route chosen by Streight. These horsemen were natives of this area and knew the territory, with all its quirks, as well as, or better than, the Confederates following them.

General Forrest had already begun his pursuit as Streight covered the next ten miles. Forrest personally led his scouts and escorts, flying down the road behind Streight followed by his two old brigade regiments: the 4th Tennessee leading, trailed by the 9th. Forrest had been in pursuit only a short time when he made contact with the Federal rearguard. Thus began a running skirmish, Streight's men firing and withdrawing, hoping to keep Forrest from damaging the main body. Streight, in a later report, expressed his thoughts as he began his eastward movement:

It was now about 11 o'clock, fighting having continued since about 6 o'clock in the morning. I had learned, in the meantime, that the enemy was in heavy force, fully three times our number, with twelve pieces of artillery, under General Forrest in person; consequently I was fearful they were making an effort to get around us and attack in the rear of our position, hence I decided to resume the march. Everything was soon in readiness, and we move out, leaving a strong guard (dismounted) in the rear, to check any immediate advance the enemy might make previous to the column getting in motion.[284]

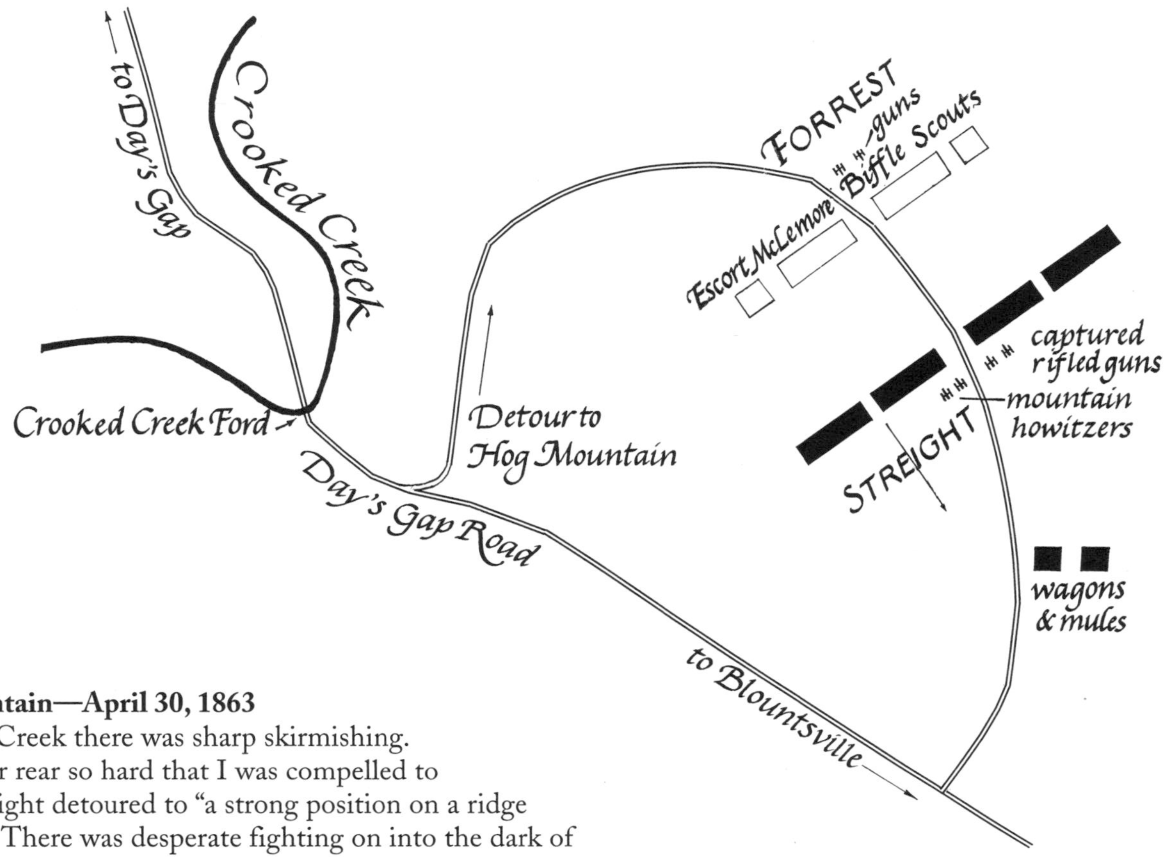
to Day's Gap
Crooked Creek
Crooked Creek Ford
Day's Gap Road
Detour to
Hog Mountain
to Blountsville
FORREST
guns
Biffle Scouts
Escort McLemore
captured
rifled guns
mountain
howitzers
STREIGHT
wagons
& mules

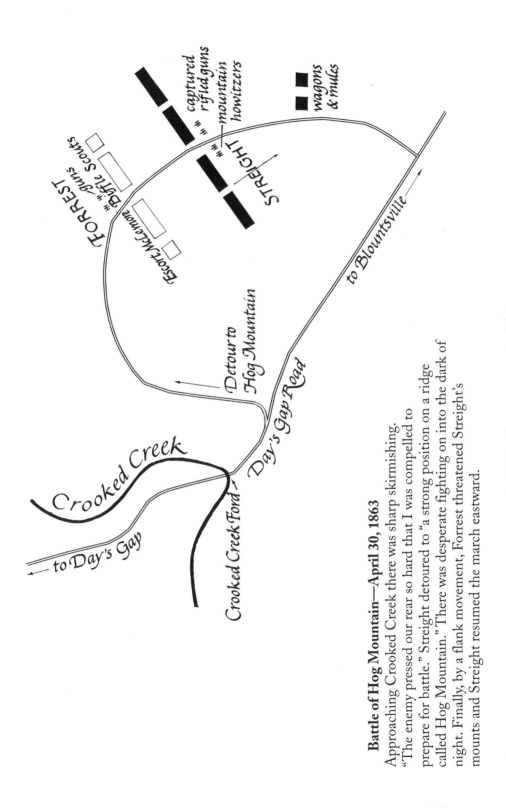

Battle of Hog Mountain—April 30, 1863

Approaching Crooked Creek there was sharp skirmishing. "The enemy pressed our rear so hard that I was compelled to prepare for battle." Streight detoured to "a strong position on a ridge called Hog Mountain." There was desperate fighting on into the dark of night. Finally, by a flank movement, Forrest threatened Streight's mounts and Streight resumed the march eastward.

Here again was the fatal Union flaw: the belief that the enemy had over-whelming numbers and the support that went with it. Had Streight been able to scout Forrest with accuracy, he would have realized that the raiders had not a three-to-one disadvantage, but a one-and-a-half-to-one advantage. That might have made him more ready for a confrontation with Forrest. But believing there were such overwhelming Rebel numbers, and knowing his pursuer was the famed Brigadier General Nathan Bedford Forrest, was enough to create caution in his every move. Still, Streight managed his movements with skill and initiative. But the moves were followed, tenaciously and relentlessly, by Forrest, "The Wizard of the Saddle."

While the Federal column was proceeding on the road toward Blounts-ville, over the saddle of Hog Mountain, they crossed Crooked Creek in column form. The last regiment in the column was the 3d Ohio, who very nearly were cut off from the regiments ahead because of the thirst of their animals. The mules and horses had experienced a rough day; they were tired, hungry and thirsty. So when the regiment started across the creek, the animals simply stopped to drink, ignoring the frantic efforts of their riders. The whole column had faced that same problem, and as the brigade slowed, the pursuing Confederates came closer and closer to the 3d Ohio, particularly Major McLemore's 4th Tennessee. Briedenthal was there and saw it all: "About two PM we were ordered to fall in and bring up the rear and we were soon under full mule-way, and all went smoothly for ten miles, when, as our regiment was in the middle of crossing a deep fork of the Black Warrior River [probably Crooked Creek], the enemy came upon our rear but some of us dismounting, succeeded in holding the enemy in check until the remainder crossed and formed upon the hill."[285]

While Briedenthal remembered the 3d Ohio protecting its own crossing, the 73d took credit for saving the 3d:

> After sundown we came to Crooked Creek, the crossing of which was found tedious owing to the delay in doing so to allow the thirsty animals to drink. The enemy pressed us severely, and came near cutting off the Third Ohio, which was bringing up the rear. After crossing, Colonel Hathaway took the Seventy-Third into position, where it dismounted, formed into line, advanced a short distance, and poured a heavy volley into the enemy's ranks, stopping them long enough for the Third Ohio to cross.[286]

(The Ohio sergeant remembered the time as being after sundown, but other sources say it was somewhat earlier.) Streight then put his brigade in line up and down the river, poured several volleys into Forrest's line, and retired.

As Forrest harried the rear and brought more and more pressure on the column, Streight felt he had to form in line of battle again. He did this in a naturally defensive position, on a ridge called Hog Mountain. Hog Mountain was two miles past past Crooked Creek, the scene of the fierce skirmish earlier. Protecting the rear, Captain David Smith and his 1st Alabama, with his little handful of men, kept the enemy at bay for more than two hours; but the skirmish and the pressure from Confederate scouts had made it clear to Streight that he needed to reform his battle line. Streight's report explained, "Sharp skirmishing commenced at Crooked Creek which is about 10 miles south of Day's Gap, and finally the enemy pressed our rear so hard I was compelled to prepare for battle. I selected a strong position, about one mile south of the crossing of the creek, on a ridge called Hog Mountain. The whole force soon became engaged (about one hour before dark)."[287] Crooked Creek ford was some two hundred feet below the Days Gap battlefield, but beyond the ford, the terrain immediately rose again to the Days Gap level, making the last mile an uphill push for the weary brigade and their relentless pursuers.

Streight then put his four guns, two mountain howitzers plus the two captured Confederate pieces, on a hill commanding the valley below. He put his four regiments in line, facing down the hill; with the mules, horses and wagons stood to the rear and down a slope.

It was almost sundown by the time Forrest had his men in place downhill from Streight's battle line. He put the Escort on the far right, then McLemore's 4th, two guns behind Biffle in the center, and scouts on the left. Forrest drew up his line, then gave the order: "Whenever you see anything blue, shoot at it and do all you can to keep up the scare!"[288] And he sent his tired troopers into battle once again.

Night had fallen when an eerie, savage battle began under a full moon, where the flashes of musket and artillery fire glowed briefly on the flushed faces of the weary but stubborn soldiers. Forrest first sent his cavalry against the Federal right, but they were repulsed. Then he tried the left without success. All the while, his artillery was crashing shot and shell into the Union men, and the howitzers and cannon from the hill smashed into the Confederate ranks below. The artillery again was directed by Major Vananda, skillfully using his four guns, firing at the flashes of Forrest's weapons.

One of Forrest's soldiers described the awe-inspiring scene:

> The pine trees were very tall, and the darkness of their shade was intense, the mountain where the enemy was posted was steep, and as we charged again and again, under Forrest's own lead it was a grand spectacle. It seemed that the fires which blazed from their muskets

were almost long enough to reach our faces. There was one advantage in being below them; they often fired above our heads in the darkness.[289]

Forrest led these two main charges. Various reports indicate at least one of his horses was shot out from under him, some reporting as many as three.[290] It was here, too, that Captain Aaron Thompson of Marshall County, Tennessee, met his death, taking a minie ball in the chest while leading Company A, 4th Tennessee Cavalry in a charge up the hill. With casualties increasing, there was terrible confusion with the surrealistic flashes of light giving the scene a jerky, spasmodic look.

The lightning of the cannon flashed at regular intervals and illumined the tight faces of men peering down the long iron of their guns; or it showed them crouching for the spring, their hats pulled low over their eyes; or it showed them looking towards that high shrill voice mounting above the roar of the powder, the shouts of men, screaming animals, and the low moans of the wounded—its sudden light burning their eyes—with his long arm and nervous fingers pointing south, oblivious to the hot lead balls curving in the dark.

Streight's men, well-officered, knew how to fight. They repulsed every charge with the stubbornness of veterans. For three hours the fighting continued, and the dark blue raiders still knelt behind Hog Mountain.[291]

Up on the hill Streight was running out of ammunition for the captured artillery, so he ordered them spiked and abandoned. He kept up a constant fire but began preparations to move out on his way to Georgia. For the second time that day, the brigade had driven off the veteran Forrest regiments, leaving Streight to continue pursuing his objective, the Georgia railroad. After spiking the guns, Streight asked for the Assistant Surgeon William Spencer of the 73d to prepare his little hospital of wounded and dying brigade members. He told him the wounded would have to be left to the enemy, as they couldn't stand the trip ahead, and the brigade was moving out.

There is no record of Spencer's rejoinder, but the twenty-nine-year-old Indiana doctor remained faithful to his charge as he watched the brigade quietly prepare to ride off to leave him with the wounded. While Spencer was the only trained medical attendant, he was supported by eight other soldiers who stayed with him to help. Four of these "nurses" came from the 80th Illinois, three from the 51st Indiana and one from the 73d Indiana. They were captured along with Spencer and the wounded, as the Provisional Brigade continued on its mission.

Forrest was reorganizing his men down below, and quiet reigned for some time, until about 10:00 PM. As the mule brigade was secretly moving out, Forrest sent his escort and part of Biffle's regiment on the two flanks of Streight, hoping to cut the horseholders and animals away from the regiments. There was confusion in the Southern ranks as McLemore's men heard commotion in the rear of the Federal line and, with the typical Rebel yell, they charged up the hill to keep the pressure on the Yanks. As they converged on the hill where Streight had been only minutes before, they found only the refuse from an old battlefield. They found a number of wagons the Federals had abandoned, the Spencer hospital and the remains of the two captured guns, spiked and demolished.

Again they met only an intrepid rear guard to challenge their arrival. Lytle's history concluded:

> The main body had skillfully escaped on their mules and horses. But Old Bedford got back his guns. They were spiked and the carriages destroyed, but this did not matter. Their physical condition had already ceased to be of any importance. The matter of possession had become purely a matter of moral ascendancy. The butternut riders buried them reverently in the sand and hurried away as the bugles sounded assembly.[292]

As the Confederate cavalry converged on the ridge, they found Dr. Spencer with his ward of broken men in blue and captured them all. Spencer kept a journal of his fearsome duties as the men lay in the field with little shelter, in unfriendly hands, hurting and afraid of what the future had in store. He said:

> *Most gallantly did our boys repel, with interest, every attempt of the Rebels to drive us from our well-selected ground. But another flank movement to counteract for which we had not the men, and our only recourse is to skillfully move out of their greedy clutches. It is rapidly and most heroically done. But our brave wounded cannot be left to the cruelties of an ignoble foe, their mangled limbs must be amputated and their bleeding wounds dressed. I am left behind for this purpose, and thus at Sand Mountain, on the 30th of April 1863, in a sparsely settled country, and in thick forests, and mountains of an inveterate foe, I find myself*
> *A PRISONER.*[293]

The doctor was an ardent Union man, and his views and attitude toward the Confederacy showed plainly in the pages of his journal. It also chronicled the few days that were spent on the littered mountaintop in Alabama, and gave the names of the men he was there to serve. The doctor counted fifty-three Federal dead and wounded in the three fights: Day's Gap,

Crooked Creek and Hog Mountain. However, using other sources as well, a more accurate figure would be eighty-four killed, wounded and captured. Spencer counted three hundred Confederate casualties, besides the prisoners who were immediately paroled and released by the Federal brigade.[294]

Of his capture, Dr. Spencer wrote indignantly:

> *With what varying emotions of trepidation and hope do I now contemplate my situation. Those brave and noble companions of my Brigade, with whom I have endured so many hardships, and upon whose brawny arms, and stalwart frames I have heretofore relied for protection, have gone, and I find myself surrounded by a mongrel set of armed men, rude and illiterate, who taunt and jeer me for my devotion to my country, and its honor, while their companions rob our wounded and strip our dead. . . . Roughly, and eagerly my captors, the "Chivalrous Southerner," now take possession of my revolver, horse and blankets, a portion of my medicines and instruments, while one rude fellow, and then another would claim my boots as "his meat," another my hat; so with my watch, money, pocket-knife, and in fact everything their curiosity, or avarice took a notion to, if found on my person.[295]*

Then he was ordered to meet with General Forrest. Forrest was in a carriage, according to Spencer, with several other gentlemen and made a very favorable impression on Spencer:

> *The general is a pleasant, good looking man, a little above the medium size, with dark eyes and a profusion of dark hair. He began by telling me "he was gratified to find I had remained with our wounded, that I would be protected from all rudeness and harm, that his surgical aid was scarce, while he was almost entirely devoid of medicine and surgical appliances etc." In fact, a few minutes conversation with the General, after being so rudely treated by his men, I felt as though such urbanity, and evidence of good breeding, and generosity to our unfortunate wounded was worthy a better cause than that of destroying "the best government on earth."[296]*

However, subsequent conversations with Forrest caused the doctor to suspect that he was being set up to encourage him to answer questions as to Streight's strength, plan and mission. Forrest complimented the Provisional Brigade by telling him, "Well Sir your Hoosier soldiers fight well Sir, d——d well Sir and Colonel Streight has a fighting devil in him, bigger than two yokes of oxen."[297]

In return, Spencer had some grudging admiration of his captors: "I found the men and officers had great respect for General Forrest which was intermingled with a little wholesome fear, and altogether he makes a better fight with his ragamuffins than one would suppose."[298]

After the conversation ended, and Forrest had departed in his pursuit, Doctor Spencer went back to work. Working with the simplest tools, in open country with limited lighting, he amputated the leg of Andrew Pyle, 51st Indiana; the right arm of Robert Crandall of the 73d; and most tragically, the left arm and right hand of Private (James) Augustus J. Farris, 73d. The left leg of Lieutenant John Welton had been amputated at Days Gap, before the brigade left, by Surgeon S. F. Myers of the 51st Indiana. It must be a testimony to the medical skills of all the doctors that all these amputees survived.[299] There were other wounds to bandage, and a watch set on those who could not be helped, to ease their last few hours. It was difficult duty, but necessary for both captives and captors.

Lieutenant Roach was more critical and considerably more passionate as he described the Rebel treatment of the wounded:

> It was with the feeling of deepest regret that we left here in a hostile country, soon to fall into the hands of a merciless foe, our brave and wounded comrades. But the necessities of war are imperative; consequently when the command *forward* was given, we were compelled to bid adieu, and leave here in the dark mountain ravine, in which our hospital was located, the brave but unfortunate men who had fallen by our sides in the late severe conflict. The treatment experienced by these men after the enemy advanced and made them their prisoners, was inhuman beyond expression. Every ounce of the bread, meat, sugar, coffee &c., left for their subsistence, was immediately taken possession by Forrest or Roddey's unfeeling troopers. [Roddey was then at Decatur, not at Hog Mountain.][300]

He described the Confederate ideas of "swapping prisoners"; the blue clads came out on the short end each time. In defense of the Southern treatment, the cavalry usually foraged for their subsistence, and having such easy pluckings available probably lent itself to some excesses. But even before this expedition, their commander, General Van Dorn, had taken Forrest to task for his excessively possessive feelings toward pre-empting any booty available.

In order for the Confederates to move out and leave the Federal soldiers behind, they required a parole be given by all Union soldiers. The form of the parole was as follows: "We, the undersigned members of Colonel Streight's Brigade Soldiers of the United States Army, hereby pledge our sacred honor, not to take up arms, give aid or information, which could be detrimental to the Confederate States of America, until regularly exchanged so help us God!" On the back of this parole was a permit to pass their lines, Vis, "under the above circumstances, the within named men are permitted to pass our lines." It was signed by Major Chas. W. Anderson, A.A.G., for Brig. General Forrest.[301] It was also signed by sixty members of the brigade: four from the 3d Ohio, eighteen from the 51st Indiana, thirteen from the 73d Indiana, sixteen from the 80th Illinois and one from the 1st Tennessee (Alabama), plus the eight "nurses."

The wounded included several who died during the day and a few who died in the days to come. One of those was newly promoted Lieutenant Colonel James W. Sheets. One Confederate history reported, "While Sheets was mortally wounded, Forrest's brother was desperately wounded. The Indiana colonel was left in the hands of his captors, and his lifeless body was consigned to a coffinless tomb. He died as brave men wish to die—at the front, with his face to the foe."[302] Actually, Sheets died on June 28, 1863, after being cared for by Mrs. Colonel Davis in Danville, Alabama, until his death. By coincidence, Sheets' hometown was Danville, Indiana. Sheets' bravery was genuine; he was wounded as he led his regiment, the 51st Indiana, in the charge that resulted in the Confederate rout at Days Gap.

Among those killed in the three battles of April 30 were twenty-year-old Solomon Swaney, twenty-three-year old Frank A. Haughey and Benjamin Riley of the 3d Ohio; Enoch Rhodes, Samuel Clark, John Coshow, Ethan Kendall and Silas Osborn of the 51st Indiana; Robert Jackson of the 73d Indiana; and John Horn, Captain Edmund Jones and Adjutant James C. Jones of the 80th Illinois. In addition, there were seventy-one Union soldiers wounded and missing, some of whom would not survive their wounds or their captivity.[303] None of the 1st Alabama Cavalry was killed that day. The only two battle deaths in Forrest's command that were identified were Lieutenant H. H. Oates and Captain Aaron Thompson of the 4th Tennessee, although there were obviously many others.

While the Forrest division was gathering the spoils of war from Dr. Spencer's hospital and its patients, Colonel Streight took his brigade down the road toward Blountsville. Streight had ordered the 73d to act as rear guard, and Streight stayed with that unit until the last of the troops had withdrawn. As the last regiment formed in column and headed east, two regimental doctors were taking last-minute care of the wounded, just before the Rebels arrived in Streight's recently abandoned camp. Dr. (Major) W. H. Peck from the 3d Ohio and Dr. Henry R. King, Assistant Surgeon, 51st Indiana, busy with the wounded, missed the order to move out. They finally discovered the brigade had pulled out, and started on horseback down the road. It was only then that they became aware that the troops they were passing were unfamiliar, and discovered they were passing a Confederate regiment. Dr. Peck was well mounted, and when the Confederates discovered they had two Yankees in their midst, Peck out-ran them. Dr.

King was not as well mounted, nor so lucky; he was taken prisoner by the 4th Tennessee, or Forrest's escort.[304]

Later, Dr. King wrote an article for the Indianapolis paper, in which he said, "After burying the dead and caring for the wounded [at Days Gap], Colonel Streight again took up his line of march for the South, and had advanced about twelve miles when he was again overtaken by General Forrest, who had been heavily reinforced by a brigade of well mounted infantry with a battery of six pieces under the command of Colonel Roddey."[305]

Once again the figures were inflated. Continual reports of non-existent reinforcements weighed heavily on Streight and his decisions, inaccurate as those figures were. Forrest may have had nine hundred men compared to Streight's 1,400, but it is doubtful that with casualties and stragglers the Confederates could muster eight hundred. In that same article, King referred to the "superior numbers" of Forrest at Crooked Creek and Hog Mountain.

When Dr. Peck reached the rear guard of the 73d, he reported immediately to the colonel that Forrest was close behind the column. It was then nearly 11:00 PM, still the night of April 30, when Streight made another effort to discourage Forrest while the main force of the brigade moved out. Streight's report described one of the last actions of the day:

> The moon shone very brightly, and the country was an open woodland, with an occasional spot of thick undergrowth. In one of these thickets I placed the Seventy Third Indiana, lying down, and not more than 20 paces from the road, which was in plain view. The enemy approached. The head of his column passed without discovering our position. At this moment the whole regiment opened a most destructive fire, causing a complete stampede of the enemy.[306]

The Southern memoirs were somewhat different. Forrest had sent out a scout, Private Granville Pillow, knowing that Streight's main weapon was ambush; his scout discovered what he thought was a party off the road ahead. The scouts were alert to the possibility of attack. Three scouts, volunteers, were sent out to draw fire, with the rest of the advance just behind:

> The distorted shadows of three horsemen fell across the sand, into the piney woods, as Old Bedford's volunteers rode into the moon's full wash of light. They rode very carelessly, but their eyes were not careless. They were fixed in alert paralysis upon the tarnation thicket ahead. They saw dark shadows behind the thicket rise from a prone position, and a few flashes from the metal on the Illinoisan barrels; then wheeled to the rear and, throwing their bodies well over the sides

of their mounts, rode safely back to their buddies.[307]

With that knowledge of the Union location, Forrest silently brought McLemore with the artillery up to almost point-blank range of the Union concealment, while Biffle's men moved around to the left of the raiders. After a few shells and a ragged volley from Forrest's artillery, Colonel Hathaway pulled his men back, racing, if mules could race, toward Streight's disappearing brigade.

The final ambush came at 2:00 AM, when Hathaway again concealed his troops in the underbrush near the road. According to Reverend (Private) Whitsitt of the 4th Tennessee Cavalry, this time it was more effective, but both sides were really too exhausted to make any follow-up attempt. "At two o'clock the next morning when most of our command had fallen asleep on horseback, we were ambuscaded at the ford of a difficult mountain stream and caused some losses, especially among the animals. We in our turn were thrown into a degree of confusion here, but they were too frightened to press their advantage."[308]

Mathes, in his biography of General Forrest, evaluates that night's work: "It was as gallant and stubborn a fight on both sides there in that far off mountain desert as was ever made by American soldiers and men."[309]

Many years later a newspaper in Memphis published an account of the battles of April 30:

> The account of this prolonged and desperate battle conflict on the barren mountain of northern Alabama has been handed down through several generations. The battle was one of peculiarly weird grandeur. The thunder of artillery, peals of musketry, and the multiplied reverberations from mountain to valley mingled with sharp words of commands, cries of the affrighted and wounded animals, added to which was a splendor in lurid splashes of rapidly served artillery and the blaze of muskets, which excites admiration, even in that moment of fiercest passion.[310]

It was almost 3 AM when Forrest felt confident enough to call a halt, have his men rest, eat, and sleep for a few hours. Streight's worn-out crew, now deeply concerned about their future, marched on into the moonlight, headed for Blountsville and hopefully some respite from Forrest's nagging pursuit. Whitsitt observed that at the positions which had been occupied by the Yankee riders, scraps of paper were found, evidences of the concerns about capture. "It looked as if every man in their column must have employed the leisure afforded by that stop to tear up all the private letters found upon his person. It was clear that their alarm had become serious and would help us much if we could keep it up."[311] It had been a very long day.

CHAPTER 11

FRIDAY MAY 1

BLOUNTSVILLE, ALABAMA

At the battle of Days Gap, the two forces had battled at the crest of Sand Mountain at an elevation of just over 1,000 feet above sea level, but the road dropped down to the six-hundred-foot level in the forty-mile route to Blountsville. All the way to Blountsville the countryside was open woodland and virtually uninhabited, with little food or forage to sustain any force. Streight's report explained, "I had hopes that by pushing ahead we could reach a place where we could feed before the enemy would come up with us, and by holding him back where there was no feed, compel him to lay over a day at least to recuperate."[312]

So the brigade kept up the march all night, coaxing their exhausted mounts along. The lead elements arrived at Blountsville, forty-three miles from Days Gap, at 8:00 AM on May 1. It was a bedraggled lot of soldiers who straggled into the small Alabama town, sore from their bumping up and down on skimpy saddles and weary from their all-day fight and all-night ride. They had been without a real rest for twenty-eight hours, and their meals had been whatever they could grab from their haversacks during the march or waiting to fight. Briedenthal's journal entry said, "This morning we are still on the road, and are in such haste to get to our destination, if possible, without further molestation, that we are not allowed time to stop to either feed or water our mules, but are hurried through streams midsides to the stock, without allowing them a taste."[313] In the past twenty-four hours, a number of their mules had given out on the rough march, and several had been killed in the persistent skirmishing. That left some of the men unmounted once again, one more reason the column had slowed to a walk as they began to relax, hoping that Forrest was far behind.

The citizens of Blountsville were planning some May Day festivities, but these activities soon took a distant third place to, first, the arrival of the men in blue and, second, Forrest's cavalry appearance a few hours later.

In Blountsville the Federals were looking forward to a rest, some food and a chance to get off their boney mounts. In the column were six wagons with the equipment, rations, ammunition and other necessaries for the brigade, but the wagons' agonizingly slow progress was another impediment to the mobility of the raiders. Streight, in order to speed up the brigade, decided to keep only one wagon with the column, taking the contents of the remaining wagons and dividing it among the pack mules and their teamsters.[314] That posed another problem:

> Of all the men in the Seventy-Third we had but one who had had experience in loading a pack-mule and tying the "diamond hitch," and that one was Colonel Hathaway himself, who in several trips he had made in Texas with trains of pack mules had learned the rather complicated art of properly securing baggage on these refractory animals. He called his teamsters up, and in a short time taught them how to do this job, with the result that there was less trouble with the pack train of the Seventy-Third than that of any of the other regiments of the brigade.[315]

After all the goods had been redistributed from wagons to animals, the excess wagons and goods were set afire, to prevent their becoming of any benefit to the Streight pursuers.

Along with the wagons and supplies that were left behind were a host of Negroes who had been following the raiders ever since they entered Alabama. This had become a problem to the extent that Colonel Streight, ardent Abolitionist that he was, finally had to call a halt to the refugee mass. The 73d Indiana history explained, "Their presence delayed us and became such an impediment that Colonel Streight was compelled to issue an order, prohibiting them in our lines as they greatly impeded our march and made our own defense much more difficult."[316]

Streight availed himself of the city's corn supply, feeding some to his animals and some to his famished troops. Later the townspeople tried to provide the Forrest cavalry with what was left as they witnessed the clash of Union rearguards and the Confederate advance party when the Federals left town. Again, Streight successfully traded new, fresh animals for his worn-out creatures, leaving few animals for Forrest to find. "It was the liveliest day in the history of Blountsville and the pretty Queen of May was neglected."[317]

By this time, on the morning of May 1, Streight's men and animals had been without sleep or rest except for brief snatches for too long. They were tired, sore from their mule mounts, and hungry, in spite of the brief rest and cold rations they had been able to find in Blountsville. They had just begun to relax, load up on some food and unsaddle, when Forrest appeared, skirmishing sharply with the Alabama cavalry in the rear.

Unfortunately for Streight, the Union rest was a short one, only two hours from arrival until "Boots and Saddles" sounded for the worn-out blueclads. They had found a substantial amount of corn and forage, and even some replacement mounts, but that did little to help the fatigue the ragged troopers felt.[318] Captain Smith's rearguard delayed the Confederates enough so that the brigade was able to get out of town in good, if exhausted, order. The short rest and a cooked meal had briefly revived the Midwesterners, but more struggles awaited them as they cleared the town.

Forrest was able to rest part of his men while a small portion kept punishing Streight's men in the rear of the column. While casualties on both sides were few, the harassment of the unexpected attacks kept the Union column off balance. Some of the advantages lay with the Union troopers, who could find a good, bushy spot by the road, settle behind it for an ambush, and drop one or two Confederates before mounting up and racing for the main body. This kept the pursuers from gaining too much on the elusive Streight.

However, at Blountsville Forrest was so close that the Union wagons hardly had a chance to burn before they were pounced on by the Rebels, who had forced the 1st Alabama rear guard to abandon the town. The Alabama Union troopers were proving themselves to be both courageous and inventive as they repeatedly locked horns with Forrest's advance guard, gaining valuable time for Streight's forces at Days Gap, Crooked Creek, Hog Mountain and again here at Blountsville. The Confederate arrival in Blountsville was sudden and boisterous. "As the smoke rose from the burning wagons, Gen. Forrest charged into the village at the head of his escort company and a portion of Starnes' 4th Tennessee. They drove Captain Smith's rear guard through and out of town in a cloud of dust and into Streight's main column."[319] Then the Confederate cavalrymen went back to douse the flames and recover some of the scarce provisions still intact, which were desperately needed by the Southerners. One of the 9th Tennessee troopers wrote that "the wagons were loaded with provisions for the men—mostly—but we found large quantities of ladies' clothing and silverware and household goods of various kinds that they had robbed the unprotected citizens of in the valley below."[320]

Forrest gave his men a breather in Blountsville, but they picked up Streight's trail early on May 1. It was not a difficult trail to follow: "Immediately the pursuit was renewed, and for 10 miles the roadway was strewn with saddles and bridles and boxes of crackers from which the Confederates drew a hasty ration; mingled with all this there was also crockery and kitchen utensils, blankets, shoes, and plated wear, and there were seen scattered around, embroidered skirts and other items of female apparel, taken in sheer wantonness. . . ."[321]

One of Forrest's men was puzzled about Streight's leisurely pace. "Colonel Streight seemed to have no proper ideas of what a cavalry soldier can endure. Possibly his men, having been only recently promoted to saddle, were galled and wearied by the novelty of the exercise. He was taking his ease as if no enemy were near when we found him at Blountsville next morning."[322]

By the time he reached Blountsville, General Forrest's temper was just barely under control. He had seen three pitched battles; he had been defeated in the first and in the second and third—Streight had escaped. These were not experiences he cherished. Near Blountsville an agitated scout of Captain William Forrest's group rode in, asking for the general. When he found him, he told him in great excitement that he had stopped in a blacksmith's shop to reshoe his horse. While he was there he overheard a local describing a column of 2,000 Yankees riding just north of Forrest, not more than four miles off. An eyewitness to Forrest's temper recalled:

> Forrest said, "Did you see the Yankees?" The man replied, "I did not see them myself, but while I was in the blacksmith's shop a citizen came galloping up on horseback and told me he had seen them."
>
> He had scarcely delivered himself of this piece of information when General Forrest, with both hands, seized the astonished soldier by the throat, dragged him from his horse, and shoving him against a tree near the roadside, proceeded to bump his head vigorously against the rough bark of the trunk. Having sufficiently punished the unreliable scout, this overbearing leader of men, who, when he found it necessary for the good of his command, constituted judge, jury, and executioner, said, "Now, damn you, if you ever come to me again with a pack of lies, you won't get off so easily!" Macbeth, springing upon the messenger with unpleasant and uncertain news, with that fierce denunciation, "The devil damn the black, the pale-faced loon" was not more ungovernable nor unreasonable than was Forrest in his furious rage.[323]

It was typical of this man whose rage ran just below the surface. The anger could be directed at anyone who displeased him, white or black, officer or enlisted man, Yankee or Rebel. It was this thinly veiled ferocity that kept his men in line, and sufficiently afraid of him that any order he gave would be promptly followed, lest the wrath of the general fall upon them.

It was Forrest's use of his veteran cavalry during this pursuit that allowed him to continue to harass Streight at all hours of the day and night. Up until the Days Gap battle, the Forrest division had been pushed hard, riding all the way from Spring Hill, Tennessee, fighting at Town Creek, then Days Gap, Crooked Creek, the ambushes at Hog Mountain and the late night bushwhacking of Hathaway's men on the 30th. But now that he had Streight boxed in, he could rest a portion of his command, and require the rest of his dwindling force to keep on Streight's tail, snapping at him whenever possible. Then he would rest those men and rush forward the "rested" troops. While no one got a whole night's sleep at any time in the pursuit, they did manage to get a few hours rest from time to time. Forrest, though, was losing men at a constant rate, due to the grueling pace, through desertion, casualties, sickness and animal breakdown.

Streight had his own problem; he had to keep all of his regiments moving at about the same pace, which meant no one slept or rested unless they all did; after the all-night march they were all nearing complete exhaustion. There was a definite incentive not to straggle, with Confederate cavalry minutes away, just behind the Yankee rear guard.

As they left Blountsville, the two forces maintained their eastward march toward Rome, on the road to Gadsden, requiring all of the strength and stamina of the men on both sides. One psychological advantage of the Forrest column was the appearance of women along the line of march, cheering for their Confederate protectors, as recounted in the *Confederate Veteran* after the war:

> Comrades, those girls caused us to gain victories we would have lost. I remember the morning we gave Streight that glorious licking at Day's Gap on Sand Mountain, in Alabama, in the spring of 1863, when he [Streight] made the raid through Alabama. Forrest had on his war jacket, and that meant fight. We came to a farmhouse where two young ladies were in the yard, and as we passed them they waved their bonnets and began to sing 'Dixie Land'. The boys yelled and yelled. The yanks doubtless concluded that Bragg's entire army was after them.[324]

While there was considerable Union sentiment in those hills, there obviously were many who favored secession.

It was ten miles from Blountsville to the Locust Fork of the Black Warrior River, Streight's next obstacle, and every foot of the ten miles was contested by Forrest's harassment of the rear elements of the Yankee column. While the pursuers were aggressive, the rearguard Yankees kept them cautious by posting sharpshooters in roadside bushes. "These hidden marksmen would hold their fire until the gray-clads were almost upon them. This type of fighting curbed the Confederates' ardor."[325] As one biographer explained, "All these advantages of the pursued, Colonel Streight, an able man as well as brave, with a command of real soldiers, exploited with skill and persistence."[326] By then, Streight was persuaded that another pause to fight would be necessary if he were to cross the river at Royal Ford. The river was high, swift and deep, and he knew that a crossing would pose a real threat if Forrest were allowed to approach the brigade while the Yankees crossed.

In this stretch of Alabama east of Blountsville, two young Southern girls became heroines, at least for the moment. Sisters Celia and Winnie Mae Murphree were at their sister-in-law's home near the ford at Black Warrior River. According to local legend, the girls had been sent to help their sister-in-law, Arminda Murphree, whose husband, Lieutenant Isaac Murphree, was off with the army. Arminda had just given birth to a baby girl, and a rather large jug of spirits had been provided as an anesthetic, but apparently not much of it was used.

As Streight was crossing the Black Warrior, he dispatched three men to find any horses in the area, and rejoin the column near Walnut Grove. The story is that the Murphree girls provided the three soldiers with mint juleps, laced with morphine, as the Yankees were searching their house. The second drink must have done the job, since they fell asleep and were taken prisoner by the girls. Early on May 2 the two young girls appeared at Forrest's camp with three horses, driving the three soldiers ahead of them. The two girls "were poor, dressed in homespun and barefooted, though clean and neat. They said they would be willing to go on with the troops, but hardly thought their services were at all necessary. The General giving each a horse, they went off smiling and proud."[327] The Murphree family also had five sons, all of whom were in the army; only two would survive the war. Lieutenant Isaac was not one of the survivors.[328] The General would be given an assist the next day by another young woman, an ardent Southerner, Emma Sansom.

As the Yankees moved toward the Black Warrior River, Streight formed a heavy line of skirmishers to protect the troops as they crossed the river. The skirmishers actually pushed the weary Southern cavalry back, letting the tired Midwesterners cross the fast-running stream, using the rocky ford to get across. During the crossing, two mules were lost, drowning as their sure-footed hooves failed them. The unfortunate mules were heavily laden with boxes of hardtack; once they slipped into the rapid waters, they went down immediately, never to come up again. The line of Union skirmishers did their work well; as the howitzers of Streight's artillery rained shells on the Southern cavalry, the skirmishers formed up with their regiments, and Streight moved on. It was just 5 PM as the last of the animals and men crossed, and the raiders' march was resumed.

While Streight kept his brigade on the march, Forrest crossed his men over the Black Warrior, using the same Royal Ford, but decided to rest his overtaxed horsemen. Their pursuit was turning into a nightmare of hunger, fatigue and frustration, and Forrest sensed it. He knew that Streight had little chance of escape, but he also knew he had to keep pressure on the invaders to keep them from spoiling the countryside. With that goal in mind, he sent Biffle to follow Streight with one hundred of his men, with the promise to let them rest when he could. The rest of his division collapsed in their camp near the river, and slept their first good sleep in three days. Some of the Confederates weren't too tired to salvage some of the mule load that rested in the river. They pulled up the soggy hardtack, finding it almost edible. One of the rescuers called out to the sleepy Tennesseans: "Boys, it's wet and full of mule-hairs, but it's a damn sight better than anything the old man's a-givin' us now!"[329]

According to one historian, while they were resting, Forrest walked among his men, then spoke to them about their mission. "After great difficulty he lined them up, and he spoke to them, warm words full of sympathy for their troubles, bold words to feed their pride; then his voice changed and it rang among them, calling for all who were willing to follow or fall in this, the last lap of the race. They forgot how dry-tired they were, and their hoarse throats shouted the right answer."[330]

It now seemed to be a matter of which force could stay awake longer, and the animals were feeling the agony as well as the troopers. To make matters worse, the road had turned uphill again. The highest point of the expedition, 1,110 feet, was between the Black Warrior and Gadsden. After crossing the river, Streight took the road to Gadsden, as most of the Forrest group snatched a few hours of sleep. But Streight knew his force was unable to continue, and at midnight on May 1 he halted. While most of the brigade slumped to the ground almost as they dismounted, asleep when they hit the ground, Briedenthal's Company A of the 3d Ohio, plus two other companies, drew picket duty. "After unsaddling our mules, our company, with two or three more, went out on picket; consequently we had but little sleep."[331]

At this time, the Union soldiers began to realize that their mission was virtually impossible to achieve, and that escape was not possible. "It now became plain that our expedition could not accomplish the task set for it, nor could we reach our own lines in safety, and the only thing to do was press on as far as possible and do what we could against their military resources."[332] But Streight still was determined to make his own private war on Forrest, and vowed to press on toward Rome. It was a relief to grant the few hours rest to his men, but he knew that before long, Forrest would be on him again. He had crossed the river, but he was far from out of the woods.

John Brown, 73d Indiana

Captain William Wallick,
51st Indiana

Emma Sansom

Major William L. Kendall,
73d Indiana

Soldiers from Craig Dunn Collection

Capt. John H. Richley, 73d
Indiana

Chapter 12

Saturday May 2

Gadsden, Alabama

As Forrest rested his men on the banks of the Black Warrior, he was in constant motion, seeing to the many details of command. There was no rest for the general as he looked to his men and equipment to be completely prepared in the final stages of the pursuit. He dispatched Biffle, with a few companies of the 9th Tennessee Cavalry, to nip at Streight's heels as he headed east on the road to Gadsden, some twenty-five miles away. He knew he had done everything possible to cage the wounded Union brigade, with Edmonson's 11th Tennessee, recently joined by the 53d Alabama of Roddey's Brigade sealing off any escape route to the north.[333] Tired as his own regiments were, he knew Streight was just as weary and that his exhaustion was mingled with dwindling hope and fewer choices than Forrest. So shortly after midnight he set out with his escort and scouts to relieve Biffle and let him get some rest, as he brought up the rest of his force.

Streight had crossed the river and kept his column on the march, but his midnight rest, eleven miles from the Black Warrior, was only for a few hours. Briedenthal commented, "We are well, but tolerably sore."[334] As the brigade fell immediately into a trance-like sleep, Briedenthal kept watch. "At daylight we were again on our way, rode two miles, fed the animals and got breakfast, consisting of good ham, coffee and crackers; it being the second feed in forty eight hours."[335] He also noted that their commissary had become increasingly selective and found that ham was the most plentiful and easiest meat to find.

Not all the Union troopers were being fed; as the rearguard Alabamians dismounted to eat breakfast, Forrest and his escorts were on them again, and a brief fire fight flourished as the lead Union troops forded Will's Creek. Streight made no effort to hinder the Rebels in his rear, content to cross the stream and gallop, (or the closest the animals could come to a gallop) toward Gadsden. Here, bad luck played another dirty trick on the Indiana colonel, although he did not realize it at the time. As his mules waded the Black Warrior River, and then the deep, swift Will's Creek, the hasty packing of the ammunition failed to keep it dry, so much of the ammunition Streight would need was soaked and useless. He later reported, ". . . and, to add still more to my embarrassment, a portion of our ammunition had become damaged in crossing Will's Creek, which at the time was a very deep fording."[336] Another lucky stroke for the South.

The Union force managed to get across the stream with no casualties, leaving a small ambush to worry the Tennessee troopers. The result of the crossing, however, was that Streight was forced to leave about twenty-five infantrymen plus some fifty Negroes, and, according to one source, some women dressed in Federal uniforms, all of them too weary to continue.[337]

A short distance away, the brigade came to Black Creek, only about four miles from Gadsden. Streight's report says only, "We proceeded in the direction of Gadsden without further interruption, with the exception of small parties who were continually harassing the rear of the column, until about nine o'clock the next morning, May 2, when the rearguard was fiercely attacked at the crossing of Black Creek, near Gadsden. After a sharp fight, the enemy was repulsed."[338]

Streight arrived at Black Creek with Forrest's remaining regiments just behind. The Northern ambushes were the only deterrent to the Rebels, except for bridge-burning to slow the pursuit. These tactics were designed not to stop, but only to slow the relentless Tennessee cavalry. After the crossing at Will's Creek, the next major physical barrier was Black Creek, which had a single bridge across its impressive width. It was a crude, uncovered, single-span, linking the towns of Blountsville and Gadsden by the main road; it was the only available bridge within miles. Another bridge about two miles away was deemed unsafe to cross, and had been closed for some time. Since the only way to get from the west bank to the east was by boat or by bridge, Streight was given one of his last hopes. If he could use this bridge to cross his brigade, then burn the bridge, he was convinced it would give him at least a half day's lead on Forrest, and some real hope of getting to Rome and cutting the railroad. By now he seemed to give no thought of escape; his focus was solely on his mission.

Actually, Streight's route had again been easy for Forrest to follow because of the discarding of items the troopers felt were not important: blankets, clothing, cook-stoves. Anything that wasn't immediately usable was dumped by the side of the road, giving considerable help to the impoverished Rebels, both in tracking the Yankees and in replenishing their supplies.

Fresh mounts were still a major concern. As Streight cleared an area, he foraged and seized numbers of healthy animals which were "purchased" from the locals in the usual way: outright confiscation, a government IOU, or, in the case of known Loyalists, Yankee cash. So as Forrest followed the barren countryside, he found no mules or horses except those pitiful discarded mounts unfit for travel, which had been "traded" by Streight's men for healthier animals.

This lack of mounts, as well as fatigue, had slimmed the Confederates' numbers drastically. The pace had weakened the pursuers as well as the pursued. As Forrest gave his men a brief rest, he knew that many of his

horsemen, valiant as they were, could go no further. As they rested, he selected the only two horses that were capable of pulling two artillery pieces.
He then asked for volunteers to continue, and, in an unusual display of com-
passion, ordered the drop-outs to take the two cannon back to Decatur. He
had at that point about six hundred men left. But as he was picking up the
Streight trail once more, Forrest's luck returned. Along the road there appeared several ladies whose spouses and friends had been taken off by the
Federals. They showed their grief in wails and sobs, wrenching at the hearts
of the Tennesseans with pleas for their recapture. This glimpse of Southern womanhood in desperate need of help tugged at their pride, and gave
them renewed strength to carry on. The presence of these ladies was probably equal to a hot meal and a bath as they spurred on toward Gadsden.[339]

One of the Forrest biographers described the formidable creek and the
setting:

> Black Creek is a crooked, deep, and sluggish stream with precipi-
> tous clay banks and mud bottom. It has its source on the plateau of
> Lookout Mountain, the southern limit of which range is less than one
> mile to the north. Only a little farther away, in a series of precipitous
> falls and whirling cascades, pure and crystal while a mountain stream,
> leaping from rock to rock it falls from its high estate to mingle with
> the stained and muddy waters of the lowland.[340]

Although the rear elements of the Federal column were hazed and harassed by Forrest's escort, the forward section arrived at the bridge, crossed
over, and set up their little mountain howitzers on the east side of the river.
Even as they crossed, rails were being torched and flaming timbers piled on
its span; the bridge almost immediately became an impassable inferno. As
the flames mounted and the bridge crashed into the creek, clouds of dust
appeared from the west and riders rapidly pulled into view. The first rider
on the scene wore blue, and came on at a full gallop. Right behind him came
the gray-clads, and as the lone Yankee saw the flaming bridge, he pulled up
short, threw up his hands and was captured, reportedly by Nathan B. Forrest
himself.[341] Forrest was stymied for the moment, as the Yankee howitzers and
a skirmish line opened fire from the east bank. And here was born a story
that elevated one young Alabama girl to heroic status. Her tale was told by
any number of books, memoirs and veterans' publications. This is the story
of Emma Sansom.

Just two hundred yards away, near the main Gadsden-Blountsville Road,
was a lone farmhouse. It was the home of the Widow Sansom and her two
teenage daughters, Emma and Jennie. Her son Rufus, who was with the
19th Alabama Infantry, on May 2 was in Gadsden on sick leave from a
Georgia hospital. The ladies were alone, the senior Sansom having died in

1859. It was sixteen-year-old Emma who came to the general's rescue, allowing him to continue his pursuit of Streight with minimum pause. The story is told in a variety of publications, but Henry Wyeth, in his Forrest biography, insists that the following is the statement he took from Emma, then Mrs. Christopher B. Johnson, after the war:

We were at home on the morning of May 2, 1863, when about eight or nine o'clock a company of men wearing blue uniforms and riding mules and horses galloped past the house and went on towards the bridge. Pretty soon a great crowd of them came along, and some of them stopped at the gate and asked us to bring them some water. Sister and I each took a bucket of water and gave it to them at the gate. One of them asked where my father was. I told him he was dead. He asked me if I had any brothers. I told him I had "six." He asked where they were, and I said they were in the Confederate Army. "Do they think the South will whip?" "They do." "What do you think about it?" "I think God is on our side and we will win." "You do? Well, if you had seen us whip Colonel Roddey the other day and run him across the Tennessee River, you would have thought God was on the side of the best artillery."

By this time some of them had began to dismount, and we went into the house. They came in and began to search for fire-arms and men's saddles. They did not find anything but a side-saddle, and one of them cut the skirts off that. Just then some one from the road said, in a loud tone, "You men bring a chunk of fire with you, and get out of that house." The men got the fire in the kitchen and started out, and an officer put a guard around the house, saying, "This guard is for your protection." They all soon hurried down to the bridge, and in a few minutes we saw smoke rising and knew they were burning the bridge. As our fence extended up to the railing of the bridge, mother said, "Come with me and we will pull our rails away so they will not be destroyed." As we got to the top of the hill we saw the rails were already piled on the bridge and were on fire, and the Yankees were on the other side, guarding it.

We turned back toward the house and had not gone more than a few steps before we saw a Yankee coming at full speed, and behind were some more men on horses. I heard them shout, "Halt! and surrender!" The man stopped, threw up his hand and handed over his gun. The officer to whom he surrendered said, "Ladies do not be alarmed, I am General Forrest; I and my men will protect you from harm." He inquired, "Where are the Yankees?" Mother said, "They have set the bridge on fire and are standing in line on the other side, and if you go down that hill they will kill the last one of you." By this time our men had come up, and some went out in the field, and both sides commenced shooting. We ran to the house, and I got there ahead of all.

General Forrest dashed up to the gate and said to me, "Can you tell me where I can get across that creek?" I told him there was an unsafe bridge two miles farther down the stream, but that I knew of a trail about two hundred yards above the bridge on our farm, where our cows used to cross in low water, and I believed he could get his men over there, and that if he would have my saddle put on a horse I would show him the way. He said, "There is no time to saddle a horse; get up here behind me." As he said this he rode close to the bank on the side of the road, and I jumped up behind him. Just as we started off mother came up about out of breath and gasped out: "Emma, what do you mean?" General Forrest said, "She is going to show me a ford where I can get my men over in time to catch those Yankees before they get to Rome. Don't be uneasy; I will bring her back safe."

We rode out into a field through which ran a branch or small ravine and along which there was a thick undergrowth that protected us for a while from being seen by the Yankees at the bridge or on the other side of the creek. This branch emptied into the creek just above the ford. When we got close to the creek, I said, "General Forrest, I think we had better get off the horse, as we are now where we may be seen." We both got down and crept through the bushes, and when we were right at the ford I happened to be in front. He stepped quickly between me and the Yankees, saying, "I am glad to have you for a pilot, but I am not going to make breastworks of you." The cannon and the other guns were firing fast by this time, as I pointed out to him where to go into the water and out on the other bank, and then we went back towards the house.

He asked me my name, and asked me to give him a lock of my hair. The cannon-balls were screaming over us so loud that we were told to leave and hide in some place out of danger, which we did. Soon all the firing stopped, and I started back home. On the way I met General Forrest again, and he told me that he had written a note for me and left it on the bureau. He asked me again for a lock of my hair, and as we went into the house he said, "One of my bravest men has been killed, and he is laid out in the house. His name is Robert Turner. I want you to see that he is buried in some graveyard near here." He then told me good-bye and got on his horse, and he and his men rode away and left us all alone. My sister and I sat up all night watching over the dead soldier, who had lost his life fighting for our rights, in which we were overpowered but never conquered. General Forrest and his men endeared themselves to us forever.[342]

True to her word, Emma and her family buried eighteen-year-old Robert Turner in a grave next to her father, and there he rests today in a little plot that is now in the median of US Highway 278, just outside Gadsden. One interesting note about Emma's account was that her mother seemed to be more concerned with the decorum of her daughter's behavior rather than the danger of Emma mounting up to help the general. The moral codes of the 1860s were difficult to ignore, it seems. Emma's account may be embellished slightly, and more dramatic than the event itself, but there are a number of references to the deed which bear out the fact that she did, indeed, lead Forrest to the ford, allowing him to stay hot on the Streight trail, and she did so at some peril to herself. Another version allowed that bullets came so close they actually hit her skirts, to which she replied, "They have only wounded my crinoline."[343]

Several other sources referred to another part of the incident which she does not mention. "At the same time, withdrawing her arm, the dauntless girl turning around, faced the enemy, and waved her *sun-bonnet* defiantly and repeatedly in the air. We are pleased to be able to record that, at this, the hostile fire was stopped; the Federals took off their own caps and waving them, gave three hearty cheers of approbation! Remounting, Forrest and Miss Sanson [sic] returned to the command, who received her with unfeigned enthusiasm."[344] Perhaps it was Northern chivalry, but it could be possible that the firing stopped because Streight was content to move on toward Rome, leaving a few in the rear to keep up the firing.

Within thirty minutes of Forrest's arrival at the ford, he had his artillery in position and had forced the Yankees left on the east bank of the creek to withdraw and drive on after the brigade, already on the road to Rome. But before the general left, he returned once again to the Sansom house, asking what more he could do for her family. Emma asked that her brother, on medical leave from the 19th Alabama and captured by Streight earlier, be returned to his home. Forrest's reply: "It shall be done before 10 o'clock tomorrow morning." He was that confident, even with the depleted, exhausted remnant of the 1,700 men he had started with in Spring Hill just over one week earlier.[345] The general then requested a token of the episode, a lock of Emma's hair. It was given to him with admiration and gratitude for the Southern general's arrival and the saving of the Sansom home.

One other version, colored by loyalties and the story mixups of the time, was told of the incident by the 51st Indiana historian, Hartpence: "But among a lot of prisoners captured by our men that morning, was one named Sansom, a low-browed brute; who, in common with the others, as was the custom, was immediately paroled; and who, as soon as he was set at liberty, made his way direct to Forrest, and piloted him to a ford, where the whole rebel force soon crossed."[346]

This is the note allegedly written by Forrest and left at the Sansom home:

Hed Quaters in Sadle
May 2, 1863
My highest regardes to Miss Emma Samsom
for hir gallant conduct while my forse was
skirmishing with the Federals across Black
Creek near Gadisden Allabama
N. B. Forrest
Brig. Genl Comding N. Ala[347]

Further evidence of her part in the episode was the granting to Miss Sansom a gift of 640 acres from the Alabama State Legislature in 1863. Although that act was revoked by the first Reconstruction Legislature, that revocation was rescinded in 1899.[348]

The Confederate river crossing began as soon as the artillery had cleared the Yankees from the other bank. Major McLemore's men led the way, down the steep slopes and across the muddy bottom, and scrambled up the eastern slope. The artillery crossed as well, using ropes and double teams of horses, with the men carrying the ammunition high on the backs of their mounts to avoid the problem of wet powder faced by Streight.[349] As soon as they were across, the general selected about three hundred of his best mounted troopers for the chase, telling the rest to catch up as soon as they could. With Forrest himself in the lead, as usual, the mounted column set out after the Indiana colonel once again.[350]

Streight's weary column covered the four miles to Gadsden in just over an hour, arriving about 10:00 AM, surprising the locals with their sudden arrival. Being in a prosperous town gave Streight a chance to "trade" more of his broken steeds for fresh ones. On the way into town, Briedenthal wrote of an incident on the road involving the continual trades of horse/mule flesh:

> Just before we came to town we witnessed a scene partaking largely of the serious and the comic, more particularly largely of the latter. One of the boys, it appears, had exchanged horses with a gentleman and a lady, something after the manner the Irishman traded linen with the clothes-line. And when we came along, the farmer was setting in the gate-way sending forth the following lamentation, "I have no children, but I have brothers in the army," (he mistook us for secesh) "boo, hoo, hoo," and similar expressions in the most doleful sounds that ever issued from any blubbering booby, whilst "better half" was standing back regarding the newly acquired "hoss" of the genus pendent-eared gentry in an altogether different mood from that of her

husband. Her curses were not "loud" but, judging from the animated gesticulation and the vinegar visage of the termagant, they were "vasty deep"; and take this scene in all its bearings, I should pronounce this "swop" to be an exchange under pretext, and will afford our tender-hearted and charitable sympathizers at home an opportunity to go into hysterics over the uncharitableness of this "Abolition war," etc., to the end of Billings-gate.[351]

The author's bias added considerable color to the tale.

Another incident showed that not all of the local livestock were made available to either Streight or Forrest as they came through the northern Alabama territory. A local minister, Reverend J. W. Cullum of Noah, Alabama, recalled:

> I was then living in North Alabama, and nearly in sight of the road Streight traveled. On that morning I had been called to conduct a funeral service over the remains of a very dear friend, Thomas Barbree, a brother of Rev. Dr. J. D. Barbree, of Nashville. I had nearly reached the place, a distance of eight miles, when I encountered an old and very wealthy citizen, who was under great excitement, moving his mules, horses, cattle, bacon, and negroes into the woods. Upon asking him what was up he cried out, "Yankees! Yankees!" and told me that three thousand had camped at Daniel Hodge's the night before. Of course our funeral congregation was broken up. On arriving at home I saw that my wife and a half-grown negro boy had our old blind gray horse and were trying to move to a place of greater security some shelled corn we were saving for bread. A sack had come untied and the corn had spilled, and they were standing over it in a good deal of trouble. It was good news that the Yankees had swept by and that Forrest was close after them.[352]

The Union column stayed only briefly in the town, looking for more animals. It was long enough to do some damage: "We destroyed four thousand dollars worth of good flour, five hundred stand of arms, and the ferry boat."[353] They also took, and pardoned, a number of Rebel officers and torched the bridge over the Coosa River in Gadsden.[354] This again caused some delay for Forrest, but the Federal column's progress was slow after Gadsden, and the gap between the two columns did not increase.

In spite of the recent horse-trading, Captain Smith, commanding the rearguard, warned that many of the men were straggling and being gobbled up by the Rebel cavalry. Streight reported, "Many of our animals and men were entirely worn out and unable to keep up with the column; consequently they fell behind the rear guard and were captured."[355] His report continued, " It now became evident to me that our only hope was in crossing the river at Rome and destroying the bridge, which would delay Forrest a day or two and give us time to collect horses and mules, and allow the command a little time to sleep, without which it was impossible to proceed."[356]

What had begun on April 30 at Days Gap had turned into a marathon march, interspersed with fighting that cost Streight in terms of casualties, time and energy; and the gap between the blue and the gray had closed to a matter of just a few hours. Even though the Indiana colonel had no military training, the tactics Streight used—ambushes, snipers and stealthy withdrawals—were textbook uses of troops being pursued. Forrest's single tactic was harassment and avoiding pitched battles, since he was outnumbered in almost every confrontation. In spite of Streight's ability to denude the country as he passed through, Forrest had consistently closed the gap between the two. In short, it was a well-fought and well-executed example of escape and pursuit. But the saga had not ended, and Streight continued to elude the Southerners.

Several miles past Turkeytown, about twelve miles from Gadsden, was Blount's Plantation, which appeared to Streight to offer food, forage and a defensible position.[357] Earlier, Streight had heard from scouts that a significant force was to his left, with the obvious intention of getting in front of the column. His scouts had discovered the 11th Tennessee and parts of the 53d Alabama riding parallel to the brigade, just to the north; however, their mission was to keep the Yankees south of the Tennessee River, not to move toward the invading brigade. But with their presence known, Streight was concerned that he might be cut off if the Southern force moved in front of him. He decided it would be necessary to march all night the night of May 2 to prevent any of Forrest's forces getting ahead of him. But to march all night, the colonel knew he had to rest and feed his men, even if it meant a pitched battle with the Tennessee cavalry. He determined that the Blount Plantation was the place to stop.

Capt. Joseph J. Westlake, 73d
Indiana, Logansport, Indiana

Pvt. Wilbur E. Gorsuch, Co. C,
73d Indiana Infantry(musician)

S. S. Duning, Co. H, 51st
Indiana

Capt. Alfred Fry, Co. A
73d Indiana

CHAPTER 13

SATURDAY MAY 2

BLOUNT'S PLANTATION—JOHN WISDOM

As Forrest left Gadsden, he sent a courier toward Rome to alert its citizens to the danger that they faced with the advance of the Union brigade. The courier's mission was to urge that Streight be held off until Forrest could get there to help defend the town. But unknown to Forrest, another local legend was born as a Gadsden citizen took it upon himself to ride to Rome, much as Paul Revere rode to Concord in April some eighty-seven years earlier.

Forty-two-year-old John H. Wisdom lived in Gadsden and was exempt from the Confederate Army because of his duties as a ferryboat operator in Gadsden and a sometime mail carrier for the Confederate government. He lived with his family on the banks of the Coosa River near Gadsden, where he worked the ferryboat east of the main Gadsden bridge. On May 2, 1863, he had driven his buggy about six miles from Gadsden to deliver a sack of corn. When he returned to the ferry, he found that the Union soldiers had cut a hole in his ferryboat and it was lying beneath the water at his dock. On the west bank of the river his neighbors shouted that the Union troopers had come by his place shortly before he got back, on their way to Rome, Georgia.

Wisdom pondered his next move, and ultimately decided to drive to Rome and warn them that the Yankees were coming. Not only was he originally from Rome, but his mother still lived there; probably his concern for her was a significant factor in his decision to drop everything and ride to Rome. After he had fed and watered his horse, knowing the sixty-seven-mile ride would be an ordeal for the animal, he left the ferry dock on the east side of the Coosa River about 3:30 PM in his two-wheeled buggy.

The horse made it only twenty-two miles, to Gnatville. Wisdom knew he had to find a fresh animal to make the trip in time to warn the Romans, but he had difficulty finding anyone who was sympathetic to his problem, until he came to Nancy Hanks, who loaned him her one pony, slightly lame, in return for holding his horse and buggy. The pony made it only about five more miles to Goshen, before it refused to go any farther. In Goshen he found Simpson Johnson, who not only furnished him with a horse, but rode on with him to a friend of Johnson's, Reverend Joel Weems, in Spring Garden, eleven miles away. Weems gave him a mount, this time a mule, and fed both Wisdom and Johnson, sending them on their way to the next stop at Cave Spring. There, Wisdom was turned down by at least one resident when he asked to trade the mule for a fresh horse. He finally found the home of John Baker, who, appreciating his determination to reach Rome, loaned him a horse.

His ride almost ended shortly after he left Baker's. Wisdom's own version stated, "North of Cave Springs, while going down a long hill in a sweeping gallop in the dark and over a rough road, Mr. Baker's horse fell down, throwing me full length into the road ahead of him. I soon recovered, mounted the horse and proceeded a distance of twelve miles, to within six miles of Rome, after stopping several times to try and get a fresh horse."[358] Next he rode to "a man named Jones," still six miles from Rome. Jones gave him a fresh mount and also rode into Rome with him.[359] "I arrived in Rome a few minutes before twelve o'clock that night, making the ride of 67 miles in eight and a half hours, including the stops for changing horses and the time I was delayed when the horse fell down with me."[360]

John Wisdom must have been tired and more than a little uncomfortable. He wryly described his progressive use of five horses and one mule, "each rougher riding than the last one."[361] But his work was not finished when he reached Rome. He found Mr. (or General) George S. Black, who ran the Etowah House Hotel, and told him the Yankees were near. Even though it was then after midnight, Black asked Wisdom to ride up and down calling to the people that the Yankees were coming. That being done, his work was finished, and "... he went to the home of his mother, who lived in Rome, and went to bed."[362] The others in town spent the rest of that night preparing for the defense of the bridges and roads that led into Rome. There were a few troops in town, with a limited number of able bodied men still not in the Confederate service, and some convalescing wounded.

Despite a number of later histories that insist Wisdom was part of Forrest's troop, or that he knew of Forrest's pursuit, Wisdom himself declared, "It has been erroneously stated that I was sent by General Forrest from Gadsden to Rome to advise the people of the coming of the raiders. This is incorrect, for I knew nothing of General Forrest being in pursuit of the raiders until he marched into Rome..."[363] Had Wisdom not completed his ride when he did, the city would not have had time to defend itself and the outcome of the raid might have been different, but the luck of Forrest held firm, leaving Streight in even more trouble.

As Wisdom was beginning his remarkable effort, Streight's troops were assembling in the yard of the Blount Plantation, gathering corn and feed for the horses and lighting fires to cook for the men as they prepared for another grueling night march. No sooner had the fires been started and saddles removed than Forrest's scouts clashed with Smith's rear guard. Far from unexpected, the early sounds of battle had spurred the Yankee colonel to set up an ambush, much as he had done before. The road across the farm was wide, bending first to the left and then to the right, between planted fields, then passing through a thatch of pines. A Forrest biographer, utilizing Streight's report, gave this version of the fight which was published years later in the *Alabama Historical Quarterly*:

> Forewarned of the Reb's approach, Streight had deployed his men to insure that Forrest received a hot reception. The terrain selected by Colonel Streight for this delaying action possessed a number of advantages. The Gadsden-Rome road, the axis of Forrest's advance, was bounded by a dense thicket of second growth pine. These thickets extended to a depth of about 20 yards. As the road neared the ridge where Streight had established his battle line, it veered abruptly to the left. One hundred yards beyond it turned sharply to the right and ascended the ridge, where the Federals were deployed. Open fields lay to the right and to the left of the thickets, which flanked the road.
>
> Streight's skirmishers had thrown down a worn fence, using the rails to erect a barricade across the road at the point where it veered to the left. The Federals hoped to force the Confederates into the open field to the right of the road. Sharpshooters were posted in the scrub timber on both sides of the road, ready to rake the oncoming greyclads. Soldiers from the 51st and 73d Indiana, supported by the two mountain howitzers, held the center of Streight's line; the 80th Illinois assumed responsibility for the right flank and the 3d Ohio for the left.[364]

Almost as soon as Streight had placed his men on the ridge, the Confederates swept down the road, past the sharpshooters and skirmishers, and on toward the ridge. First the Indiana regiments bore the brunt of the attack; after the first charge was driven off, the next wave hit the 80th Illinois and 3d Ohio. After several more thrusts, beaten back by the two little howitzers and the rifle fire, the Southerners retreated to a ridge opposite and massed their men. During the action, the first of the day's disasters struck the Federals, with a single bullet to the chest of Colonel Gilbert Hathaway, who fell and died within minutes, despite attendance by Surgeon Seth Myers. The colonel had been with his adjutant on the right of the 73d; he had just gone to find Major Walker and was giving encouragement and instructions to his men when he was hit. A regimental history reported the men's anguish at the colonel's death:

> It was in this engagement also, that the gallant Colonel Gilbert Hathaway, of the 73d Indiana, fell with a mortal wound, and in a few minutes expired. The Union army possessed no braver nor more valu-

able officer than he. To our devoted brigade, his loss was irreparable. Those of them who yet remain will remember how cheering and inspiring was his presence in their midst; how his coolness steadied them, amid greatest excitement; and his voice of encouragement was a herald of victory. His character so frank and open; his bearing so modest, and so full of simplicity, conciliated and captivated all hearts, and made everyone who knew him his devoted friend.[365]

This testimonial was not from his own regiment, the 73d, but from the 51st Indiana. Hathaway's loss decimated morale and numbed the spirit of the raiders, as well as Streight himself. He had now lost the regimental commanders of both his Indiana regiments, Colonel Sheets of the 51st, Streight's old regiment, and Hathaway of the 73d, and he felt very much alone. The shot that took the life of Colonel Hathaway was a remarkable one, coming from some six hundred yards away and reportedly fired by a 4th Tennessee private, Joseph Martin.[366]

Hathaway's death and burial were also recorded in a Confederate history:

This Federal hero, leading his men in a charge, fell with his face to the foe, crying out, "If we die, let us die at the front," and there he went down, covered with the glory and honor which fame always accords to the brave. There was only time for comrades to request a decent burial for the brave Indiana colonel who had died so far away from home, and had been cut down in the full pride of his splendid career. These officers had known different experiences than the Confederates. They had been accustomed, when men of rank were killed, to handsome coffins and the consoling ornaments and trappings which robbed death on the battlefield of some of its terrors. The owner of the plantation was asked to provide a metallic case for the dead soldier. He mournfully said, "There are no metallic cases in this country." "Then give him a plain pine coffin," pleaded the Federal officer, now exposed to and endangered by the fire of the advancing Confederates. "We have no coffins," replied the man, sadly shaking his head. "Then take some planks and make a box and bury him and mark his grave." "You have burned all my planks," replied the man, "and I have nothing with which to make even a box." "Then," he pleaded once again, with the bullets whistling around his head and the Confederates immediately in sight, "wrap his body in an oil cloth and bury him, for God's sake, where he may be found!" And this the magnanimous planter agreed to do. He faithfully kept his pledge, and in the Alabama garden he gave sepulture to the gallant soldier. The Federal officer, with his enemies at his heels, and with the Confederate bullets buzzing about his person, waved the dust of his comrade a last sad adieu, and putting spurs to his horse galloped away and left the dead hero with his enemies to make and guard his tomb.[367]

Streight's later report acknowledged the loss: "His loss to me was irreparable. His men almost worshipped him, and when he fell it cast a deep gloom of despondency over his regiment which was hard to overcome."[368]

Streight's second blow was even more devastating to the brigade, the discovery that his ammunition had been damaged and was, in many cases, useless. Although the damage had been done two days before in the crossing of Will's Creek, it was at Blount's Plantation that he first learned of the calamity. Success now seemed even more distant; Rome and the Union Holy Grail were still more than fifty miles away.

A grisly incident happened at the plantation, involving Private Charles McWilliams of the 51st. (After the battles at Stones River in December 1862, he and Bilheimer of Company C had been detailed to the 8th Indiana Artillery, but when the raid started they were returned to the 51st.) At Blount's plantation, while McWilliams was serving the howitzers, "he had his head shot off by a rebel cannon ball, while faithfully performing his duty."[369] While no reliable statistics indicate casualties in this clash, the Confederates list two killed and six wounded.[370] Union losses were considerably heavier; Briedenthal recalled, "We lost more in killed here than in the other two engagements."[371] One fatality was Private Charles Stafford of the 3d Ohio. The twenty-seven-year-old died of his wounds on May 2.[372]

During this engagement a young Confederate trooper of the 4th Tennessee, William Haynes, was captured by Streight's men and was hustled immediately to the colonel for questioning. Streight had no clear idea of the size of Forrest's force, and so was hoping to learn something from the Confederate sergeant. Haynes' answers played a significant part in Streight's analysis and strategy. When asked how many men Forrest had, the Confederate began to name the various brigades that were on the field: Forrest, Roddey, Starnes, Armstrong, Whitfield and others whose names he couldn't remember. He was the perfect man for this type of bluff, and evidently very convincing. Believing again that he was heavily outnumbered, after the interrogation, Streight turned to his officers and said, "Gentlemen, they have us!"[373]

As Forrest's men were forming on the ridge, Streight picked two hundred of his best men to send on to Rome in an attempt to protect bridges and crossings for the rest of the brigade, and possibly occupy the city. The men selected were chosen primarily by the condition of their mounts, and were taken from all regiments. Rome was some sixty miles south of the Confederate lines, and few troops were expected to be there. The leader of the group was Captain Milton Russell of Company A, 51st Indiana; high hopes and expectations followed him as he led his men up the road toward Rome.

On the way, Russell was to cross the Chattooga River on the ferry and hold the crossing while waiting for the rest of the brigade, sending most of his party to Rome. The rest of the Streight brigade, still unfed and without rest for themselves or their animals, were to press on and follow the advance party. As the party approached the Chattooga River, Corporal William B. Gibson, of Company A, and Russell's guide started to swim the river on horseback. Gibson made it to the other bank, but his horse took exception to the swim and began to twirl around and around. Gibson slipped off the saddle to let the horse have his way, but found himself unable to swim with all his equipment, soaked and full of water, pulling him under. Captain Marion T. Anderson of the 51st Indiana saw the corporal disappear from sight; he jumped on the old ferryboat, and, with the assistance of a trooper on the ferry, steered the boat toward the spot where Gibson had disappeared. "Placing himself on the forward part of the scow, the captain watched for the reappearing of the corporal; when plunging his arm full length into the water, he succeeded in catching the drowning man by the hair, raising him out and taking him to shore."[374]

One of the men selected to go with Captain Russell was James Lawson Brown of the 80th. In his diary he told of one more piece of bad luck:

> We left the command at 10 o'clock PM and started for our destination about 60 miles distant. Next morning at 8 o'clock about 100 of us reached the bridge across the Coosa river two miles from the foundries we were after. The other 100 had fallen by the way, their horses just falling in the road. The rest of us just run over them and left them. Only one stop was made during the night that was in crossing a small river in an old flat boat which was used as a ferry boat—the old man who owned the boat thought all the time that we were Rebels. When the last load was crossed over a big hole was cut in the bottom of the boat and started it downstream.[375]

That hole in the boat was another nail in the coffin of the raid.

Back at Blounts Plantation with Russell on his way, and the Confederates quiet on the opposite ridge, Streight withdrew cautiously to a thicket half a mile to the rear of their position, posting his men in ambush to wait for the Rebel advance. Forrest was suspicious of all of Streight's moves, having been caught several times in the previous days, and this time he smelled another trap. He sent his men on a flanking movement, prompting the Yankees to pull back and begin the move to Rome, down through the town of Centre. As the brigade moved out, a portion of the 73d remained to cover in case of attack. They sensed that Forrest was about to charge again, so they set fire to two buildings on the premises, lighting up the sky for some distance; that seemed to forestall any immediate Rebel charge.[376] Briedenthal indicated that part of the 3d Ohio stayed behind as well: "Late in the afternoon the greater portion of the command was sent forward while the Third Ohio was left behind as usual. After leaving our animals at the front, with every fourth man, we then burned the outbuildings, and the wall of the fences, down to one string, for protection. We then deployed out and awaited the rebels' approach; but in vain for they would not bite at the 'Yankee' hook."[377] That night, May 2, 1863, would determine the success or failure of the raid.

Forrest was now certain he would win the grueling contest, believing that Streight's men were almost totally exhausted. With this assurance, he allowed all but a small group of his scouts to camp, rest, eat and relax. For the next ten hours all of them took full advantage of the break; minutes after they stopped, silence fell over the entire camp. The rest not only brought relief to the men in camp but allowed those left behind in Gadsden to catch up and beef up the diminished numbers of the Forrest pursuit.

The inflated numbers of Rebel troops reported by young Haynes, plus the disturbing presence of the Confederates on his left, seemingly trying to get in his front, made Streight believe that another forced night march was required. He knew the risk; in his own words he said, ". . . though the command was in no condition to do so, . . ."[378] A third straight all-night march was almost the prelude to failure.

Their progress this time was pathetically slow. Streight reported, "I then decided to withdraw as silently as possible, and push on in the direction of Rome, but as a large number of the men were dismounted, their animals having given out, and the remainder of the stock was so jaded, tenderfooted, and worn down, our progress was necessarily slow; yet, as everything depended on reaching Rome before the enemy could throw a sufficient force there to prevent our crossing the bridge, every possible effort was made to urge the command forward."[379] Streight still had hope, in spite of all his setbacks.

Night had closed in on the Union column, which moved almost in a trance as the march continued on toward Centre, only a few miles from the plantation. As they approached the town, the scouts reported that Forrest had placed a roadblock in Centre; this report only strengthened Streight's decision to keep moving. In reality, Forrest's men were sleeping soundly near Blount's Plantation; the Federal scouts had seen some Home Guards who were not even aware of Streight's units.[380]

In order to by-pass this Confederate roadblock, Streight sent a substantial force to skirmish with the Confederate units in Centre, while he took the rest of the brigade on a roundabout route, joining the main road again some three miles past the town. Soon his skirmishers rejoined him, and the mood began to change to one of hope and optimism as they headed down the road to the ferry crossing of the Chattooga River. Here they hoped to sink the ferryboat and stall Forrest long enough to insure that they would reach Rome and destroy the more significant bridge there, which crossed the wider and deeper Coosa River. Streight was sure that would give him enough time to find new mounts, destroy the railroad, and do other damage to the industries of war.[381] Still, the men were tired, dead tired, almost past exhaustion, as they struggled on.

They had covered almost nineteen miles when they reached the Chattooga ferry and began a search for Russell's guard and the boat. Their hearts sank as they realized the boat was gone and there was no way to cross. Captain Russell had done the unforgivable: his failure to guard the ferry crossing had allowed Confederate citizens to sneak other boats away from the dock and hide them downriver. There were no boats for the Federals to use to cross the swift Chattooga. That could have been the final straw to the weary Streight, but he felt so close to success that he sought out his local guides, Unionist sympathizers who knew the area, and asked for solutions. The only solution appeared to be to head farther upstream to Dykes' Bridge and cross there. The now despondent column headed for Dykes', but it was the middle of the night, and they were in unfamiliar surroundings.

Off a fork to the left of the main road was the Round Mountain Iron Works. Streight was elated to find that at last he could do some actual damage to a Confederate war plant. Briedenthal's Company A, 3d Ohio, was detailed to destroy the Works.

> We then filed to the left and took the road leading to it, and came to it in a short time, where we dismounted and placed a guard over the animals, and the rest of us proceeded to destroy the mammoth establishment. It was designed originally for smelting iron, but has, within the last year, been undergoing great additions, until they had it almost completed for manufacturing a variety of the munitions of war, such as cannon, shell, etc., and was worth several millions to them. But through the agency of fire, applied by us, with the hearty cooperation of the negroes, who threw the first brands into their own sleeping-berths, we soon had the "heaven and earth" illuminated with the conflagration of one of Dixie's most valuable establishments.[382]

The 3d Ohio may have found their way, and the fire-light may have helped them get out of the area, but the rest of the brigade was floundering about in their mind-fogged daze, trying to find Dykes' Bridge. The area surrounding the Iron Works had been burned and gutted for fuel for the Works, and in place of the forest that used to be there was a charcoal-blackened, endless series of wagon ruts leading off in all directions. Wagons from the foundry had been used to take wood to the plant and to return with iron, crossing the open charred ground with little attention to a road of any kind. The scouts of Streight's command became confused and bewildered, leading the column off in several directions before they were able to decipher the land and once again head for the bridge.[383] During that frustrating time, units became separated, disoriented and confused in the pitch black night, causing more time delays before the right path could be found and the whole brigade controlled. It was a real-life version of a nightmare.

It is difficult to imagine the state of the brigade: exhausted, virtually starving and struggling just to stay in the saddle, passing over a miserable, surrealistic landscape of blackened ground. It was almost daylight when the bridge came into sight, undamaged by any action and usable for the swift crossing of the Yankee force. As soon as they had crossed, the torch was put to the timbered bridge to keep it from serving the same purpose for Forrest, who, as everyone knew, would be along soon. Even though there appeared to be little reason to hope that Forrest would be held up long enough for the Federals to get away from him, there was an immediate need to rest, water and feed the mounts and the bedraggled troops as well. Not the least of the problems were the animals, whose condition matched the troopers. Streight's report summarized: "Large numbers of the mules were continually giving out. In fact, I do not think at that time we had a score of the mules drawn at Nashville left, and nearly all of those taken in the country were barefooted, and many of them had such sore backs and tender feet that it was impossible to ride them...."[384] After three nights of riding, fighting and walking, without food or forage, the condition of the brigade was such that it was no longer a functional fighting unit; it was a group of stumbling automatons intent only on survival.

Time was running out for the beleaguered Provisional Brigade and its colonel. The irony of the moment was that on this same May 2, another Union raiding force under Colonel Benjamin Grierson was completing a startling raid down south through Mississippi, briefly cutting off communication for the Southern forces at Vicksburg, tearing up railroads, burning supplies, and drawing Confederate cavalry from all parts of Mississippi. Grierson had taken three regiments of cavalry south from La Grange, Tennessee, and with two of the three regiments, successfully completed his mission which began on April 17 and ended in Baton Rouge, Louisiana, on this date, May 2. He was part of the same Army of the Tennessee that provided General Rosecrans with the Dodge troops, although he finished his raid with General Nathaniel Banks' Department of the Gulf in Baton Rouge. His men, too, arrived in Baton Rouge exhausted, starved and saddle-sore, but were treated to a hero's welcome by Banks, and received plenty of food and rest. Streight's men on May 2, unlike Grierson's, had little to look forward to as dawn broke on May 3.

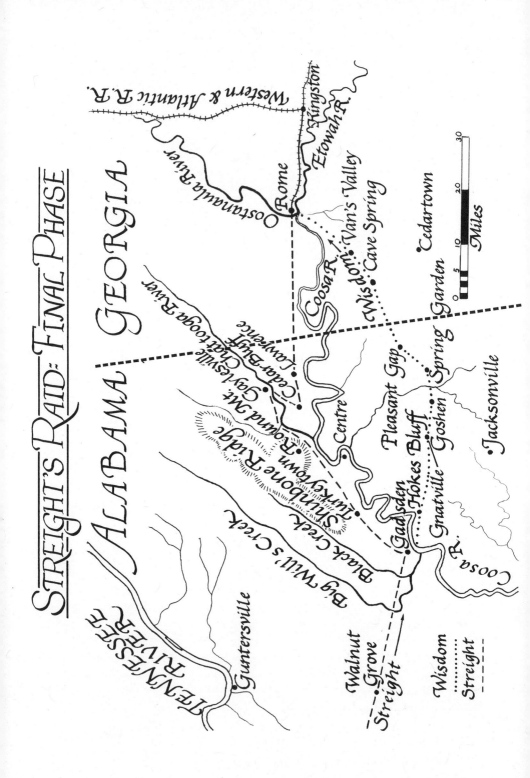

STREIGHT'S RAID: FINAL PHASE

TENNESSEE RIVER

ALABAMA   GEORGIA

Guntersville

Walnut
Grove
Streight

Big Will's Creek

Black Creek

Sind Mt.
Sandbone Ridge
Gaylesville
Round Mt.
Turkeytown
Cedar Bluff
Lawrence

Gadsden

Hokes Bluff

Pleasant Gap

Gnatville
Goshen
Spring Garden

Jacksonville

Centre

Coosa R.

Wisdom
Cave Spring
Van's Valley

Rome

Oostanaula River

Etowah R.
Kingston

Western & Atlantic R.R.

Cedartown

Wisdom ·········
Streight - - - -

Miles
0 5 10 20 30

CHAPTER 14

SUNDAY MAY 3

ROME, GEORGIA

It was after midnight May 2 when Rome received word from John Wisdom that the war was coming to Rome. As the hours pushed on toward dawn, the town prepared for Streight's arrival. The city of Rome had sent away its young men in the two years of war that preceded Streight's arrival. There remained, as has been said, some Confederate convalescent soldiers in the area, but the militia force was an untrained selection of under-and-overage men who had no real concept of the military or of combat. This was the manpower situation about one o'clock, as the word spread like wildfire through the city.

General George S. Black, the hotelier, was the head of the local militia, but there had been little interest in practicing the military skills usually associated with militia, so the group bore little resemblance to an organized force. When he was confronted with Wisdom's news, he set out to fortify the city.

Rome was a city built on two rivers, the Etowah coming from the east and the Coosa flowing north to south. As the river comes in from the north, it is called the Oostanaula, but when it joins the Etowah it becomes the Coosa.[385] The road from Alabama came toward town from the west, and in order to get into the city from the west, it was necessary to cross one of the city's two bridges, the bridge across the Coosa. The main city defense was centered on the covered bridge which crossed over the river on the Alabama Road.

As the church bells rang the alarm, crowds began to gather at the railroad station, looking for a way out of town. With all the noise of bells ringing, shouted warnings, and requests for help, Rome had become bedlam. One report indicated, "Within thirty minutes after his arrival, John Wisdom was in all probability the only man in Rome asleep."[386] One locomotive was on its way to Kingston, Georgia, but was to be back by dawn with other trains and troops. Another report gave more credit to the railroaders, saying, "The engineers of the Rome Railroad made trips into the countryside warning the people and bringing the planters who responded to the call to arms. They brought their squirrel rifles, muskets, and muzzle loading shotguns."[387]

The Coosa River was the highway of several steamboats which were threatened by the alarm; three of them: *Laura Moore, Alphretta* and *Chero-*

kee cut loose their lines and sailed upriver out of harm's way.[388] One of the residents made this entry in his war journal for May 3: "This morning at 2 o'clock, news came by Mr. Wisdom that the Enemy had destroyed his boats on the Coosa River at Gadsden, and also burnt the Depot or Warehouse at the same place, that it was done yesterday about 2 o'clock PM. The news created quite an excitement; a train left by 1/2 past 4 for Kingston, families commenced moving out, also the Civilians to arms."[389]

Much of the activity was providing combustible materials to be placed on the bridge over the river. The bridge was packed with bales of straw and saturated with turpentine in case the Yankees came close enough to threaten the town. Two cannons were placed on the riverbanks to cover the approach, and other roads had cotton bale barricades in case the troopers came from another direction. The following week the local paper made its report on the activity:

> The first intimation the people of Rome had was the arrival of Mr. John H. Wisdom, from Gadsden, giving information of the rapid approach of the Federals. Tremendous excitement, and be it said to the discredit of some, much liquor was wasted, doubtless to screw up their fighting point. By 8 PM [should be AM] two cannon, with barricades of cotton bags, were mounted and placed in position on the river bank. The citizens from the country flocked in with their rifles and squirrel guns, and there soon were enough to make a pretty formidable fight, if they had been under any sort of organization. But the organization amounted to as near none as possible.[390]

The tempest of activity in those early morning hours was a result of ignorance and the belief that Rome would stand—or fall—on its own. The citizens of Rome knew nothing about Forrest's presence nearby until his couriers arrived, well after Wisdom's alarm had been sounded. Wisdom knew nothing of Forrest's pursuit of Streight, so his warning of a Yankee column approaching had no reassurance of help at hand. Before Forrest's courier arrived, it was thought the closest Confederate troops were those under Bragg some sixty miles north.

One of the Confederates officers in Rome that May day was Lieutenant C. W. Hooper, of Stonewall Jackson's brigade, who was recruiting soldiers for the eastern commands. As one of the few experienced officers in the territory, General Black sought Hooper's assistance in raising a company of home guard troops. Hooper was able to gather fewer than two hundred men on such short notice, but it was enough for one company of reasonably efficient scouts under Hooper's leadership.[391] As scouts and videttes were being sent out at different intervals in different directions, Hooper's company was sent out toward the Alabama border, searching for the lead elements of the Yankee raiders.

The whole experience in Rome that night was caricatured in a rendition of the experience by "Bill Arp" (in real life Major Charles W. Smith) in the *Southern Confederacy* newspaper in Atlanta. This is a small portion of his story:

> *The yeomanry and the melishy jined a squad of Confederate troops and formed in line of battle. They were marched across the Oustanawly River, and then the plank of the bridge torn up so that they couldn't retreat. This were done, however, at ther own valyunt request, because of the natural weakness of the flesh. They determined, jintly and sevrally, firmly by these presents,* to do sumthin.
>
> *Two cracked cannon, what had holes in the ends, and two or three on the side, were propped up between the kotten bags, and pinted dead straight down the road to Alabam. They were fust loaded with buckshot and tacks, and then a round ball rammed on top. The ball were to take the raid in front, and the bullets and tacks to rake 'em in the phlanks. These latter it was supposed would go through the cracks in the sides and shoot around generally. Everybody and everything determined to die in their tracks,* or do sumthin.

Old Bill might have exaggerated slightly, but it was obvious from the papers that confusion did reign in those hours as they waited for the onslaught.

The *Southern Confederacy* on May 4 published a letter from a Rome Railroad conductor to a Mr. Stilwell, which supported the fact that reinforcements really were bound for Rome:

> *Kingston, May 3d, 1863*
>
> *Mr. C. H. Stilwell—Dear Sir: I learned this morning that the Yankees were below Rome, and that our men needed reinforcements. I then ran the train to Rome from this place to carry about seven hundred men, and have just returned, having learned the following particulars: General Forrest has overtaken the enemy at Gaylesville, Cherokee County, Alabama, about twenty miles west of Rome, and the courier stated that an engagement had taken place. The courier left before the fight closed, therefore we can't tell the result. I have a dispatch from General Forrest to General Bragg, asking for a force to be sent to Rome to check them. Their advance came within eight miles of Rome this morning and drove in our pickets. They number two hundred. Their whole force is about fifteen hundred. We have the bridges guarded, and feel confident of our ability to hold them. Mrs. Stilwell is at Oliver's. The bullets flew thick around your house, but your family are all*

safe. We do not fear any attack between here and Rome. The enemy burnt Noble's Iron Works. We need more men. If Forrest fails to check them, then good bye Rome.
    C. A. Smith
    Conductor of the Rome Railroad.392

The actions of the conductor were reminiscent of the performance of another Georgia railroad conductor whose persistence in pursuit doomed the Andrews Raid, just one year earlier.

While the townspeople spent the night preparing for an attack, the advance party of Streight's brigade, under Captain Milton Russell, rode all night. Their pace, determined by the condition of their animals and their men, was agonizingly slow. After crossing the Chattooga on the ferryboat without incident, they had moved on toward Rome. It was early on Sunday when they arrived close to town, camping at Shorter's plantation, just west of the recently fortified bridge across the Coosa. They had hoped to arrive some four hours earlier, before any alarms could be given and any reinforcements could arrive. They cautiously approached the city. Roach describes their advance:

> As Russell made his way toward Rome, he stopped a mail carrier headed for Gadsden, and convinced him to avoid trouble by returning to Rome.
>
> He at first declined accompanying "our boys" but the Captain assured him that the "Yankees" were but a short distance behind, and that if he continued his route, he would undoubtedly fall into their hands. It needed no further argument to induce him to "change front" and proceed with our men in the direction of Rome.
>
> Whether the Captain will consider it a compliment or otherwise, I will state that the rebel "post-boy" supposed he was one of Forrest's Colonels, consequently was very familiar and talkative, and furnished him with much valuable information concerning the numbers and disposition of the troops and defenses of the city. It is difficult to imagine his surprise and consternation when our men were attacked by the rebel pickets sent out from Rome—he turned instantly pale as a corpse, and tremblingly gasped that he "guessed the Yankees had already got him." [393]

The local Confederate newspaper gave a slightly different version of the approach of the scouts:

> About 9 o'clock AM a small body of the enemy's advance (about 200) reached the environs of the city, and were actually bold enough

to dismount and feed their horses almost in sight of the city. They picked up all the horses and mules in the neighborhood, took some citizens prisoners and reconnoitered the defenses of the city. Learning that we were prepared with artillery, they bivouacked and seemed to await the arrival of the main body.[394]

Another chance meeting that influenced the outcome of the raid was an encounter between Captain Russell and an elderly black lady, balancing a load of laundry on her head, who approached the Yankees as they made camp just outside Rome. Their conversation was overheard and later reported by a young Alabama resident, R. L. Lindsey, who had been taken prisoner as he drove his buggy on the Gadsden-Rome road. Russell questioned the woman thoroughly about the situation in Rome, and about its defenses. "General Forrest and this old woman saved the scalps of that crowd of old men and boys lined up behind their breastworks, effectively cut off by the stuffed bridge from retreat" was the analysis of one local historian.[395]

In the conversation, the lady convinced Russell that thousands of Confederate regulars were stationed in Rome, with more arriving with each train coming into town. Russell could see the fortification on the bridge, and make out the cannon, and his interrogation was enough to convince him that the town could not be successfully attacked.

The Yankees were always ready to believe that the Rebel numbers were greater than their own, and therefore usually made decisions based on inaccurate estimates of the enemy, encouraging excess caution. Had Russell arrived earlier, and had he found a shoal ford just a mile north of the bridge and marched his men into Rome, ignoring the defended bridge, he probably could have captured the city, its munitions factory and railroad.[396] But he did not. He went back to Shorter's house, called "Thornwood," and waited.

As the morning wore on, couriers arrived from Forrest, encouraging the Romans to hold off the raiders, that he would be there to help before long. That news was a relief to the city and they became considerably more confident of their future. What the Confederates did not know was that Russell had sent a courier back to Streight citing the reasons he could not take Rome: bridge defenses, number of troops, no fords and, the primary reason, the condition of his men.[397] The courier bringing this news to Streight brought the worst news that Streight could have received. Until that moment the Indiana colonel had expectations that Rome could still be taken, and the mission completed.

Lawrence, May 3, 1863

CHAPTER 15

SUNDAY MAY 3

RAID'S END—CEDAR BLUFF, ALABAMA

The sun was just rising as the last of Streight's brigade crossed Dykes' bridge over the Chattooga and set fire to its timber planks. The column must have been a picture to see: bedraggled, charcoal-dust covered, filthy from all the days and nights without a chance to bathe, riding on little donkeys or mounted on horses unfed for days, or, in many cases walking on blistered, aching, bleeding feet. It certainly would have been hard to tell a Confederate column from a Yankee force. Not only was their condition unkempt, but they were asleep in the saddle, or on their feet if a mount had given out. Streight's force could hardly be called any kind of a military unit by this time, but the regiments could still strike fear in the hearts of any neighborhoods through which they passed, looking like evil personified.

A drawing of Streight's men on this morning shows them neatly dressed and in disciplined, prone skirmish lines, but in truth they were virtually asleep as they finally halted near the Widow Lawrence's farm, and in most cases simply lay where they dismounted, so tired were they. They had crossed the bridge soon after daybreak, and the colonel knew they could go no further, although he was concerned about closing the distance between Russell and the main column.

By nine o'clock there was no more postponing. "The boys were so overcome with drowsiness that they would go to sleep on their animals; for we had not slept more than six hours in the last seventy-two, and had fought three general engagements, and rode one hundred and fifty miles."[398] So Streight called for a halt, hoping that firing the bridge had allowed him enough time to rest a bit, feed and water, and still stay ahead of his pursuers.

Near Blount's plantation the Confederates were awakened at sunrise and ordered to mount up. Ten hours of sleep had worked wonders on the Rebel troops. The men who had been almost incoherent with fatigue were now bright-eyed and revitalized, ready to roll on toward Rome and Streight. When General Forrest ordered them to move out, the entire command rode forward with an enthusiastic Rebel yell.

With virtually fresh men and horses, Forrest took his diminished force on the trail of the Yankees and covered the route up to Dykes' Bridge in less than three hours, the same distance that Streight had covered in his all-night marathon. The only bad news was that his two regiments, scouts and escorts were now down to just over five hundred men, but these were the toughest men, the ones who had kept up for reasons of pride or self-respect. This time his scouts knew the roads; the march over the difficult charcoal beds was in daylight and the column moved with some precision. As the column came to the ashes of Dykes' Bridge, Forrest galloped up and surveyed the river. He wasted no time, but ordered the men to strip, carry the ammunition over by hand, and haul the cannon with ropes across the muddy bottom. It took just an hour, and the Confederates were back in the saddle, horses hitched up to cannon, and ammunition all dry.

At some time in preceding days, Streight must have addressed his men, emphasizing the critical importance of the raid, and their part in the grand scheme of Union strategy. The Official Records cite a communication between Lieutenant General William Hardee in Bragg's camp in Tullahoma, Tennessee, and General Bragg on May 8, 1863: "I heard from Mr. Erwin, who arrived yesterday, that Forrest, in the pursuit of the enemy, was near enough on one occasion to hear Colonel Streight, the Federal commander, exhorting his men to stand up to their work; that his expedition was one of four on the military chess-board, and if it failed it would materially interfere with the success of the others."[399] The reference probably was to Grierson's Raid; Grant's move down the Mississippi; an infantry probe into Mississippi; and Streight's Raid.

It was just after nine o'clock on May 3, on a bright Sunday morning, when Forrest's advance party overtook the Yankee column, cooking its breakfast over open fires in an area aptly named "Straight-Neck Precinct."[400] The few buildings in the area marked the Lawrence farm, not far from Gaylesville, Alabama. The first sound of guns heard by the brigade became the sound of a stake being driven into the heart of the raid. But reflex action required the colonel to form his line of battles just behind the smoking breakfast fires, with the officers trying to rouse sleeping troopers covering the ground. The sketchy line was formed with the Yankees on their bellies behind a ridge but in an open field. "However, no amount of shaking and yelling could wake more than half of the soldiers, most of whom were dead to the world."[401] It spoke volumes about their condition to realize that the sounds of firing, bullets zipping by, and other noises of battle failed to waken those lying prone on the ground.

Forrest sent McLemore around the left, Biffle to the right, and his own scout and escort in the center, as he ordered his skirmishers to open fire on the Union brigade. Lytle's history went on to say: "His line, in crescent shape, fringed a wooded ridge. This was most opportune. It masked the exact number of troops he brought to the field."[402] No exact figures are known as to his real strength, but it did not exceed five hundred and was reported in one place as low as 420.[403] In the middle of the area was a significant hill, where the center of Forrest's line stood and added even more protection from Streight's view. It further masked his numbers and his movements.

Tired as he was, Streight tried to absorb his situation. Word had just been received from Russell that the Rome bridge was heavily defended and could not be taken; he was virtually out of ammunition for both his howitzers and the rifles of his men; everyone was in a state of exhaustion; and he learned from the scouts that the force on his left was still dogging his route. He had no escape routes, and he still believed that Forrest had vastly superior numbers. Nevertheless, he reacted swiftly and formed his line facing Forrest and ordered skirmishers to return the Confederate fire. But even as the bullets whizzed overhead, the Midwesterners fell asleep on the hard ground, lying on their stomachs, facing the enemy. Streight's report said, "The command was immediately ordered into line, and every effort made to rally the men for action, but nature was exhausted, and a large portion of my best troops actually went to sleep while lying in line of battle under a severe skirmish fire."[404]

Forrest used a new tactic at Cedar Bluff; "Bluff" was an appropriate term, as the Confederate general hornswoggled the invaders into surrender. Instead of a vicious mounted charge, he chose to keep his skirmishers firing, but sent a flag of truce under Captain Henry Pointer across the field toward Streight's center. The surrender demand issued to Streight was "in order to stop the further and useless effusion of blood."[405]

Streight had been convinced that the bridge over the Coosa into Rome was the key to any possible success of his mission. His officers shared that view. As Captain Pointer waited, Streight summoned his officers to a council to discuss possible surrender. The colonel made it clear that it was not possible to take the bridge in Rome. Streight reported, "Most of my regimental commanders had already expressed the opinion that unless we could reach Rome and cross the river before the enemy came up with us again, we should be compelled to surrender. Consequently I called a council of war."[406] He then set forth their predicament and they discussed any possible options. The colonel concluded,

> As I have remarked before, our ammunition was worthless, our horses and mules in a desperate condition, the men were overcome with fatigue and loss of sleep, and we were confronted by fully three times our number, in the heart of the enemy's country, and although personally opposed to surrender, and so expressed myself at the time, . . . I yielded to the unanimous voice of my regimental commanders, and at once entered into negotiations with Forrest to obtain the best possible terms I could for my command. . .[407]

(Again there was the misconception that Forrest had vast numbers of men. By now Forrest was the underdog three to one, but Streight still believed his was the smaller force by the same ratio.) There are several variations in the reports of those negotiations, but the scenario is generally the same, although not acknowledged by Streight. The brigade commander requested a meeting with Forrest, and rode out under his own flag of truce to meet him. According to Forrest's later version of the meeting, Streight refused surrender unless Forrest could show him the superior strength that Streight believed he had.

At this juncture a section of Ferrell's battery, the only artillery Forrest had in reach, galloped up in full sight. When Streight protested against movement of troops nearer a certain ridge while negotiations were going on under a flag of truce, Forrest sent Captain Pointer to order the artillery back. The alert young captain, responding to a covert nod from his commander, enlarged upon the order to such an extent that the same two guns appeared, disappeared and reappeared at so many points as to seem almost a column of artillery.[408]

As Forrest described the scene afterwards, he was standing with his back to the guns, while Streight faced them. "I seen him all the time we was talking," Forrest was quoted as having said, "looking over my shoulder and counting the guns. Presently he said, 'Name of God! How many guns have you got? There's fifteen I've counted already!' Turning my head that way, I said, 'I reckon that's all that has kept up. . .' "[409]

The infantry regiments used the same tactics; McLemore and Biffle shifted their men in and out of sight as the negotiations between the two commanders continued, sending couriers from non-existent units. Streight pressed Forrest once again: he would surrender if he could see that Forrest outnumbered him, but Forrest maintained that would be an insult to his men, and refused to parade his troops, knowing full well what the results of such a parade would be. Forrest then offered Streight some refreshments, a drink or two. Captain Pointer made a "pointed" suggestion that he should accept the drink as it might be his last. The play-acting of the Rebels was without flaw, and the cumulative effect of troop movements and banter led the colonel to believe that surrender was his only option.

Finally Streight was convinced, and they began to set out the terms of surrender. It was agreed that:

1. Each regiment would be permitted to retain its colors.
2. The officers were to retain their side-arms.
3. Both officers and men were to retain their haversacks, knapsacks and blankets; and all private property to be respected and retained by the owner.
4. Both officers and men were to be paroled and sent north within ten days.[410]

These terms, agreed upon by both sides, concluded the negotiations and Streight rode back to his brigade.

Still Streight had doubts about the strength of the Confederate force. If Gen. Forrest were lying, he would look foolish. On the other hand, if the Rebel command was as large as it seemed, continued resistance could only be a waste of the lives of his men, and he would become known not only as a fool, but as a butcher of his own command. Streight decided to leave the final decision up to his subordinate officers. He returned to confer with them, and they voted unanimously to capitulate. The Confederate cavalrymen waited nervously as the Federal force nearly three times their number stacked their weapons.[411]

Streight's report then stated simply, "And at about noon, May 3, we surrendered as prisoners of war."

The raid was over, just twenty-one miles from its goal. But the ripple effect was just beginning.

Forrest was not out of the woods yet. If Streight were to discover he had vastly superior numbers, the Yankees could probably still whip their Southern pursuers. So when Streight requested that his men be allowed to mount up, ride to an open field and stack arms, Forrest had no real choice except to agree even though he still feared a fight. Private Whitsitt of the Forrest 4th Tennessee remembered the scene:

The place was crowded with undergrowth, and Streight proposed to march down the road until they should find an open field suitable for the business of laying down his arms. Forrest gave assent, and in a few minutes we were in the road, which shortly became a lane with immense fields of growing cotton on each side. That was the longest lane I ever traveled. It may have been a mile, but it seemed ten miles in length. Streight had about fourteen hundred and fifty men, and we had about four hundred and seventy-five in line. We were drawn up on both sides of them, and every man of them carried a loaded rifle and some likewise loaded pistols. If they had concluded to renew the struggle, it is difficult to understand how any of us could have escaped alive. Forrest galloped up and down the column and busily gave orders to couriers to ride to the rear and order imaginary regiments and imaginary batteries to stop and feed their animals and men. But the regiment of Starnes [McLemore] and Biffle and Ferrell's Battery, which had been depleted to skeleton proportions, were the only available troops within one hundred miles.

Finally, the lane came to an end, and there was a field of broom sedge on the right-hand side. Colonel Streight led the way, and his troops shortly formed in line. Then at the word of command they dismounted, stacked arms, remounted and rode away. There was an inexpressible sense of relief when they parted company with their arms and ammunition; but we did not venture to suggest the fewness of our numbers until we had delivered them safely to the keeping of the guards whom the government had dispatched to Rome to receive them.[412]

Before they formed to stack their weapons, Briedenthal wrote that one of the 3d Ohio took his Henry rifle, which had been presented to him by a previous regimental commander, and ". . . broke it and stuck it in a mud-hole. I bent mine, as did others, so they would shoot, like old Blackburn's rifle—around a tree or a hill!"[413] The stacking ritual greatly relieved Forrest, knowing that without weapons, the Yankees were truly his prisoners.

Forrest quickly segregated the officers from the men, assigning Colonel Biffle and the 9th Tennessee to watch the enlisted men, while he gathered the officers with McLemore's 4th Tennessee. It is not entirely certain when Streight discovered the true size of Forrest's remaining troops, but when he found the real strength to be considerably less than his own force, he was outraged; he asked to have his arms back so they could have another crack at their harassing pursuers, but Forrest simply laughed and replied, "Ah, colonel, all's fair in love and war you know!" and the matter was finished.[414]

According to several regimental histories, Streight was allowed to make a brief speech to his men before they were all separated. Streight thanked them for their endurance and faith and wished them well in the future. He ended by "calling upon them to give three cheers for the Union, which were given with a burst of enthusiasm. General Forrest was present, but made no objection to this as he respected brave men wherever found, and had gained a great victory over these."[415]

The story of the surrender is hard to verify exactly. Forrest himself told parts of it some years later; newspapers, memoirs and other sources set forth embellished accounts of the surrender and reactions to it. However, the fact remained that Streight with his 1,400-plus men surrendered to Forrest who had fewer than six hundred. Streight had little choice; his men were exhausted, animals worn out, two regimental commanders dead, ammunition useless and escape cut off. But it was a humiliation for U.S. arms.

One of the Southern ladies who lived near Cedar Bluff wrote about her memory of that day: "Their arms were stacked a half mile from our house and the hungry men poured in. The large gate was opened in front of our house and wagons and tents were taken into the grove. Every negro on the place was put to work with pot, oven and skillet cooking for the exhausted soldiers. I continued serving till midnight, serving one table after another."[416]

The Streight force would enter Rome, but not quite as they had expected to. They would be the vanquished, not the victor. The Yankee enlisted men were marched only part of the twenty-one miles to town, where they were permitted to rest and camp for the night. "... marched thirteen miles, and saw more citizens than we had seen for the last one hundred miles. I cannot account for this difference in the population upon any other hypothesis than this: that those behind, hearing the 'Yanks' were coming, had done like the old Negro—'taken to the hills.'"[417]

Then the age-old practice of barter began for the men who had been trying to kill each other just hours before. Briedenthal explained, "Many of the boys sold their penknives for five dollars, and rubber blankets for ten dollars, they, (the rebs) jocosely remarking that the 'blockaders' were upon them. On the other hand we paid fifty cents for corn cakes made of unsifted meal, with no salt in them and dried by the fire, and no larger than a common sized biscuit."[418] He compared the Yankees to "lost Sheep," wandered from Father Abraham's fold, who have fallen into "wolves in sheep's clothing." But after supper they lay down and peacefully went to sleep.

The officers were shepherded down the road to Rome by McLemore's men, led by Forrest himself. They were only a few miles from Rome when the column ran into Captain Russell's advance force coming back from Rome. After Russell decided the bridge was too tough a nut to crack, he sent his courier to his commander, mounted his force and headed back for the main body. James Lawson Brown wrote in his diary, "After skirmishing with a lot of home guards and convalescent soldiers until late in the afternoon we gave up the idea of crossing the river and started back on the same road we came—going back two or three miles we met General Forrest and regiment of cavalry with Colonel Streight and his staff they having surrendered early in the morning."[419] In an earlier entry, Brown had related, "On May 1st, Gen Rhody came up with Forrest here with reinforcements making his force about 8000 men while we had less than 2000." [420] The old game of overestimating continued. Private William W. Wallis of Company F, 80th Illinois, wrote home on May 26: "When within three miles of the Georgia Line we met three rebel brigades with nine cannon placed all ready for us."[421]

Russell was astonished to see the Yankee column with Confederate outriders guarding the leaders of the brigade. Streight called to him that he must surrender as the brigade had done. Russell acquiesced. With tears in his eyes he claimed he preferred death to surrender, but was given no chance to die, so he surrendered the last of the brigade. Numbers differ slightly, but in all approximately 1,650 Yankee soldiers with their arms, animals and wagons, had been taken out of the fight. Forrest with the Union officers rode as fast as their still-weary mounts would take them, reaching Rome about 6:00 PM on Sunday. As the Forrest guard and the blue-coat officers came into sight of the city, the old cannons, brought down to the river for defense of the city, were both fired in salute as a tribute to Forrest, but someone forgot to unload the pieces. "Insisting on firing an artillery salute, shotted guns were discharged with such carelessness, and in the direction of the very road of General Forrest's approach to the town, as barely to miss him."[422]

The town had been notified of Streight's surrender; the early-morning terror had been forgotten, and the scene was one of pure joy. The streets were filled with citizens anxious to see both the hero Forrest and the beaten Yankees. Many anecdotes have surfaced about what may or may not have happened on the streets of Rome during the celebration. One, in particular, was repeated in a number of publications:

Now that there was no danger from them, the Romans offered Streight and his raiders the hospitality of their town. But the brave, unfortunate commander of the Mule Brigade, as he thought about the ruse which had been practiced upon his credulity, could not enter into the spirit of the entertainment. Captain Anderson, his face shiney and his flaxen hair all cleaned after his march, saw the Colonel's glum looks. He went over, and in a brotherly fashion, laid his heavy arm about the raider's shoulder.

"Cheer up, Colonel," he said, "this is not the first time a bluff has beat a straight." [423]

It is true that the raiders were treated reasonably well in their short stay in Rome. The officers were put up in the Etowah Hotel that Sunday night, although some had to sleep on the floor. The men camped on the ground miles outside of town, but, with no guard duty, picket or other duties to perform, they all, officers and men alike, had their first full night's sleep in four days.[424]

On Monday May 4, the 11th Tennessee Cavalry and parts of the 53d Alabama came riding into town from the north, having heard about Streight's capture. They had been the ever-present force that kept Streight looking over his left shoulder, waiting for that moment when the left flank would be hit. Soon after they arrived, the Federal enlisted men rode into the city about 10:00 AM and were stared at by many as the first live Yankees they had ever seen. The treatment was not totally cordial. Briedenthal wrote of one unpleasant incident:

They offered several insults, but we did not accept them, but exhibited our indifference and independence by standing aloof upon our dignity, with one notable exception worthy of recital. Some man had bawled out, "So you came to take Rome, and Rome took you," which one of the boys retorted with "The h—ll you did! I can't see it in that light, for when our two hundred and fifty advance came within range of the city, not one of your skulking citizens could be found, and had we orders to take this place, we would have taken it. You talk of taking us! Forrest took us; you take nothing! You belong to the Royal Stand-backs, who are the last in and first out, when there is any fighting to be done!" The citizen vanished.[425]

The initial attitude of the Romans seemed to include the prisoners in the festivities, probably because Forrest insisted in providing decent housing and food. Mrs. George Ward who lived in Rome wrote, "He told us that his prisoners were coming into town, and he wanted them to have rations. He said, also, that his own men had been riding hard . . . and he wanted something for them to eat at once."[426] Even Lieutenant Roach acknowledged, "We remained in Rome until Tuesday morning, May 5, under orders of General Forrest, who, to his credit be it said, furnished us with sufficient rations for our subsistence, and also with comfortable quarters."[427] A Southerner veteran remembered long after the war:

When the prisoners and the Confederate Escort were within four miles of Rome, the high hills which adjoined the place were filled with militia scouts, who evidently intended to carry out General Forrest's request to prevent the enemy from entering Rome. As the Confederates entered Rome with the prisoners, the streets were alive with its citizens, including many refugees from Tennessee, and some two thousand men in hospitals, who turned out to welcome and greet their deliverers. Every honor was given to officers and men and unstinted hospitality, which embraced even the Federal officers to some extent.[428]

"Bill Arp," writing in the Atlanta *Southern Confederacy*, and in his own way, summed up the events in Rome:

Well, Mr. Editurs, you know the sequil. The Generul bagged 'em and broght 'em on. The planks were put back on the bridge. The river bank infantry countermarched and fired a permiscous volley in token of jewbilee. One of the side-swipin cannon went off on its own hook, and the ball went ded through a house and tore a buro all to flinders. . . .

By and by the Comanchy Skouts and pickets all cum in, and shuk ther ambrosial locks and received the congratulations of their friends. Then began the ovashun of fair women and brave men to Gen. Forrest and his gallant boys. Bokays and tears were all mixed up promiskous. Big chunks of cakes and gratitude were distributed generally and frequent. Strawberries and cream, eggs and inyuns, pies and pancakes–all flew around amazin, for everybody was determined to do sumthin. Gen. Forrest subsided and General Jewbilee tuk command, and Rome herself again. The 4 pronged forks and silver spoons ros from the dead and even the old hen what one of our city aldeman had burried with her head out was disinterred and sacrificed immediately for the good of the kountry.

Thus hav ended the raid, and no loss on our side. Howsumever, I suppose that Mr. Linkhorn will keep "peggin' away."

Yours truly and immensely,

THE ORTHOR

Adjective General of Yeomanry.[429]

The treatment of the prisoners in Rome varied, according to different sources. Private Wallis wrote on May 26, "After this surrender they took all of our blankets, canteens, haversacks and half starved us."[430] Briedenthal thought that treatment by Forrest's men was decent, but exposed to the citizens of Rome, nothing was sacred. On May 5 he wrote, "Thus far we have been treated well the enemy—I mean by the soldiers, by Forrest's men especially, who have used us as a true soldier will treat a prisoner."[431] That attitude did not include the townspeople: "On their march they were reviewed by citizens, who lined the road curious to see the 'Yankees,' this being the first command to penetrate so far into their country. Many of them were very insolent and disagreeable. The guards were otherwise, being courteous and respectful, showing the difference between 'stay-at-homes' and those in actual service."[432]

As soon as they were out of Forrest's control, treatment became harsh, and the surrender terms agreed to by Forrest gave way to the bitterness of the locals, getting their first look at the enemy. By the time the Federals left Rome, they had little left in the way of personal possessions. "[A]s we passed out, the officers (home guards) stripped us of our oil and wool, blankets; and those that had their overcoats on their arms had to leave them; haversacks, canteens, tin cups, platters, knives and forks, watches, finger-rings, penknives and some had their money taken from them. All this was 'private property.' So much for Southern faith."[433]

For the men of the brigade, the events moved routinely, if not swiftly, toward their return to the north. The official notice that they were free for reassignment came in a release issued by Colonel William H. Ludlow, the Union's Agent for Exchange of Prisoners, on May 30, 1863: "I have the honor to report that the following officers and men have been declared duly exchanged as prisoners of war since the announcement in General Orders, No. 117 dated May 9, 1863." The list included, "All the officers and enlisted men of the Fifty-first Regiment Indiana Volunteer Infantry, of the Seventy-third Regiment Indiana Volunteer Infantry, of the Third Regiment Ohio Volunteer Infantry, of the Eightieth Regiment of Illinois Volunteer Infantry, and of the First Tennessee Cavalry, forming part of Streight's brigade and captured near Cedar Bluff, Ga., about the 1st of May, 1863." [434] The order had a few flaws; one, the officers of these regiments had not been exchanged; two, Cedar Bluff was in Alabama, not Georgia; and three, the capture was May 3, not May 1. The future of the brigade officers was still under consideration as the exchange process was underway.

The only officers who were being exchanged were the surgeons and the chaplains. On May 28 Surgeon S. F. Myers of the 73d reported that he was in Annapolis after being exchanged, as well as surgeons Wilson Pottenger, 73d; Henry King, 51st; and W. L. Peck and T. C. Clasen, 3d Ohio.[435] The rest of the officers, including Surgeon William Spencer, who was captured after being left behind with the wounded at Day's Gap, still resided in Libby Prison in Richmond.

When Forrest and Streight concluded their negotiations, they both believed that the Federal officers and men would have a short taste of life behind the Rebel lines, then be exchanged and go back to their home states in short order. That was the usual way of doing things when whole units were captured. But even as the two agreed on the fourth surrender condition, that officers and men would be paroled and exchanged within ten days, the rules were changing.

EPILOGUE

General Forrest was feted in Rome, and a big celebration was planned for May 6. However, he was ordered out on the 5th, so missed the big party; he was given a beautiful horse named "King Philip" by the Southern citizens, and another by citizens of Rome. King Philip survived the war and was put out to pasture, then died in 1873. The Confederate Congress in February 1864 issued a "Thanks of the Confederate Congress to General Nathan B. Forrest and the men of his command" for this capture, Chickamauga and West Tennessee service.[436] He was promoted to Major General December 6, 1863, and Lieutenant General on February 28, 1865. Forrest survived the war but did not prosper in business and died in Memphis in 1877.

Lieutenant Gould of Forrest's artillery was transferred to another unit as soon as the campaign ended. In a moment of anger, he confronted Forrest and after a few hot words Gould shot the general. Forrest, badly wounded, still managed to hold Gould, open his pocket knife and stab the lieutenant, who lived for only two days. Forrest recovered.

Emma Sansom married an Alabama soldier, C. B. Johnson, and moved to Texas in 1879, raised seven children, and died at fifty-three in 1900. There is a monument to her memory in downtown Gadsden at the foot of the Coosaw River bridge.

John Wisdom returned to Gadsden and lived there until his death in 1909 at eighty-nine, leaving seven surviving children. The grateful citizens of Rome gave Wisdom a silver service valued at $400, $400 in cash, and sent $400 to Mrs. Hanks who had loaned him the lame pony.[437]

Colonel Hathaway was buried on Blount's farm, and his body was eventually shipped back to his wife in Indianapolis for permanent burial, but not until December 8, 1866.

Indiana's Roll of Honor summarizes his fifty years of life: "As a lawyer, he was successful; as a citizen he was esteemed for his honesty and uncompromising integrity; as a neighbor and a friend, he was beloved for his generosity and fine social qualities; and as a Christian soldier he feared only his God."

Colonel Sheets disappeared from the records. Nothing is known of him, except that he was buried "in a Southern grave."

Up until 1949 the graves of a number of men killed at Blount's Plantation were well marked and well tended, but sometime around 1950 they were plowed under and lost to history.[438]

Dr. Spencer resigned from the 73d Indiana and became Surgeon of the 10th Tennessee (Northern) Infantry; he survived the war.

Celia Murphree married John C. Renau in 1864. He had been wounded in the Confederate Army at Nashville; they raised six children and remained in Alabama. Celia died at age fifty-eight in 1899.

Winnie Murphree married Asa Bynum, a Southern soldier, and they moved to Ellis County, Texas. No record of their deaths survive, but they were buried near their Texas home.

Captain Edmund Jones of the 80th Illinois, killed at Days Gap, had been captured and paroled in October 1862 in Kentucky, and had been promoted to command of Company F in December 1862.

Captain Anderson and Corporal Gibson, of the Chattooga River episode, both survived the war.

Casualties of the raid are difficult to determine. In Streight's report, written almost eighteen months after his capture, he estimates a loss of fifteen officers and one hundred thirty men killed and wounded during the raid. Bragg made no report of Forrest's losses, and few records exist to form an estimate.

The dead from the April 30 battles were interred by Dr. Spencer in a small graveyard in what is now Battleground, Alabama. The cemetery mentioned by Spencer as "Union Burying Ground" no longer exists, but some locals believe that the Days Old War Cemetery might be it. "Mr. Staples (contributor) said that his father told him that Streight's soldiers fired on the Confederates near Days Gap and a skirmish ensued. Some were wounded and died. The bodies were placed in a barn over night and carried the next day to the present site."[439] The cemetery is just northwest of Battleground, just over the line into Morgan County.

A monument next to Alabama Highway 9 near Cedar hollys springs, Alabama, marks the surrender of the raiders. "This marks the place where Gen. N. B. Forrest and 322 men captured Colonel A.D. Streight with 1466 men May 3, 1863."

The 51st Indiana and 73d Indiana were reorganized and reassigned to the Army of the Cumberland in December 1863. The 80th Illinois was sent back to Nashville about the same time. The 3d Ohio was reassigned to guard duty in Tennessee. The companies of the 1st Middle Tennessee rejoined the 1st Alabama Cavalry and operated in northern Alabama for the remainder of the war.[440]

At the time of the raid, the state government of Georgia had decreed that any troops raised in Georgia should be used only within the state, but after Streight's Raid, Forrest offered Hooper's company a chance to stay with his cavalry division in Tennessee. Eighty-six members of the company elected to stay with Forrest. The company did excellent service and stayed with Forrest until he surrendered in Gainesville, Alabama, May 11, 1865.[441]

CHAPTER 16

APRIL 30 TO MAY 5

DAYS GAP, ALABAMA—THE WOUNDED

Dr. William Spencer was the only real doctor left behind with the Streight wounded at Days Gap on April 30. He was assisted by eight volunteer "nurses" to attend to the needs of the wounded. There were fifty-three casualties; some were slightly wounded, some critically, but all needed some care and encouragement as the Confederate cavalry surrounded them. Spencer counted six who died, and other records indicate at least two others who died of wounds after release by the Confederates; one of these was Colonel Sheets. The list of wounded was painstakingly recorded with the names, regiments and, in some cases, wounds.

The injured soldiers were lucky; the twenty-nine-year-old Indiana doctor had had a good deal of medical training, graduating from Jefferson Medical College, and also served as an adjunct professor of Medicine and Surgery at Cincinnati College of Medicine and Surgery. His medical experience was far greater than his military experience; he had been in the 73d Indiana less than thirty days when they left Nashville.

According to Spencer and Lieutenant Roach, the Rebel cavalry decided that captured goods were theirs for the taking, and a methodical stripping of the wounded, and the supplies left with them, began almost at once. Dr. Spencer's journal is decidedly prejudiced as he indignantly recounts his stay behind enemy lines: "But their bottomless Confederacy is founded on a system of lies, as black as sin. Can we suppose they propagate their wicked scenes without lying even to one another?"[442] The doctor digresses on occasion to scold the Southerners for their many sins.

It was difficult for the brigade to abandon their own people, wounded and helpless, so they left as many provisions for them as was possible. Sadly, the wounded would not have the provisions for long. The 51st Indiana regimental history strongly condemned the exploitation of these weak and injured men by the Rebels:

Not only was the bread, meat, sugar and coffee taken, but even the medical stores and instruments were carried off; leaving our poor, wounded boys in a half-naked and starving condition. Even combs, pocket-knives and other articles of use were forced from the helpless sufferers by those gallant and chivalrous representatives of that most phenomenal "uprising of the people," whose souls have been fed on the fallacious conceit that one of their half-caste soldiers was equal to five Northern pure-blooded freemen. They were, in villainy.[443]

This regimental history also recounts that the wounded were subject to the agonies of lying untreated. Their wounds and their fractures were untended, as the tide of battle moved on and the Confederate troops, except for the guards, moved out after Streight. "In consequence of such brutality, many laid there and suffered horrible agony from undressed wounds and starvation, until death put an end to their misery."[444] That may have been an exaggeration of the situation, but it certainly was an unhappy plight for those left behind. The plundering of the Yankees was understandable, given the shortage of all goods, medical and otherwise, that plagued Southern troops, and most particularly the Forrest troops who had been in action for almost two weeks with little chance of resupply.

One saving grace for the injured was the presence of friendly civilians, who made every effort to provide the little extras that made survival possible. Although the Confederate guards tried to keep the Yankees from the reach of the Loyalist Alabamians, there were numerous cases of civilians being able to surreptitiously slip a ration or some other item of comfort to a wounded soldier. "The loyal citizens would gladly have afforded all the comfort and relief in their power; but the brutal rebel guard would not allow the poor sufferers to receive a cup of milk even, nor a piece of bread, from that source. The ingenious tact of woman occasionally was too much for the vigilance of the rebel sentinel; and some of our boys were the grateful recipients of some kind of favor, or of some article of food smuggled to them."[445]

On the morning of May 1, Spencer brought his helpers together to bury the dead in the Davis Church Yard; then they managed to carry all the wounded back to Days Gap, the scene of the earlier fighting. Spencer makes no mention of how that was accomplished, but simply states that the wounded were moved.[446] Spencer records that fifty-three Union soldiers were killed, wounded and captured. By actual count of the various regiments in their daily reports or their histories, in addition to the fifty-three on Spencer's list, there were at least twelve other deaths at Days Gap and Crooked Creek.

For the next eight days the wounded lay outside, with little or no cover or shade, with the hot Alabama sun beating on them. It was a full-time effort to keep dressings and wounds clean, to keep the flies and other insects, as well as maggots, from inflicting even more unhappiness on those too helpless to move. During the battle and after, Dr. Spencer and the brigade staff amputated limbs of four of the soldiers, and all four lived to be discharged from the service. Two of them, members of the 73d Indiana, were listed as still living in a publication of the 1900 reunion of the regiment held in South Bend, Indiana, September 5 and 6, 1900. One of the two was Corporal James J. Farris who had his left arm amputated, and shortly afterward his right hand.[447] The other amputee from the 73d was Robert Crandall who lost his right arm at Days Gap.

While the damaged Yankees lay on the field in Days Gap, Spencer noted,

> *Citizens, men, women and children, for many miles around, came to see "the wounded Yankees," and at the end of the second day we saw these thoughtless creatures carry off the last remnant of our before too scanty supply of army bread, and bacon, which had been left to us by our friends at their departure. Now all those requiring amputations, and other surgical operations, had been treated and the wounds of each as often dressed as necessary. How true "The blast is tempered to the shorn lamb." We would have suffered for the substantials of life, but for the fact that there were many Union women, as well as old men and boys, in the mountains round about us. These would occasionally visit us bringing a bucket of buttermilk, some corn bread, and perhaps some honey or stewed dried apples. These angelic creatures have our perpetual blessing, and, as I write, I rejoice with them, that through the vigorous policy of General Rosecrans, their homes are now permanently within our lines, where the reign of terror and despotism will never again reach them.*[448]

On May 2 Charles W. Anderson, Forrest's adjutant general, came to Spencer with the parole form, and it was signed by all members of the Yankee hospital then under the doctor's care. Spencer himself was given "a protection paper" which is quoted as follows:

> *Surgeon William Spencer of the United States Army, is in charge of the Wounded of Colonel Strait's Brigade, Officers and Soldiers of the Confederate Army, will in all cases, and under all circumstances respect his rights and personal liberty in the performance of his duties to the Wounded of his Command.*
> *By command of Brig. Gen'l Forrest*
> *Davis Gap Chas. W. Anderson*
> *May 2, 1863 Major & a.a.g.*

The parole meant little on the day it was signed; there had been no procedures for releasing anyone, and besides, few of them were able to be moved. However, at the end of the eighth day, May 9, the battalion guarding the hospital, Major Wheeler's Battalion of Colonel Roddey's Regiment, pulled out to rejoin Roddey, who was headed for Tuscumbia, and, according to Spencer, "with them went the last of our contentious guards."[449]

The Confederate troop movement meant more to the wounded than they knew. It meant that those loyal mountain people could open their homes to the injured Yankees, and they did so generously. The same day that the guards left, a large number of "Union folks" came in ox-carts, wagons and buggies, offering to take the wounded into their homes.

> *With these our wounded were carefully removed as possible, and by midnight were distributed by one's, two's, and three's according to the abilities of the proprietor or the severity of the wound, to the farmers among the valley below where Wheeler's men had been camped. I was surprised at the unreserved expression, now on every hand, for the Union. Men, Women and Children, with few exceptions, espoused Colonel Streight's cause and hoped, "Streight would continue to <u>larrap</u> (in their peculiar paraphrase) Forrest, twice a day until his whole command was destroyed, or the Confederacy gutted."*[450]

It was these poor people of the mountains who had struggled with the war, holding to their beliefs in the Union in spite of some cruel oppression by the Confederate Home Guard. This was one of their first opportunities to show their sympathy for not just the Union cause, but the soldiers who offered up their lives and limbs for that same cause.

Spencer acknowledged the importance of these Union sympathizers:

> *Justice, to those noble hearted spirits who took into their homes our wounded, from their uncomfortable position on the battlefield, demands (in-as-much as their homes are now permanently located within our lines) a tribute of respect. This perhaps cannot be more fittingly done than by giving to the public their names, as well as the names of those to whom they exhibited so much kindness while helplessly wounded and left alone in the enemy's country.*

> *Simon Witham (Orderly Sergeant) Co. I 73d Indiana was taken care of by Mr. Joseph Staunton (an old citizen).*
> *A.V.H. Foote Co. F 73d Indiana, James J. Farris Co. K 73d, Andrew Pyle Co. F 51st Indiana, Henry B. McCauley Co. F 80th Illinois [probably Henry B. McCaseley Co. I 51st Indiana] were taken care of by Mr. James Gipson.*
> *Captain James Sheets commander 51st Indiana and Lieut. John A Welton Co. E 51st Indiana were cared for by Mrs. Colonel Davis.*
> *William House Co. D 80th Illinois by Turrentines.*
> *James Moroney Co. F 51st Indiana by Mr. Thomas Wallace.*
> *Francis M. McIntosh Co. B 80th Illinois by Mr. J. F. Wood.*
> *Lieut. Edwin Reed Co. I 3d Ohio by A. H. Harris.*

Cyrus Lowthain Co. B 51st Indiana and Henry E. Huntley Co. B 73d Indiana by Mrs. Minter.

John Holm Co. D 80th Illinois by Levi Crawford.

Robert Crandall Co. F 73d Indiana by James P. Roberts.

James Hamsom Co. G 80th Illinois by Ellis Stringer.

Samuel B. Keeler Co. A 80th Illinois by Jackson Wilhite.

Wm. W. Gallagher Co. F 80th Illinois and James H. Jenkins Co. A 80th Illinois by William Morris.

One of the most poignant was the case of Thomas D. McCulloch of Co. D 1st Tennessee Cavalry (1st Alabama Cavalry). Shot in the lung, he was taken to his mother's home in Decatur, Alabama, where he died soon afterward.[451]

To Spencer, these citizens, still in Rebel country, were the true heroes of the raid. While Spencer was among these loyal citizens of Alabama, it began to shape his thinking of Southern attitudes, and how they might be changing. While these mountain people were, for the most part, non-slaveholders and people of meager means, they were still Alabamians and represented a portion of that Southern state.

> *It is a fact beyond dispute or doubt, and becoming more palpable every day that people of the slave states, the great mass, the non slave holder, the "bone and sinew" of the country, are really opposed to the institution of Slavery, and in favor of getting rid of it; that they are becoming more and more of this way of thinking every day; and that they are likely to accept the President's plan of reconstruction or reunion—not tardily, reluctantly and as the least of two evils, but willingly and gladly, as the best of all plans."[452]*

Apparently Spencer really believed that attitudes were changing in the South, as he was undoubtedly influenced by the Union sympathizers in that area. Those views, however, were rare in other parts of the South.

By May 19 Spencer found his mission at an end, and he left his wounded soldiers in their citizen homes:

> *The wounded men now no longer need my assistance. Good nursing is all they require, and I can no longer delay reporting myself as ordered to the Provost Marshall at Decatur, Alabama. I accordingly take a hasty farewell of my wounded friends, as well as those whose loyalty has so long stood the test—I take a last lingering look at the "Union burying ground" in Davis' Church Yard; vividly I again see the heroism in battle of those whose remains lie here. I am reminded of individual suffering and death of each. I shed a silent tear o'er their graves and bid them farewell forever.[453]*

Spencer's ordeal, however, was not finished. It would be many months before he would see his Indiana home again. Spencer left for Decatur, Alabama, to report to the Confederate authorities and was sent to Libby Prison to join the rest of the brigade officers.

Four of Spencer's nurses were from the 80th Illinois: James McCaughan, Benjamin F. Davison, Henry Miller and Nicholas B. Jones. Three were from the 51st Indiana: Floyd Dickinson, John Misner and W. E. Stafford. And one was from the 73d Indiana: Wm. Hammerly. All were captured with Doctor Spencer. Spencer's summary of his patients was, "These men will all recover, with the exception of two, and for these I can do nothing that nurses cannot do."[454] Which two he referred to is uncertain, but they might have been Colonel Sheets and Recruit Reuben Huls or Private James McCullock. Not mentioned was another Jones from the 80th Illinois, Captain Edmund Jones, commanding Co. F, killed April 30, apparently no relation to Nicholas Jones.

Hartpence, in his history of the 51st Indiana, told the story of Private William P. Jelf of Company C:

One of the sad incidents of the fight at Day's Gap was the wounding of Wm. Jelf, of Co. C. After the first fire, the command arose to make a charge; when the Rebels fired, he fell. At the same moment Lieutenant-Colonel Sheets and another man fell, immediately behind him; and all were supposed to be mortally wounded. Calling John P. Smith to him, Jelf delivered to him a silver watch, with a small chain attached, with a request that if he got through safely, he would take them to his mother. As John P. anticipated search and robbery by the Rebels, in case they were captured, he tore the chain loose, throwing it away, and concealed the watch on his person. Soon afterward, securing a pone of corn bread, about the size of his hand, he carefully cut out a circular piece of the top crust, then removed just enough of the inside to receive the watch, replaced the disc of crust, and on examination, after capture, so innocently exposed the corn pone, as to entirely elude discovery; and so he carried the watch through all the vicissitudes of subsequent imprisonment and exchange, to Jelf's home in Indiana, where he delivered it in good condition to Jelf's mother. Charles Cox, who was among the last who saw Jelf, gave him a canteen of water, and left him with the citizens to die. Jelf recovered slowly; and when John P. returned to camp at Indianapolis, he was almost the first person he met.

"For God's sake! Will," said John P., "go to your mother as soon as you can. I have just been to see her, and I told her you were dead!"

Jelf hastened home, and the meeting to his grief-stricken mother, as though he had been raised from the grave; rejoicing her crushed heart beyond measure![455]

While the wounded suffered, and in some cases died, as the result of their wounds, other troopers suffered as well. Twenty-three-year-old Private Henry Beauchamp of the 80th Illinois had been sick in the Paducah hospital for weeks, and finally succumbed to typhoid pneumonia on May 7. Army life was too much for thirty-seven-year-old Henry D. Chandler, 80th Illinois, who never got past Nashville on the raid. He was left there and died of congestion on April 23. Private Samuel McCullough, twenty-three years old, of the 80th Illinois, never even got on the boats; he died in Nashville on April 10, the day before the brigade left town. Private William G. Rogers, of the 80th Illinois, died April 17 in Murfreesboro of consumption. Private William H. H. Smith, of the 80th Illinois, just twenty years old, made it as far as Ft. Henry, but died there April 19.

The problem of the missing in action is not confined to recent wars. Even in this minor engagement, men disappeared, never to be heard from again. Some of the "Missing in Action" were later accounted for, but not many. Private Absalom Baggs of the 80th Illinois was listed as missing April 30 at Days Gap. His last service record entry was "died in rebel hospital Huntsville, Alabama, May 8, 1863." Henry Bird and Shannon Carr of the 73d Indiana were still listed as missing in June 1865. Bird was a wagoneer; he and Carr disappeared and were never heard from again. (See Chapter 9). Bird's children were awarded a pension in 1875. John Charles, twenty-three-year-old private of the 80th Illinois, was listed as missing at Days Gap; no further record.

There were fifty-four sick and wounded who were sent directly to Libby Prison in Richmond, in the care of the Georgia Medical Director and Private Peter Phillippe. They were confined there but exchanged shortly afterward.[456]

The records that still exist after 130-plus years are amazing, but they do leave gaps that allow the use of imagination to fill the unexplained history of the thousands of troops involved in Streight's Raid.

The 73d had a reunion in 1900, and published a list of known survivors to that time. Those who were listed on the 1900 reunion roster are marked with an asterisk below. (Other regiments published no such list after the war ended, so it is assumed that the men resumed their normal lives, restricted in many cases by the permanent effect of their wounds.)

SPENCER'S CASUALTY LIST

T. Taylor—3d Ohio—Shot in head—Died.

John R. Creshaw (Coshow)—Co. B 51st Indiana—Eighteen-year-old farmer—Shot in hip—Died.

John Horn—Co. C 80th Illinois—Shot in head—Died.

Washington Parker—Co. F—51st Indiana—Shot in lungs—Died.

Robert Jackson—Co. E 73d Indiana—Eighteen-year-old blacksmith from New York—Shot in eye—Died.

William House—Co. D 80th Illinois—Shot in right knee—Mustered out 1865.

Frederick Neighouse—Co. D 80th Illinois—Shot in hand—Volunteer Reserve Corps October 1864.

John F. Holm—Co. D 80th Illinois—Shot in nose—Discharged disability—October 20, 1863—He was seventeen years old when wounded, lost his right eye, "ball passed through the nasal bone and supposed to be lodged in the orb of the eye."—Died at seventy.

James P. Smith—Co. F 80th Illinois—Shot in heel—Mustered out 1865.

John Mackey—Co. F 80th Illinois—Shot in thigh—Drowned December 1863.

James Hamsom—Co. G 80th Illinois—Twenty-five-year old shoemaker—Shot in shoulder—Volunteer Reserve Corps February 4, 1864—Sent to Knoxville, then Richmond, Va., then paroled and exchanged—He was put on limited service because of wounds and transferred to Veterans Reserve Corps September 1864.

Samuel B. Keeler—Co. A 80th Illinois—Shot in thigh—Died July 8, 1864.

James Kells—Co. I 51st Indiana—Shot in head—No record found

George W. Farris—Co. I 51st Indiana—Shot in pectoral muscle—Mustered out December 1864.

Jacob B. Richeson—Co. I 51st Indiana—Shot in thigh—Mustered out 1865.

Henry B. McCaseley—Co. I 51st Indiana—Shot in thigh—Discharged, wounds.

James McCourt—Co. I 51st Indiana—Shot in cheek—Discharged September 9, 1863, wounds.

Washington Turner—Co. F 51st Indiana—Shot in hip—Mustered out 1865.

Andrew J. Pyle—Co. F 51st Indiana—Amputated leg at thigh—Discharged September 23, 1863, wounds.

Harrison Owens—Co. C 51st Indiana—Shot in thigh—Discharged April 1864, wounds.

William H. Jeff (Jelf)—Co. C 51st Indiana—Shot in neck—Mustered out 1865.

*Wm. G. Cook—Co. D 73d—Shot in throat.

George Brown—Co. A 73d Indiana—Shot in knee—Discharged October 29, 1863, wounds.

Jacob Hosier—Co. B 51st Indiana—Shot in side—Mustered out December 1864.

William H. Williams—Co. H 51st Indiana—Shot in neck—Discharged.

Cyrus Lowthain—Co. B 51st Indiana—Shot in head—Mustered out 1865.

Adrian V. H. Foote—Co. F 73d Indiana—Shot in side—Discharged February 11, 1864, wounds.

*Augustus J. Farris (James)—Co. K 73d Indiana—Twenty-eight-year-old farmer—Left arm and right hand amputated—Discharged October 19, 1863, wounds—Medical & Surgical History describes double amputation, leaving thumb on right hand. Farris married, had one child, and died in 1926. His compensation was $8 a month in 1863, had risen to $72 a month when he died.

*Henry E. Huntley—Co. B 73d Indiana—Shot in thigh—Discharged December 26, 1863.

Patrick Griffin—Co. B 51st Indiana—Shot in leg—Veterans Reserve Corps January 14, 1864.

*Robert Crandall—Co. F 73d Indiana—Twenty-two years old—Right arm amputated—Discharged July 28, 1863, disability—He was taken to Richmond, Va., then paroled. Married in 1866 and had twelve children—Died in 1923 at eighty-three.

*Samuel Witham—Co. I 73d Indiana—Shot in spine—Discharge October 1862(63?), wounds.

James D. McCullock—1st Tennessee [Alabama] Cavalry—Twenty-six-year-old farmer—Shot in lung—Taken to mother's house and died—Service record shows he was taken to Richmond, confined in the hospital, and died there February 26, 1864, of diarrhea.

Lieutenant Charles W. Pavey—Co. E 80th Illinois—Concussion spine—Captured, escaped, mustered out 1865—Became successful businessman, and promoted to general in the National Guard—Died at seventy-four.

Captain (Lieutenant Colonel) James W. Sheets—51st Indiana—Shot in hip—Died June 28, 1863.

Lieutenant John A. Welton—Co. E 51st Indiana—Twenty-three-year-old farmer who was an unusual 6' 1" tall when he enlisted in November 1861—Left leg amputated below the knee—Resigned June 20, 1864.

J. A. Stafford—Co. F 51st Indiana—Shot in hip—No record.

Captain Albert Carley—Co. E 73d Indiana—Shot in thigh—Captured, "Drowned in the Catawba River, near McCullohs factory, in the state of South Carolina, on the 20th day of Feb. 1865."—His pension file shows his wife could not, or would not, care for his children and was denied pension for them.

Lieutenant James C. Jones—80th Illinois—Twenty-one-year-old adjutant—Shot in hip and bowels—Died.

*Hallen Greeg [Probably Allen Gregg]—Co. E 73d Indiana—Mustered out 1865.

Edwin Reed—Co. I 3d Ohio—Shot in the Crest of the Ilium—Recovered from wound while in Libby Prison, escaped, but died of pneumonia in Annapolis in 1865.

James M. Haskill—Co. I 3d Ohio.

R. H. Allen—Co. I 80th Illinois—Mustered out 1865.

Solomon Sheeney [Swaney]—Co F 3d Ohio—Died.

Francis F. McIntosh—Co. B 80th Illinois—Veterans Reserve Corps December 1863.

W.[William] W. Gallagher [Gallagly]—Co. F 80th Illinois—Adjutant General of Illinois—"Died of wounds in St. Louis, Missouri, May 1, 1864." [Service record shows hospital stay until discharged for disability May 1, 1864. "Gunshot wound of right ankle . . . Ball lodged causing anchylosis of joint."]

James H. Jenkins—Co. A 80th Illinois—Mustered out June 1865.

Lorenzo B. Seargeant—Co. H 73d Indiana—Discharged October 12, 1863, wounds.

James Moroney—Co. F 51st Indiana—Mustered out December 1864.

John Misner—Co. K 51st Indiana—No record.

*William Page—Co. E 73d Indiana—Discharged February 10, 1864, wounds.

Robert Hulls [probably Reuben Huls]—Co. D 80th Illinois—Shot twice through right and once through left thigh—Died of wounds May 15 at Sand Mountain.

CHAPTER 17

MAY 3 AND ON

AFTERMATH

Streight's Union troops were prisoners, subject to conflicting procedures for release or incarceration. As soon as the brigade had stacked its arms and the surrender was complete, the officers were separated from the men, and their destinies differed substantially. In a somewhat unique development, the officers fared much worse than their men.

The Confederate authorities had yet to determine whether the raid was a genuine military excursion, or whether it had undercurrents of inciting slaves to insurrection, or just spying. As soon as Streight's capture was reported, telegrams began to fly from Richmond, Montgomery and other areas requesting some harsh treatment for these "guerrilla warriors."

The officers were brought into Rome first on the night of May 3. The enlisted men stayed in camp outside Rome until the following day, arriving in the city on the 4th. They were afforded reasonable treatment, fed, as requested by General Forrest, and given such shelter as was available while under Forrest's guard. However, when the citizens of Rome took charge, things became more tense. The historian of the 51st Indiana indignantly reported that they were, ". . . enduring every insult that such a low, ignorant, unprincipled, ill-born people only could invent. The vile creatures crowded around the cars, the women flaunting themselves in the most indecent manner; and all boasting of the superior chivalry of the South."[457] While they rested in Rome on the 5th, the Federals were given paroles, in which they promised not take up arms against the South until exchanged.

PRISONER'S PAROLE

I,................................of Co..of the United States Army, captured by Brig. Gen. Forrest, solemnly swear before Almighty God, the Sovereign Judge, that I will not bear arms against the Confederate States Government, nor help, aid or assist, either directly or indirectly, any person or persons, in making war against the same, until regularly exchanged as a prisoner of war, and that I will not, at any time, communicate to any person, information received within the Confederate lines, detrimental to the same.

Sworn and subscribed to before me at
   (Prisoner's Name)
          A. Inspr. Gen.

On May 5 the brigade officers and men prepared to board railroad cars to their first destination, Atlanta, Georgia. Just prior to the boarding, the Romans relieved the enlisted men of most of their possessions, and skimpy rations of boiled fat pork and corn bread were passed out, ". . . but as bad as it all was everyone took it good naturedly, entering into friendly talk, exchanging jokes and experiences with the guards."[458] At about 11 AM the cars, boxcars with no seats, left for Kingston, Georgia, where they made their first stop, then went on to Marietta and finally, at 8 PM, the cars arrived at Atlanta. The men were herded to an open common area while the officers were quartered in the City Hall; a few days later the men were taken to a central military prison. Members of the 73d vowed that the few days spent in Atlanta were the toughest days of their war-time experiences. "Upon their arrival in Atlanta the enlisted men were again corralled in an open field without shelter, or even blankets or overcoats, they having all been taken from them. The weather turned suddenly very cold and wet."[459]

The men started on their way to Richmond at 8 PM on May 7, after two days of exposure to weather turning colder each day. In spite of the miserable weather and accommodations, Sergeant Briedenthal started every day's journal entry with, "I am well and in exuberant spirits. . ."[460] The trip to Richmond, in overcrowded and bare box cars, was broken only by the arrival in Knoxville, where they had the good fortune to be placed under the guard of the 54th Virginia Infantry. (Briedenthal says it was the 24th.) These guards ". . . kindly divided their rations with our starving boys. This was a most gracious thing to do, and proved that even out of Sodom some good might come."[461]

When the men arrived in Richmond on May 11, they were taken immediately to Belle Isle, an island prison camp in the middle of the James River. There was little shelter from the increasing cold, and rations were thin, or non-existent. Exhausted by the experience of the preceding weeks, the men had little reserve strength to meet all the problems of prison life. One of the men, Private Tilman McDaniel, of Company C, 51st Indiana, lost his grip on reality in the cold and miserable camp, stepped over the "dead line," and was shot dead by the guards. He was placed in an unmarked mass grave in Richmond.

Compounding the prison problems was the arrival of hundreds of prisoners taken in the Battle of Chancellorsville, who arrived at Belle Isle about the same time as Streight's brigade. This meant even shorter rations.

The one redeeming feature of the men's prison life was that it was short. On the 15th of May, the brigade's enlisted men marched thirty-five miles, from Richmond, through Manchester, then down the Petersburgh Road to City Point. After a miserable night there on the 16th they boarded the five steamers provided and headed for the Parole Camp at Annapolis, Maryland. From there it would take considerable time to get back to their homes and reassigned to their regiments, but once the veteran Provisional Brigade members set foot on Maryland soil, their troubles virtually ended.

There were some, however, who were not able to get to their homes as soon as the others. Sergeant Simon Witham had been wounded and left with Dr. Spencer at Days Gap. On August 5, 1863, he was still in Annapolis, and wrote to Governor Morton:

Sir, I wish you to get [me] together with some two or three others of the 73d and 51st Indiana Regiments out of this place, we are wounded and some of us will probably never be fit for Service we think it hard after going through the hardships that we have to be used as we are here. I came in here on 3d of July. I was then able to walk around am still able to walk and I wish to come to Indianapolis.
Simon Witham

PS We are in the Hospital[462]

While the enlisted men endured the trial of brief imprisonment, the officers had a different fate. They were taken to Atlanta at the same time as the men, but stayed there several days after the brigade left. They arrived in Richmond on April 16; as they were winding their way to the Southern capitol, discussions were being held in Confederate circles as to the fate of the raiders. The men had been processed through the usual channels, but on May 8 Governor John Gill Shorter of Alabama was fuming at the Richmond government, saying that his state should decide the fate of some of the prisoners.

Among the prisoners captured by General Forrest I understand there are two companies of Alabamians who have enlisted as such in the army of the enemy, and having been engaged with known enemies of the State and the Confederate States in acts not justified by any rule of war or by necessity have been captured on the soil of Alabama not only levying war against the State, but instigating slaves to rebellion and committing deeds of rapine and destruction upon the property of its citizens without the excuse which can pertain to military necessity or the course of war. . .

I respectfully request that these marauders be delivered up to the authorities of this State for trial by her civil tribunals for their acts of violence and rapine against our citizens and the treason against the State whose citizens they claim to be.[463]

After a meeting with President Jefferson Davis, Confederate Secretary of War James Seddon replied to the governor on May 23:

On inquiry here I find there was no Alabama regiment (so-called) among the prisoners, but of a so-called Tennessee regiment there were two companies which are believed to have been composed of Alabamians. The privates had before receipt of your letter been sent off under the cartel. Some of the officers of these companies as well as of the other regiments captured by General Forrest remain and they will suffice perhaps to exhibit the determination of the Government and serve as exemplars of the punishment which will be visited on such crimes.[464]

Another, later report to Governor Shorter from Seddon was somewhat more brusque and not so conciliatory:

Sir: The official reports of General Forrest relative to the operations in Alabama and Georgia resulting in the capture of a body of the cavalry of the enemy near Rome, Ga., have been received. It does not appear from these reports that any slaves were associated as soldiers with the enemy's troops and if there were any Alabamians enlisted among them they made their escape before the capture. The probability is that your Excellency has been misinformed on the subject.[465]

In spite of Forrest's report that the Governor had no basis to discriminate against these officers in any exchange program, it soon became apparent that in Richmond no decision had been made about the raiders, and Streight's officers, still being held in custody, would be in a special class. It was this indecision that would cause the brigade officers months of prison time. In Seddon's response, the Alabama scouts were correctly identified as Alabamians serving in a Tennessee unit, having been assigned to the 1st Middle Tennessee Cavalry before the raid began.

But as this scene was being played out in Richmond and Montgomery, the pawns in the political game, the brigade officers, were en route to Richmond from Atlanta. According to the *Richmond Enquirer*, their stops in Atlanta and Augusta were not so unpleasant as the stops made by the enlisted men. A local paper huffed, "At Atlanta and Augusta the officers of the robbers and marauders who were recently captured near Rome by Gen. Forrest were permitted to go about at will, taking their meals at hotels, visiting the barrooms in the latter city, and inspecting the condition and situation of affairs as if they were making their trip through our country a matter of business or pleasure."[466]

Whatever "pleasures" they received on the trip ended abruptly when they arrived in Richmond and were taken off the cars and marched to Libby Prison. Even as they arrived, they were optimistic about the future, feeling that within days they would be on their own way north. In Richmond they found that their men had already passed through, and the officers expected that they would soon follow. They had no knowledge of the high-level meetings and the politics that were deciding their fates. "We were informed by the rebel officials, that we would be detained there a few days, perhaps three or four, awaiting a flag of truce boat from Fortress Monroe to convey us North; we were indeed most gloomy."[467] But when other prisoners, captured after they had been, were called out for the next boats, the brigade officers became concerned. They soon found that they were being considered as special cases, and were informed by Commissioner of Exchange Robert Ould that they were to be sent to Alabama to be tried for inciting slaves to insurrection.[468]

The refusal to exchange these officers breached the cartels involving exchange; this and other factors caused the exchange system to break down. Few exchanges would take place from then on.[469] Word spread rapidly that Streight was not going to be exchanged, nor were any of his officers. On May 11 Governor Morton of Indiana already knew of the situation, having read about it in the "Rebel papers," and wrote Secretary of War Edwin Stanton, asking that some Confederate hostages be kept to gain leverage for Streight's exchange. He gave a slightly different twist to the Alabamians presence in the brigade:

In July, 1862, Colonel A. D. Streight, Fifty-first Regiment Indiana Volunteer Infantry, with his regiment left Decatur, Ala., and marched over the mountains some twenty-five miles below that place to the relief of a number of Union citizens who had been obliged to abandon their homes and seek refuge in the mountains, and while there Colonel Streight succeeded in enlisting about 400 of these Alabamians in his regiment. They were regularly mustered into the service and have been doing service ever since.

Some days since Colonel Streight, with the permission of General Rosecrans, left with a mounted brigade for the purpose of cutting off General Bragg's communications—which they partially succeeded in doing, but were defeated and captured near Rome—and the account from the rebel newspapers states that "the men were paroled except the four companies of renegade Alabamians who were sent to Richmond."

Now I take it that this is a direct and palpable violation of the cartel. These men are regularly mustered into the Fifty-first Regiment Indiana Volunteer Infantry, and I respectfully ask that 800 prisoners may be selected from those now in our possession and held for the safety of these loyal Alabamians.[470]

That request was acknowledged by the War Department on May 15 without comment.

Later, the governor of Illinois, Richard Yates, added his weight to the matter in a May 25 communication to Secretary Stanton:

> A number of citizens of Alabama, now residents of this State, have addressed me by letter asking me to interest myself in securing for citizens of Alabama, relatives and friends of theirs captured with Colonel Streight's command, the rights and immunities of prisoners of war. These men have claims upon the Government in this regard of the highest character. They have run fearful risks in their devotion to the Union and the Government should never desert them in their peril. Their lives are in danger but should a hair of their heads suffer instant retaliation should be enforced.[471]

Other incidents taking place would add to the controversy. On May 15, the Union executed two Confederate officers as spies in Sandusky, Ohio. As a result, Confederate Commissioner Ould telegraphed Lieutenant Colonel William Ludlow, Union Agent of Exchange, the following message:

> The Confederate government has ordered that two captains now in our custody be selected for execution in retaliation for this gross barbarity. This order will be speedily executed.
>
> Your papers refer to other cases of parties condemned to death upon the same charge. They are some five or six in number.
>
> In view of the awful vortex into which things are plunging I give you notice that in the event of the execution of these persons retaliation to an equal extent at least will be visited upon your own officers, and if that is found to be ineffectual the number will be increased.
>
> The Great Ruler of nations must judge who is responsible for the initiation of this chapter of horrors.[472]

The Confederates lost little time in selecting officers, by a drawing of names from a box containing the names of all captains in Libby. It was the misfortune of Captain John M. Flinn of the 51st Indiana to be one of the two selected; Captain Henry W. Sawyer of the 1st New Jersey Cavalry was the other. The Union quickly retaliated by selecting, not by lottery, but by name, two Confederates to be executed if the Union captains died. The two Southerners were W. H. F. "Rooney" Lee, second son of Robert E. Lee, and William S. Winder, son of the provost marshal of Richmond.

Immediately after the two unlucky Union officers had been identified, the effect of the rapid selection of the Union captains, and the fear of immediate execution of their fellow inmates were dramatized in Dr. Spencer's journal: "The officers are now returned to the prison quarters, all except these two condemned men, whom we never expect to see again on earth. We now see from the windows, these two condemned ones conducted by the guards up town, we fear to execution. The whole prison are mute with grief and horror at this tragic calamity to two of our most esteemed prison associates."[473] Whether the threat of retaliation was effective in the Confederate execution plan or not, in spite of many nervous moments experienced by the pawns in these moves, none of the four officers was executed.[474]

Captains Flinn and Sawyer were not the only hostages being held in Richmond. Spencer himself became a hostage. He was picked to be a hostage for a Confederate Dr. Green, of the Southern navy, who had been selected as a hostage for Dr. William P. Rucker of Virginia. Rucker was held in Libby ostensibly for murder, horse theft and treason, all of which were stoutly denied by Rucker and his attorney. Spencer had waxed philosophic on the subject of being held hostage: "We who are threatened conditionally with hanging have ceased to have much fear upon the subject—or rather much thought and discussion with reference to the probabilities, in our several cases, have hardened our sensibilities in that particular."[475]

In the next months, Streight was not a complacent prisoner, nor was he a quiet one. He sparked some controversy by writing to the Confederate Secretary of War, James A. Seddon, complaining bitterly about conditions at Libby. In a letter dated August 30, 1863, he stated that he and his officers, ninety-five in number, had personal money taken from them by prison officials in violation of Forrest's surrender condition.[476] He also described ration deficiencies and unsanitary prison accommodations and asked the secretary for ways in which his officers could purchase better living conditions. The Confederate prison authorities had confiscated $3,400 from him when he was taken to Libby. There followed a number of correspondences to and from various Richmond authorities as to the solution. There is no record of any decision that benefited the colonel in his plea for the return of his money.

In a bizarre twist, some Union officers, including one of Streight's own, took exception to his August 30 letter to Seddon, and wrote a rebuttal to prison authorities. "And, in conclusion, permit me to bear testimony of the kind and courteous treatment we have received at the hands of all the officers connected with the prison."[477] The letter was signed by recently promoted Major David A. McHolland of the 51st, who had become regimental commander of Streight's old 51st when Sheets was killed. A similar sentiment was expressed by Second Lieutenant James C. Jones, 35th Ohio. The senior officers who endorsed McHolland and Jones were Colonel Charles W. Tilden, 16th Maine, and Lieutenant Colonel James M.

Sanderson, First Corps. For Colonel Streight it must have been a bitter blow to have one of his own officers cloud the effect of his message to Seddon.

However, on September 18 a meeting was called of all officers in the prison to seek ways to improve their lot. The meeting was chaired by Major E. N. Bates of the 80th Illinois; the secretary appointed was Major Harry White, 67th Pennsylvania. "The meeting was attended by nearly all of the officers confined in the prison, and much feeling was manifested in the object of the meeting."[478] The assembled officers appointed a committee of three to report back to the group; one of the three was Surgeon William Spencer, who was still a prisoner. The committee's statement, "which was read to the meeting and instantly adopted with the manifestation of much feeling and not a dissenting vote," was a vindication of Streight's complaints.[479] Four resolutions were put forth:

1. *Resolved,* That the written statement addressed to Captain J. Warner, commissary of Subsistence, C. S. Army, indorsed and vouched for by Col. Charles W. Tilden, Sixteenth Maine Volunteer Infantry, and Lieutenant-Colonel Sanderson commissary of subsistence First Corps, U.S. Army, in reference to the treatment and sentiments of the officers confined here, is in every particular a gross misrepresentation of facts, and its reasonable inferences unqualifiedly false.
2. *Resolved,* That said statement is directly calculated to stifle the voice of our reasonable complaint, as truthfully set forth in the communication of Col. A.D. Streight, which they stigmatize as unjust and untrue, to mislead and deceive our commissioner for exchange of prisoners and our Government.
3. *Resolved,* That in view of the cruel and inhuman treatment of the enlisted men of our Army by the Confederate authorities which daily comes under our notice, not to speak of the indignities and deprivations to which our officers have been subjected, this action of those officers whose names are attached to the communication referred to in the first resolve meets our unqualified condemnation.
4. *Resolved,* That our thanks are due to Colonel Streight for his fearless and unselfish efforts to secure for us additional accommodations from our enemies, and that an increased amount of our rations are some of the fruits of his labors, and the course he has pursued in relation to our condition meets with our hearty approval.

The resolutions were unanimously adopted.[480]

Streight made speeches to other prisoners and wrote repeatedly to prison authorities. He even successfully smuggled a letter to Indiana Governor

Morton with Dr. Spencer when he was released. This handwritten, two-page letter described the atrocious prison conditions at Libby, but also the even-worse situation for enlisted men held on Belle Isle. The letter was a plea to have Morton use any means possible to gain exchange for prisoners, or to improve conditions. There were no visible improvements, but his continued efforts made Streight a target for the Confederate guards and prison officers.

In all his efforts, escape was his ultimate goal. In October 1863 a plan was developed which included a mass uprising of prisoners, overpowering of the guards, a march to the arsenal to arm and organize released prisoners, then on to the capital to capture Jeff Davis and his cabinet. From there they would march en mass to Union lines. It was a grand plan. To organize the effort, Streight and four other senior officers formed "The Council of Five," with Streight as the chief. Unfortunately, it involved too many of the prisoners, and the secret soon found its way to prison guards. The discovery by guards and officials killed any chance of success for such a massive plan.

In December 1863 Streight and Captain B. C. G. Reed, 3d Ohio, were offered a chance to bribe a guard and escape. The offer was made by the guard in a note to the colonel, explaining the bribe to be paid: $100 in greenbacks and two silver watches. The plan was a trap; after paying the bribe, the two officers were fired on and recaptured as they left the prison gate. For their efforts they were both put in solitary confinement, on bread and water. Streight wrote, "I have stated that we were reduced to bread and water fare; I will add that what we get for bread is of such a quality that we, as yet, have been unable to eat it."[481] The trap was thought to be a plan to murder Streight and defuse any escape plans.

Soon, though, another effort was made which had more chance for success. A tunnel was planned and constructed under the guidance of Colonel Thomas Rose, 77th Pennsylvania, and others. Upon its completion on February 9, 1864, a breakout through the tunnel commenced, with Streight one of the first ones out. Lieutenant Roach described one problem:

> The whole length of the tunnel was about sixty feet, with a diameter just large enough for a large sized man to pass through, though in one of the curvatures worked around a rock it was smaller; here Colonel Streight, who by the way is somewhat inclined toward corpulency, *stuck fast*, and was compelled to back out, and divest himself of coat, vest and shirt, when he was able to *squeeze* through, pulling his garments aforesaid through with a string after him.[482]

One hundred and nine officers escaped through the tunnel, including several other Provisional Brigade officers. Of those who escaped, forty-eight

were recaptured and two drowned in the Chickahominy River.[483]
Roach's book quotes a Richmond paper:

IMPORTANT ESCAPE OF YANKEE PRISONERS
OVER FIFTY FEET OF GROUND TUNNELLED.

The most important escape of Federal prisoners which has occurred during the war took place at the Libby prison sometime during last Tuesday night. Of the eleven hundred Yankee officers confined therein, one hundred and nine failed to answer to their names at roll-call yesterday morning. Embraced in this number were eleven Colonels, seven Majors, thirty-two Captains and fifty-nine Lieutenants. The following is a list of the Colonels and Majors.

The first one on the list was "Colonel A. D. Streight, of the Fifty-first Indiana regiment, a notorious character captured in Tennessee by General Forrest, and charged with having raised a negro regiment. . ."[484]

The actual escape was only the first part of Streight's challenge. He and Captain W. W. Scearce teamed up to cross the miles of Confederate territory to Union lines, and only by good luck and perseverance, plus the kindness of many sympathizers enroute, finally arrived in Washington three weeks later on March 1, 1864. Streight's journey after he left Libby was a pilgrimage that rivals those of ancient times. He and the captain were housed in a Union sympathizer's house in Richmond for a week, while the guards and troops searched everywhere, with numerous false alarms. Streight's reputation by then earmarked him as the principal escapee to be recaptured, so his was an especially dangerous journey. Finally, after a week hiding in Richmond, the pair, with two Rebel deserters, left Richmond, swam across the Chickahominy River in the bitter cold, and began their trek toward Union lines. Twice they were discovered by Southern soldiers, but managed to escape their clutches and continue. The weather was cold, and they had several rivers to cross, so they were virtually always cold and wet.

Toward the end of their travels, almost frozen, discouraged and pursued, the Federal officers were befriended by Negroes who fed and housed them, even as the Confederate troops searched nearby. This added strength to Streight's Abolitionist views. Roach concluded:

A long, weary, and perilous pilgrimage had been theirs. Eleven days and nights of watching and anxiety, of cold and hunger, of peril and hairbreadth escapes, of threading thickets and marshes, of crossing streams, and shelterless sleeping on the ground, of lacerated feet and frost bitten hands, of alternating hope and despair, was their varied and bitter experiences. But it was liberty they sought, and they gained it. Bravery, energy, perseverance, the kindly moon and solar star, and the negro guide, brought them safe within our lines. Freedom, friends, and the protecting folds of the stars and stripes, was their reward.[485]

Records indicate that the Provisional Brigade officers who escaped with Streight, plus Captain Marion Anderson of the 51st Indiana who had escaped earlier, and Lieutenant Colonel Ivan N. Walker and Major A. B. Wade who were actually exchanged, were the only ones of Streight's officers to gain their freedom before the war ended. Almost all the others were held until the end of the war, a period of about twenty-three months. They were kept at Libby for a year, transferred to Danville, Virginia; to Columbia, S.C.; Macon, Georgia; Savannah, Georgia; and finally Charleston, South Carolina. They were moved to Charleston to try to dissuade the Union from firing on that city.[486]

The effect of those months in prison on the men after the war is not known. Civil War individual and regimental records are helpful, but not many records exist after the war period. Pension records are sketchy, many of the veterans or their survivors never filed for pensions, and those records that exist are seldom complete. Officers, including Streight, who spent time in the Confederate prison system, later reported that many of their health problems began in Libby Prison or other Southern camps.

The release of the officers still remaining in prison marked the final event of the raid that had started two years earlier. It had brought the brigade members, officers and men, in a journey from Nashville on April 11, 1863, to numerous destinations, the last of which was Washington about April 1, 1865. They had endured the hardship of the raid, capture, prison and finally release; few would be the same again.

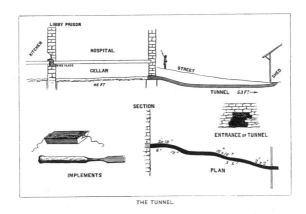

THE TUNNEL.

Epilogue

After his release Colonel Streight returned to his regiment, later commanding a brigade in the Army of the Cumberland. He was promoted to brigadier general in March 1865 and resigned a week later. He became a successful lumberman and publisher, and died in 1892 at sixty-three. His wife had him buried in the front yard of their Indianapolis home, saying, "I never knew where he was in life, but now I can find him."

Captain David Smith, 1st Alabama Cavalry, was from Alabama, enlisted in the 21st Ohio Infantry in Huntsville, Alabama, in April 1862 at thirty-seven years of age. By special act he was appointed captain in the 1st Alabama Cavalry in July 1862. He was captured and sent to Libby Prison, then taken to Alabama at the request of the Alabama governor, and taken to a number of Alabama jails. A letter from him to his wife on November 17, 1864, shows him in a military prison in Columbia, South Carolina. He was finally released in early 1865, sent to Annapolis and died there of pneumonia on April 18, 1865. He never saw his wife after leaving the 21st Ohio; she followed him in death June 6, 1866, leaving four young children.[487]

First Lieutenant William A. Curry, 3d Ohio, twenty-two years old, died in prison in Charleston, South Carolina, on September 29, 1864, of yellow fever.

The good deeds of the 54th Virginia were repaid in kind after the war when the remnants of the Provisional Brigade met the Virginia unit in Tennessee ". . . the 54th were received with genuine joy, by the remnants of the Provisional Brigade and supplied with the best of everything the camp afforded."[488]

In September 1863, after the enlisted men had been exchanged and were home on furlough, one of the 80th Illinois men wrote his wife:

You remember the soldier that had the dragoon cap on in Centralia—he and several others belonged to the 9th Ill they give up ther mules and horses to us at Tuscumbia and since we was captured they have taken some of Forests men and they had blankets whicht belonged to our Regt they said that the 80 was a good Regt and had its name up for its gallentry—long may its name be remembered and ever worthy of the prais given.[489]

A letter written June 1, 1863, to Governor Morton begged him to increase his efforts to free his son, Captain Benjamin C. G. Reed of the 3d Ohio, and the others. The father was pastor of the Market Street Baptist Church, Zanesville, Ohio. After his escape from Libby, Captain Reed was discharged from the 3d Ohio on

August 12, 1864, became major of the 174th Ohio, and, at twenty-three, was killed near Murfreesboro, December 1864.[490]

Captain John Flinn, held hostage, was never executed; regimental records show that he was released and discharged from the army in December 1864.

Colonel Sanderson was released from Libby Prison but dismissed from the service. After months of seeking witnesses, he appealed the dismissal and it was overturned, reinstating him to his rank. In August 1865, however, he was released from the service. His book written after the war bitterly criticized Streight and General Neal Dow who he felt were responsible for the army's actions in his dismissal.[491]

POSTCRIPT

As the smoke of battle cleared away, it was a time of reflection. Forrest returned with his men to Tennessee; the citizens of Rome had their celebration and settled back to normal; the raiders were taken to Atlanta and on to their own trials. The South had added much to its folklore, but the Yankee raiders were to disappear into the twilight zone of history. General Forrest was now a legend; John Wisdom had the accolades of his communities; Emma Sansom was enshrined as a genuine Southern heroine; and even the Murphree girls had their fifteen minutes of fame. The men of Forrest's division, as well as the general, were acclaimed and honored by no less than the Confederate Congress. There probably was no more apt application of the current saying, "The thrill of victory and the agony of defeat." The victors had the acclaim, plus the horses, mules, arms and equipment of the vanquished, while the conquered Yankee enlisted men faced illtreatment even in their exchange, with prison and privation for the officers. In some cases, the prison stay was a death sentence.

The famous Forrest Division continued to add to its laurels in the coming two years of war, but the four Union regiments and their leader faded from the national scene. Many Southern biographies of Forrest detail the events of the raid, while few of the histories written about Northern armies have any full account of the event. However, the accounts by both Southern and Northern historians had little criticism of the abilities of the men or their officers, either the pursuers or the pursued. The raid and its hardships proved once again the patriotic fervor of the men on both sides. Their faith in their leaders, their cause and themselves was enough to overcome the misery and exhaustion and futility of the raid. The leaders of the raid proved to be equally as capable as their troops in that two-week ordeal in northern Alabama. Although the raid failed, both the Yankees and Rebels were at their best.

James F. Cook wrote an insightful article titled, "The 1863 Raid of Abel D. Streight: Why it Failed." He cites a number of reasons for the raid's failure, but among the primary reasons was luck. It was obvious from the start that it was a high-risk effort. In all the official records and historical documents there was virtually no mention of an escape route. Only once was reference made to the raider's return across northern Alabama. That was not a viable escape route, the raiders having attracted all the attention of the Confederate forces as well as militias in those northern counties. Even in his instructions, Streight was told to make his surrender as expensive to the Rebels as he could.

The mission could have been successful, even if the brigade was captured, had they been able to disrupt the rail line between Atlanta and Chattanooga. And they did come very close to accomplishing that goal.

The first reason for the failure of the raid was the use of the cranky mule. While the various advantages of the mule were itemized, little attention was paid to the disadvantages: their lack of speed, their irritable dispositions, their stubborn behavior, and certainly their noisy presence. The brigade location was difficult to disguise when it was continually announced by the braying of hundreds of protesting jackasses. The comfort factor also favored horses, as the infantrymen soon found out. The blame for the decision to mount the men on mules probably belongs to generals Rosecrans and Garfield.

The second reason for the Union defeat was the continual delays encountered on the boat trip, rounding up the mules in Eastport, and the two days in Tuscumbia, spent foraging and selecting men for the raid. Without these delays, it is doubtful that Forrest could have been in a position to catch the brigade. So much time was consumed in searching for animals that a speedy march was impossible. The delays were, to a large extent, a result of reason number one, selecting mules for mounts in the first place.

The third reason was that General Dodge, in his screening effort, failed to continue to distract Forrest. Had he pressed the Confederates after Town Creek, and delayed the Southern pursuit of the raiders for even one day, Streight might have had a chance to succeed; but Dodge's withdrawal left the Rebel cavalry free to press Streight almost before the actual raid started. While the demonstrations and rumors that Colonel Dibrell made at Florence might have given Dodge good reason to return to Corinth, his decision to head back had been made before Dibrell's efforts began. It is even possible that Dodge felt that his presence in Corinth was of more value to his own army, the Army of the Tennessee, than it was to Streight, part of the Army of the Cumberland. It is also possible that his feint might have hindered the raid's success more than it helped. It was Dodge's move toward

Tuscumbia that caught Bragg's attention and caused him to send Forrest south. That put Forrest in the area as Streight started for Rome.

A fourth reason was the continual overestimation of the forces opposing both Dodge and Streight. Dodge's reliance on his assistant adjutant's report increased the Dodge caution, and Streight believed, even at the end, that Forrest outnumbered him substantially. More adequate scouting might have established more accurate figures. This overestimation, however, was a common Union flaw that caused the Yankees to be less aggressive than they should have been on a number of occasions.

But if these reasons were the cause of the Streight defeat, what of General Forrest's contribution? His overall pursuit and capture of Streight were textbook examples of leadership and perseverance. He personally suffered every hardship endured by his men, and prodded them to keep going long after many officers would have stopped to rest. Splitting his forces and sending small parties to harry the brigade, he made maximum use of the limited number of troops in his command. But without several lucky breaks, he might well have failed.

Early in the pursuit, Forrest's luck gave him bad weather. Heavy rains and swollen rivers helped at Town Creek, preventing Dodge from a timely crossing of his force. The continuing rain slowed Streight's lightning mule brigade to a slow walk. The wagons and plodding mules were no match for the well-mounted veteran Confederate cavalry, allowing Forrest to close the gap between his cavalry and the Provisional Brigade.

However, a major stroke of luck was the appearance of Emma Sansom. If she had not shown the ford to the pursuers, Streight might easily have gained enough time to rest and proceed to Rome. Forrest, in spite of his genius, could not take credit for the young girl's presence or her bravery. A second piece of good fortune was the Paul Revere-style ride of John Wisdom to alert the forces in and near Rome of Streight's approach. He was not sent by Forrest, but took it on himself to fly through the night to warn his old neighbors of danger. He arrived well before the couriers sent by Forrest, in time for troops to be put in place and reinforcements summoned. So Forrest could not be credited with the Rome alert, although his couriers were sent on a similar mission; it was Wisdom who gave the Romans the time they needed.

The raid was an example of courageous and determined behavior on both sides, which allowed for a certain respect between the participants. The treatment of the prisoners, while miserable later on, for the most part was courteous while under the care of Forrest. Forrest himself praised Streight as "a most excellent officer."[492]

Cook, in concluding his analysis of Forrest, says, "He was lucky, too."[493]

The effect of the raid on the fate of the war is hard to determine. It cost the Northern effort almost 2,000 men, lost for varying periods of time, plus the various animals and baggage of the brigade. Its cost in terms of human suffering was substantial, but human suffering is rarely a quantifying factor in wartime.

The strategic effect might be easier to identify. As this raid drew Forrest's and Roddey's cavalry eastward, Colonel Benjamin Grierson's highly successful raid to the south, through Mississippi, was taking place. His expedition met with little opposition and, as a result, was highly disruptive to the Mississippi defenses, even at Vicksburg. It also aided General Grant as he took his forces down the Mississippi to cross the river to attack Vicksburg on its most vulnerable south and east side. Grierson's raid distracted the few cavalry in Mississippi at that time, and it was a factor in the successful completion of Grant's complicated strategy. That strategy did pay off with Grant's capture of Vicksburg in July. Streight's move kept the Confederate cavalry occupied, and that in itself was a measure of success. The raid's only significant tactical accomplishment was the burning of the Iron Works outside Rome; that was hardly worth the loss of a full brigade.

In spite of its ending, the Provisional Brigade's effort signaled an increasing attempt to mount expeditions into enemy country, to duplicate the raids of the Confederate cavalry. The North was now using cavalry and mounted infantry in the same way the Confederacy had for two years. These new efforts would add cavalrymen to the status of heroes; names such as Philip Sheridan, George Armstrong Custer, Judson Kilpatrick and others would obtain equal status with McClellan, Hooker, Burnside and Meade, the famous names of the first two years of the war. Unfortunately, Streight would never become a household word, but in many ways he was a leader in the new approach to the Northern use of raiders. The Indiana colonel was a competent, creative, aggressive and brave leader. The only thing he lacked that spring of 1863 was luck—and several more good horses.

The formidible-looking Mrs. Abel Streight in later years.

James J. Farris returned from Streight's Raid with only one arm and a deformed hand.

When Abel Streight died, his wife buried him in the front yard of their Indianapolis mansion. "I could never keep track of him when he was alive. Now I can keep my eye on him," she said.

NOTES

For this book, as is the case with most books about the Civil War, the primary research tool is the government publication *War of the Rebellion: Official Records of the Union and Confederate Armies*. This one hundred twenty-eight volume work, published by the Government Printing Office, is a treasure store of information for Civil War research. All citations for these official records are cited as *AOR*.

Sources used for Dodge's expedition are taken primarily from regimental histories. The best of these are William W. Cluett's *History of the 57th Illinois Volunteer Infantry*; Charles F. Hubert's *History of the 50th Illinois Volunteer Infantry*; and Marion Morrison's *A History of the 9th Illinois Volunteer Infantry*. Stephen Z. Star's *Jennison's Jayhawkers* was also a valuable source.

Several fine biographies of Forrest were used for the sections on his forces. Included were Robert Selph Henry's *First With The Most Forrest*; Jordan and Pryor's *The Campaigns of Lieutenant Gen. N.B. Forrest*; Andrew Nelson Lyle's *Bedford Forrest and His Critter Company*; J. Harvey Mathes' *General Forrest*; and John Allan Wyeth's *That Devil Forrest*.

Much of the information on Streight came from regimental histories: Hartpence's *History of the Fifty-First Indiana Veteran Volunteer Infantry*; William S. Hoole's *Alabama Tories: 1st Alabama Cavalry, USA*; and Committee of the Seventy-Third's *History of the Seventy-Third Indiana Volunteer Infantry*. Another primary source was A. C. Roach's *Prisoner of War and How Treated*. Much detailed information came from Henry Briedenthal's diary, published in the *Rebellion Record*; Rucker Agee's paper "The Forrest-Streight Campaign of 1863," prepared for the Milwaukee Civil War Roundtable; and William Barton McCash's University of Georgia Master's Degree thesis, "Colonel Abel D. Streight's Raid, His Capture and Imprisonment."

The chapter on the wounded at Days Gap is almost entirely from William Spencer's journal.

PREFACE

[1] Phisterer, *Statistical Record of the Armies of the United States*, p.132.

[2] Young, *Confederate Wizards of the Saddle*, p. 455.

[3] Webb, *Crucial Moments of the Civil War*, p.189.

INTRODUCTION

[4] Streight service record.

[5] Ibid.

[6] Willett, *One Day of the Civil War*, p.12.

[7] *AOR*, Series II, Vol. V, pp. 779-780.

[8] *AOR*, Series I, Vol. XXIII, Pt. 1, p. 371.

THE RAID

[9] McCash, "Colonel Abel D. Streight's Raid, His Capture and Imprisonment," p. 9.

[10] Streight, "The Crisis of Eighteen Hundred and Sixty-One in the Government of the United States and How it Should Be Met."

[11] Nowland, *Sketches of Prominent Citizens of 1876*, pp. 505-6.

[12] Anonymous letter, August 5, 1861, *Indianapolis Daily State Sentinel*, August 6, 1861.

[13] McCash, "Colonel Abel D. Streight's Raid, His Capture and Imprisonment," p. 4.

[14] *AOR*, Series I, Vol. XVI, Pt. 1, p. 790.

[15] Dodge, *Personal Recollections of Abraham Lincoln, General Ulysses S. Grant and General William T. Sherman*, pp. 53-54.

[16] Wyeth, *That Devil Forrest*, p.132.

[17] Du Bose Manuscript.

[18] *AOR*, Series I, Vol. XXIII, Pt.1, p. 282.

[19] Ibid.

[20] Ibid.

[21] Boatner, *The Civil War Dictionary*, p. 16.

[22] Thompson, *The Free State of Winston*, pp. 73-74.

[23] Ibid., p. 73.

[24] Hoole, *Alabama Tories*, p. 121.

[25] *AOR*, Series I, Vol. XXIII, Pt. 1, p. 285.

[26] Ibid., p. 282.

[27] Fitch, ed., *Annals of the Army of the Cumberland*, p. 438.

[28] *AOR*, Series I, Vol. XXIII, Pt. 2, p. 224.

[29] Ibid., p. 213.

[30] Ibid., p. 214.

[31] Ibid., p. 244.

[32] Ibid., p. 213.

CHAPTER 1

[33] Beatty, *Memoirs of a Volunteer*, p. 184.

[34] Crawford, *Dear Lizzie*, pp. 91, 92.

[35] Garfield, *The Wild Life of the Army*, p. 255.

[36] *AOR*, Series I, Vol. XXIII, Pt. 2, pp. 213-214.

[37] Ibid., p. 285.

[38] Ibid., p. 218.

[39] Ibid., pp. 272-304.

[40] Ibid., p. 301.

[41] *AOR*, Series I, Vol. XXIII, Pt. 2, p.197.

[42] McCash, "Colonel Abel D. Streight's Raid, His Capture and Imprisonment," p. 52.

[43] Briedenthal diary, p. 337.

[44] *Nashville Union*, April 11, 1863.

[45] *AOR*, Series I, Vol. XXIII, Pt. 2, p. 188.

[46] Ibid., pp. 213, 219.

[47] Streight to Morton telegram, April 8, 1863.

[48] Hathaway to Morton telegram, April 22, 1863.

[49] Adjutant General of Indiana, *Indiana Volunteer Infantry*, p. 674.

[50] Illinois Military and Naval Department, *Report of the Adjutant General*, p. 50.

[51] Briedenthal diary, p. 337.

[52] Roach, *The Prisoner of War and How Treated*, p. 12.

[53] McCash, "Colonel Abel D. Streight's Raid, His Capture and Imprisonment," p. 54.

[54] Briedenthal diary, p. 337.

[55] Ibid.

[56] Ibid., p. 338.

[57] Scribner, *Indiana's Roll of Honor*, p. 116.

[58] *AOR*, Series I, Vol. XXIII, Pt. 1, p. 286.

[59] Roach, *The Prisoner of War and How Treated*, p. 13.

[60] Committee of the Seventy-Third Indiana Regimental Association, *History of the Seventy-Third Indiana Volunteer Infantry*, pp. 125-6.

[61] Scribner, *Indiana's Roll of Honor*, p. 116.

[62] Hartpence, *History of the Fifty-First Indiana Veteran Volunteer Infantry*, pp. 141-142.

[63] Brumfield Diary.

[64] Scribner, *Indiana's Roll of Honor*, p. 117.

[65] James Lawson Brown journal.

[66] *AOR*, Series I, Vol. XXIII, Pt. 1, p. 286.

[67] Committee of the Seventy-Third Indiana Regimental Association, *History of the Seventy-Third Indiana Volunteer Infantry*, p. 127.

[68] *AOR*, Series I, Vol. XXIII, Pt. 1, p. 286.

[69] Barnard diary, p. 25.

[70] McHolland to Morton telegram, April 14, 1863.

[71] Adjutant General of Indiana, *Indiana Volunteer Infantry*, pp. 501-2.

[72] Roach, *The Prisoner of War and How Treated*, p. 16.

[73] *AOR*, Series I, Vol. XXIII, Pt. 1, p. 242.

[74] Gibson, *Assault and Logistics*, p. 305.

[75] McCash, "Colonel Abel D. Streight's Raid, His Capture and Imprisonment," p. 63.

[76] James Lawson Brown journal.

[77] Briedenthal diary, p. 338.

[78] Society of Survivors, *History of the Ram Fleet*, p. 275.

[79] Ibid.

[80] Barnard diary, p. 27.

CHAPTER 2

[81] Garfield, *The Wild Life of the Army*, p. 256.

[82] Wyeth, *That Devil Forrest*, p. 163.

[83] *Southern Confederacy* (Atlanta), April 22, 1863.

[84] Lytle, *Bedford Forrest and His Critter Company*, p. 149.

[85] *AOR*, Series I, Vol. XXIII, Pt. 2, p. 777.

[86] Lytle, *Bedford Forrest and His Critter Company*, p. 146.

[87] Ibid.

[88] "Roddey's Old Company," *Confederate Veteran*, vol. XIII, May 1905, p. 216.

[89] Hirschon, *Grenville M. Dodge: Soldier, Politician, Railroad Pioneer*, p. 71.

[90] *AOR*, Series II, Vol. V, p. 924.

[91] Ibid., p. 242.

[92] Anonymous journal, pp. 21-22.

[93] Saunders, "Wartime Journal of a 'Little Rebel'," *Confederate Veteran*, vol. XXVIII, January 1920, p. 11.

CHAPTER 3

[94] Cohen letter to *Jewish Messenger*, April 10, 1863.

[95] Stratton letter to his folks, April 10, 1863.

[96] *AOR*, Series I, Vol. XXIII, Pt. 1, p 242.

[97] Pomeroy diary.

[98] Adjutant General's Office, *Official Military History of Kansas Regiments*, p. 95.

[99] *AOR*, Series I, Vol. XXIII, Pt. 1, p. 251.

[100] Dodd, *Annals of Northwest Alabama*, vol. IV, pp. 275-276.

[101] Morrison, *A History of the Ninth Regiment Illinois Volunteer Infantry*, p. 50.

[102] *AOR*, Series I, Vol. XXIII, Pt. 1, p. 252.

[103] Ibid., p. 246.

[104] Ibid., p. 253.

[105] Ibid.

[106] Ibid.

[107] Regimental records, 64th Illinois Volunteer Infantry.

[108] Hubert, *History of the Fiftieth Regiment Illinois Volunteer Infantry*, p. 187.

[109] Morrison, *A History of the Ninth Regiment Illinois Volunteer Infantry*, p. 51.

[110] Stratton letter, May 2, 1863.

[111] McKee diary.

[112] Ambrose, *History of the Seventh Regiment Illinois Volunteer Infantry,* p. 148.

[113] *AOR,* Series I, Vol. XXIII, Pt. 1. p. 247.

[114] Ibid., p. 244.

[115] Ibid., p. 247.

[116] Ibid., p. 249.

[117] Morrison, *A History of the Ninth Regiment Illinois Volunteer Infantry,* p. 51.

CHAPTER 4

[118] *AOR,* Series I, Vol. XXIII, Pt. 1, p. 242.

[119] Ibid., Pt. 2, p. 671.

[120] Anonymous journal, p. 4.

[121] Ninth Illinois regimental daily records, April 18 to May 16, 1863.

[122] *AOR,* Series I, Vol. XXIII, Pt. 1, p. 244.

[123] Stratton letter to his sister, May 3, 1863.

[124] Eddy, *The Patriotism of Illinois,* vol. 2, p. 60.

[125] Ambrose, *History of the Seventh Regiment Illinois Volunteer Infantry,* p. 148.

[126] Hubert, *History of the Fiftieth Regiment Illinois Volunteer Infantry,* p. 190.

[127] Cluett, *History of the Fifty-Seventh Regiment Illinois Volunteer Infantry,* p. 60.

[128] Ibid.

[129] *AOR,* Series I, Vol. XXIII, Pt. 2, p. 252.

[130] Ibid., Pt.1, p. 244.

[131] Ibid., Pt. 3, p. 215.

[132] Hartpence, *History of the Fifty-First Indiana Veteran Volunteer Infantry,* p. 120.

[133] AOR, Series I, XXIII, Pt. 2, p. 249.

[134] Briedenthal diary, p. 339.

[135] Wyeth, *That Devil Forrest,* p. 168.

[136] Pruitt, *Bugger Saga,* p. 61.

[137] *AOR,* Series I, Vol. XXIII, Pt. 1, p. 247.

[138] Ibid., p. 286.

[139] Briedenthal diary, p. 339.

[140] Regimental records, Seventy-Third Indiana Volunteer Infantry.

[141] Committee of the Seventy-Third Indiana Regimental Association, *History of the Seventy-Third Indiana Volunteer Infantry,* p. 129.

CHAPTER 5

[142] Ambrose, *History of the Seventh Regiment Illinois Volunteer Infantry,* p. 150.

[143] Briedenthal diary, p. 339.

[144] Cluett, *History of the Fifty-Seventh Regiment Illinois Volunteer Infantry,* p. 61.

[145] Ambrose, *History of the Seventh Regiment Illinois Volunteer Infantry,* p. 151.

[146] Stratton letter to his sister, May 2, 1863.

[147] McKee diary.

[148] Cluett, *History of the Fifty-Seventh Regiment Illinois Volunteer Infantry,* p. 61.

[149] Briedenthal diary, p. 340.

[150] Ibid.

[151] Committee of the Seventy-Third Indiana Regimental Association, *History of the Seventy-Third Indiana Volunteer Infantry*, p. 129.

[152] Morrison, *A History of the Ninth Regiment Illinois Volunteer Infantry*, p. 52.

[153] *AOR*, Series I, Vol. XXIII, Pt. 1, p. 255.

[154] Ibid.

[155] Pomeroy diary.

[156] Starr, *Jennison's Jayhawkers*, p. 263.

[157] Ibid.

[158] *AOR*, Series I, Vol. XXIII, Pt. 2, p. 788.

[159] Allen service record.

[160] Ridley, *Battles and Sketches of the Army of Tennessee*, p. 171; and Jordan and Pryor, *The Campaigns of Lieutenant General N. B. Forrest and Forrest's Cavalry*, pp. 250, 252.

[161] Foote, *The Civil War*, vol. 2, p. 181.

[162] Henry, *First With the Most Forrest*, p. 144. (Other sources say it was April 27, but most older histories say it was the 26th.)

[163] Wyeth, *That Devil Forrest*, p. 170; and Lindsley, ed., *The Military Annals of Tennessee: Confederate*, p. 683.

[164] John Preston Watts Brown diary, p. 110.

[165] *AOR*, Series I, Vol. XXIII, Pt. 1, p. 248.

[166] Ibid., p. 287.

[167] Ibid., p. 283.

[168] Ibid.

[169] Ibid., p. 287.

[170] McCash, "Colonel Abel D. Streight's Raid, His Capture and Imprisonment," p. 397.

[171] Briedenthal diary, p. 340.

[172] Hartpence, *History of the Fifty-First Indiana Veteran Volunteer Infantry*, p. 122.

CHAPTER 6

[173] Hubert, *History of the Fiftieth Regiment Illinois Volunteer Infantry*, p. 193.

[174] Ambrose, *History of the Seventh Regiment Illinois Volunteer Infantry*, p. 152.

[175] Wunderlich letter to his brother, May 8, 1863.

[176] Pomeroy diary.

[177] Ambrose, *History of the Seventh Regiment Illinois Volunteer Infantry*, pp. 153-154.

[178] Jordan and Pryor, *The Campaigns of Lieutenant General N. B. Forrest and Forrest's Cavalry*, p. 252.

[179] Hubert, *History of the Fiftieth Regiment Illinois Volunteer Infantry*, p. 193.

[180] Jordan and Pryor, *The Campaigns of Lieutenant General N. B. Forrest and Forrest's Cavalry*, p. 252.

[181] Hubert, *History of the Fiftieth Regiment Illinois Volunteer Infantry*, p. 193.

[182] Ambrose, *History of the Seventh Regiment Illinois Volunteer Infantry*, p. 154.

[183] Hubert, *History of the Fiftieth Regiment Illinois Volunteer Infantry*, p. 194.

[184] Kibbee letter to Cousin Hattie, May 9, 1863.

[185] Hubert, *History of the Fiftieth Regiment Illinois Volunteer Infantry*, p. 193.

[186] Cluett, *History of the Fifty-Seventh Regiment Illinois Volunteer Infantry*, p. 62.

[187] Regimental records, 81st Ohio Infantry.

[188] Bearss, "Colonel Streight Drives for the Western and Atlantic Railroad," *The Alabama Historical Quarterly*, vol. XXVI, p. 158.

[189] Ibid., p. 160.

[190] *AOR*, Series I, Vol. XXIII, Pt. 1, p. 294.

[191] Ohio Roster Commission, *Official Roster of the Soldiers of the State of Ohio in the War of the Rebellion*, vol. 2, p. 468.

[192] Smith pension record.

[193] John Preston Watts Brown diary, p. 110.

[194] *AOR*, Series I, Vol. XXIII, Pt. 1, p. 248.

[195] Jordan and Pryor, *The Campaigns of Lieutenant General N. B. Forrest and Forrest's Cavalry*, p. 253.

[196] *AOR*, Series I, Vol. XXIII, Pt. 2, p. 799.

CHAPTER 7

[197] *AOR*, Series I, Vol. XXIII, Pt. 1, p. 248.

[198] Ibid., p. 195.

[199] Ibid.

[200] Ibid., pp. 248-249.

[201] Ibid., p. 283.

[202] Lindsley, *Military Annals of Tennessee: Confederate*, p. 656.

[203] *AOR*, Series I, Vol. XXIII, Pt. 1, p. 282.

[204] Hubert, *History of the Fiftieth Regiment Illinois Volunteer Infantry*, p. 194.

[205] Jordan and Pryor, *The Campaigns of Lieutenant General N. B. Forrest and Forrest's Cavalry*, p. 254.

[206] Cohen letter to the *Jewish Messenger*, May 6, 1863.

[207] Starr, *Jennison's Jayhawkers*, p. 266.

[208] Ibid.

[209] McKee diary, pp. 13-14.

[210] *AOR*, Series I, Vol. XXIII, Pt. 1, p. 282.

[211] Ibid., Pt. 2, p. 224.

[212] Cluett, *History of the Fifty-Seventh Regiment Illinois Volunteer Infantry*, p. 62.

[213] Hubert, *History of the Fiftieth Regiment Illinois Volunteer Infantry*, p. 195.

[214] Ambrose, *History of the Seventh Regiment Illinois Volunteer Infantry*, p. 152.

[215] Hubert, *History of the Fiftieth Regiment Illinois Volunteer Infantry*, p. 196.

[216] *AOR*, Series I, Vol. XXIII, Pt. 1, p. 243.

[217] Ibid., p. 245.

[218] Ibid., p. 284.

[219] Cohen letter to the *Messenger*, May 6, 1863.

[220] Hirschon, *Grenville M. Dodge*, p. 73.

[221] Barnard diary, p. 9.

[222] Cornyn service record.

[223] Various service records.

CHAPTER 8

[224] Jordan and Pryor, *The Campaigns of Lieutenant General N.B. Forrest and Forrest's Cavalry*, pp. 255-256.

[225] Cotten, "The Williamson County Cavalry," pp. 104-105.

[226] Webb, ed., *Crucial Moments of the Civil War*, p. 249.

[227] Cotten, "The Williamson County Cavalry," p. 105.

[228] Briedenthal diary, p. 340.

[229] Ibid.

[230] Hartpence, *History of the Fifty-First Indiana Volunteer Infantry, p. 124.*

[231] Ibid.

[232] *AOR*, Series I, Vol. XXIII, Pt. 1, p. 287.

[233] Committee of the Seventy-Third Indiana Regimental Association, *History of the Seventy-Third Indiana Volunteer Infantry*, p. 132.

[234] Scribner, *Indiana's Roll of Honor*, vol. II, pp. 117-118.

[235] Committee of the Seventy-Third Indiana Regimental Association, *History of the Seventy-Third Indiana Volunteer Infantry*, p. 132-133.

[236] Duncan journal, p. 12.

[237] Briedenthal diary, p. 341.

[238] Agee, "Forrest-Streight Campaign of 1863," p. 12.

[239] Roach, *Prisoner of War and How Treated*, p. 20.

[240] *AOR*, Series I, Vol. XXIII, Pt. 1, p. 288.

[241] Briedenthal diary, p. 342.

[242] Scribner, *Indiana's Roll of Honor*, vol. II, p. 133.

CHAPTER 9

[243] Wyeth, *That Devil Forrest*, p. 174.

[244] Ibid.

[245] Ibid., p. 173.

[246] Henry, *First With the Most Forrest*, p. 146.

[247] Wyeth, *That Devil Forrest*, p. 106.

[248] Lytle, *Bedford Forrest and His Critter Company*, pp. 156-157.

[249] Committee of the Seventy-Third Indiana Regimental Association, *History of the Seventy-Third Indiana Volunteer Infantry*, p. 133-134.

[250] Lytle, *Bedford Forrest and His Critter Company*, p. 157.

[251] Ibid., p. 156.

[252] *AOR*, Series I, Vol. XXIII, Pt. 1, p. 288.

[253] Ibid.

[254] Ibid.

[255] Roach, *Prisoner of War and How Treated*, p. 22.

[256] Ibid.

[257] Lytle, *Bedford Forrest and His Critter Company*, p. 138.

[258] Mathes, *General Forrest*, p. 115.

[259] Committee of the Seventy-Third Indiana Regimental Association, *History of the Seventy-Third Indiana Volunteer Infantry*, p. 146.

260 Briedenthal diary, p. 342.

261 Roach, *Prisoner of War and How Treated,* pp. 22-23.

262 Briedenthal diary, p. 342

263 Mathes, *General Forrest,* p. 115.

264 Duncan, *Recollections of Thomas D. Duncan, Confederate Soldier,* p. 114.

265 Lytle, *Bedford Forrest and His Critter Company,* pp. 158-159.

266 Ibid., p. 159.

267 Ibid.

268 Mathes, *General Forrest,* p. 116.

269 Jordan and Pryor, *The Campaigns of Lieutenant General N. B. Forrest and Forrest's Cavalry,* p. 259.

270 Spencer journal, pp. 6, 7.

271 Ibid.

272 Hartpence, *History of the Fifty-First Indiana Veteran Volunteer Infantry,* pp. 126-127; Jordan and Pryor, *The Campaigns of Lieutenant General N. B. Forrest and Forrest's Cavalry,* p. 249; and Lindsley, ed., *The Military Annals of Tennessee: Confederate,* p. 691.

273 Adjutant General of Indiana, *Indiana Adjutant General Report . . . 1861-1865,* vol. 2, p. 501.

274 Committee of the Seventy-Third Indiana Regimental Association, *History of the Seventy-Third Indiana Volunteer Infantry,* p. 136.

275 Ibid.

276 Roach, *Prisoner of War and How Treated,* p. 23.

277 *AOR,* Series I, Vol. XXIII, Pt. 1, p. 288.

278 3d Tennessee Cavalry regimental records.

279 Committee of the Seventy-Third Indiana Regimental Association, *History of the Seventy-Third Indiana Volunteer Infantry,* p. 137.

CHAPTER 10

280 Dinkins, "Pursuit and Capture of Colonel Streight," *Confederate Veteran,* vol. XXXV, December 1927, p. 452.

281 Fisher, *They Rode with Forrest and Wheeler,* p. 40.

282 Agee, "Forrest-Streight Campaign of 1863," p. 10.

283 Webb, *Crucial Moments of the Civil War,* p. 243.

284 *AOR,* Series I, Vol. XXIII, Pt. 1, p. 288.

285 Briedenthal diary, p. 342.

286 Committee of the Seventy-Third Indiana Regimental Association, *History of the Seventy-Third Indiana Volunteer Infantry,* p. 140.

287 *AOR,* Series I, Vol. XXIII, Pt. 1, p. 289.

288 Lytle, *Bedford Forrest and His Critter Company,* p. 160.

289 Ibid., p. 161.

290 Cotten, "The Williamson County Cavalry," p. 106.

291 Lytle, *Bedford Forrest and His Critter Company,* p. 161.

292 Ibid.

293 Spencer journal, p. 4.

294 Ibid.

295 Ibid., p. 5.

296 Ibid.

297 Ibid.

298 Ibid.

299 Adjutant General of Indiana, *Indiana Adjutant General Report . . . 1861–1865*, vol. 5, pp. 509-531.

300 Roach, *Prisoner of War and How Treated*, p. 24.

301 Spencer journal, p. 7.

302 Young, *Confederate Wizards of the Saddle*, p. 463.

303 Various service and regimental records.

304 *Indianapolis Journal*, June 5, 1863.

305 Ibid.

306 *AOR*, Series I, Vol. XXIII, Pt. 1, p. 289.

307 Lytle, *Bedford Forrest and His Critter Company*, p. 163.

308 Whitsitt, "Streight's Raid," *Confederate Veteran*, vol. XXV, August 1917, p. 360.

309 Mathes, *General Forrest*, p. 118.

310 *Memphis Commercial Appeal*, August 27, 1933.

311 Whitsitt, "Streight's Raid," *Confederate Veteran*, vol. XXV, August 1917, p. 361.

CHAPTER 11

312 *AOR*, Series I, Vol. XXIII, Pt. 1, p. 289.

313 Briedenthal diary, p. 342.

314 Committee of the Seventy-Third Indiana Regimental Association, *History of the Seventy-Third Indiana Volunteer* Infantry, p. 142.

315 Ibid., pp. 142-143.

316 Ibid., p. 143.

317 Blount County Historical Society, "The Forrest-Streight Raid: A Blount County Viewpoint," np.

318 Bearss, "Colonel Streight Drives for the Western and Atlantic Railroad," *Alabama Historical Quarterly*, vol. XXVI, Summer 1964, p. 175.

319 Starnes, *Forrest's Forgotten Horse Brigadier*, p. 74.

320 John Preston Watts Brown diary, p. 111.

321 *Memphis Commercial Appeal*, September 3, 1933.

322 Whitsitt, "Streight's Raid," *Confederate Veteran*, vol. XXV, August 1917, p. 360.

323 Wyeth, *That Devil Forrest*, p. 185.

324 Youngblood, *Confederate Veteran*, vol. II, October 1894, p. 363.

325 Bearss, "Colonel Streight Drives for the Western and Atlantic Railroad," *Alabama Historical Quarterly*, vol. XXVI, p. 175.

326 Webb, *Crucial Moments of the Civil War*, p. 254.

327 Jordan and Pryor, *The Campaigns of Lieutenant General N. B. Forrest and Forrest's Cavalry*, p. 250.

328 Blount County Historical Society, *The Forrest-Streight Raid: A Blount County Viewpoint*, np.

329 Lytle, *Bedford Forrest and His Critter Company*, p. 165.

330 Ibid., p. 166.

[331] Briedenthal diary, p. 343.

[332] Committee of the Seventy-Third Indiana Regimental Association, *History of the Seventy-Third Indiana Volunteer Infantry*, p. 144.

CHAPTER 12

[333] Anonymous journal.

[334] Briedenthal diary, p. 343.

[335] Ibid.

[336] *AOR*, Series I, Vol. XXIII, Pt. 1, p. 290.

[337] Jordan and Pryor, *The Campaigns of Lieutenant General N. B. Forrest and Forrest's Cavalry*, p. 266.

[338] *AOR*, p. 290.

[339] Jordan and Pryor, *The Campaigns of Lieutenant General N. B. Forrest and Forrest's Cavalry*, p. 266.

[340] Wyeth, *That Devil Forrest*, p. 186.

[341] Ibid., p. 187.

[342] Ibid., pp. 188-190.

[343] Jordan and Pryor, *The Campaigns of Lieutenant General N. B. Forrest and Forrest's Cavalry*, p. 269.

[344] Ibid.

[345] Agee, "Forrest-Streight Campaign of 1863," p. 9.

[346] Hartpence, *History of the Fifty-First Indiana Veteran Volunteer Infantry*, p. 132.

[347] Hurst, *Nathan Bedford Forrest*, p. 124.

[348] Henry, *First With the Most Forrest*, p. 491.

[349] Starnes, *Forrest's Forgotten Horse Brigadier*, p. 75.

[350] Bearss, "Colonel Streight Drives for the Western and Atlanta Railroad," *Alabama Historical Quarterly*, vol. XXVI, p. 178.

[351] Briedenthal diary, p. 343.

[352] Cullum, *Confederate Veteran*, vol. VII, January 1899, p. 30.

[353] Briedenthal diary, p. 343.

[354] Committee of the Seventy-Third Indiana Regimental Association, *History of the Seventy-Third Indiana Volunteer Infantry*, p. 143.

[355] *AOR*, Series I, Vol. XXIII, Pt. 1, p. 290.

[356] Ibid.

[357] Agee, "Forrest-Streight Campaign of 1863," p. 12.

CHAPTER 13

[358] *Gadsden Times* (Gadsden, Alabama), July 20, 1909.

[359] Aycock, *All Roads Lead to Rome*, pp. 90-91.

[360] *Gadsden Times* (Gadsden, Alabama), July 20, 1909.

[361] Aycock, *All Roads Lead to Rome*, p. 91.

[362] Ibid.

[363] *Gadsden Times* (Gadsden, Alabama), July 20, 1909.

[364] Bearss, "Colonel Streight Drives for the Western and Atlantic Railroad," *Alabama Historical Quarterly*, vol. XXVI, p. 179.

[365] Hartpence, *History of the Fifty-First Indiana Veteran Volunteer Infantry*, p. 134.

[366] Jordan and Pryor, *The Campaigns of Lieutenant General N. B. Forrest and Forrest's Cavalry*, p. 270.

[367] Young, *Confederate Wizards of the Saddle*, pp. 469-470.

[368] *AOR*, Series I, Vol. XXIII, Pt. 1, p. 291.

[369] Hartpence, *History of The Fifty-First Indiana Veteran Volunteer Infantry*, p. 134.

[370] Dinkins, "Pursuit and Capture of Colonel Streight," *Confederate Veteran*, vol. XXXVI, January 1928, p. 17.

[371] Briedenthal diary, p. 343.

[372] Stafford service record.

[373] Cotten, "The Williamson County Cavalry," p. 109.

[374] Hartpence, *History of the Fifty-First Indiana Veteran Volunteer Infantry*, pp. 143-144.

[375] James Lawson Brown journal.

[376] Committee of the Seventy-Third Indiana Regimental Association, *History of the Seventy-Third Indiana Volunteer Infantry*, p. 147.

[377] Briedenthal diary, p. 343.

[378] *AOR*, Series I, Vol. XXIII, Pt. 1, p. 288.

[379] Ibid.

[380] Bearss, "Colonel Streight Drives for the Western and Atlantic Railroad," *Alabama Historical Quarterly*, vol. XXVI, p. 181.

[381] Committee of the Seventy-Third Indiana Regimental Association, *History of the Seventy-Third Indiana Volunteer Infantry*, p. 145.

[382] Briedenthal diary, p. 343.

[383] Committee of the Seventy-Third Indiana Regimental Association, *History of the Seventy-Third Indiana Volunteer Infantry*, p. 148.

[384] *AOR*, Series I, Vol. XXIII, Pt. 1, p. 292.

CHAPTER 14

[385] Aycock, *All Roads Lead to Rome*, p. 90.

[386] Ibid., p. 92.

[387] Mann, "Paul Revere of the South."

[388] Ibid.

[389] Norton journal.

[390] *Tri-Weekly Courier* (Rome, Georgia), May 7, 1863.

[391] "A Company Made Favor With General Forrest," *Confederate Veteran*, vol. XXII, March 1914, p. 130.

[392] *Southern Confederacy* (Atlanta), May 4, 1863.

[393] Roach, *Prisoner of War and How Treated*, p. 39.

[394] *Tri-Weekly Courier* (Rome, Georgia), May 5, 1863.

[395] Aycock, *All Roads Lead to Rome*, p. 93.

[396] Ibid.

[397] Bearss, "Colonel Streight Drives for the Western and Atlantic Railroad," *Alabama Historical Quarterly*, vol. XXVI, pp. 183-184.

CHAPTER 15

[398] Briedenthal diary, p. 337.

[399] *AOR,* Series I, Vol. XXIII, Pt. 2, p. 824.

[400] Lytle, *Bedford Forrest and His Critter Company*, p. 171.

[401] Cotten, "The Williamson County Cavalry," p. 110.

[402] Lytle, *Bedford Forrest and His Critter Company*, p. 171.

[403] Ibid.

[404] *AOR*, Series I, Vol. XXIII, Pt. 1, p. 292.

[405] Jordan and Pryor, *The Campaigns of Lieutenant General N. B. Forrest and Forrest's Cavalry*, p. 273.

[406] *AOR*, Series I, Vol. XXIII, Pt. 1, p. 292.

[407] Ibid.

[408] Henry, *First With The Most Forrest*, pp. 156-157.

[409] Ibid., p. 157.

[410] Committee of the Seventy-Third Indiana Regimental Association, *History of the Seventy-Third Indiana Volunteer Infantry*, p. 150.

[411] Cotten, "The Williamson County Cavalry," p. 111.

[412] Whitsitt, "Streight's Raid," *Confederate Veteran*, vol. XXV, August 1917, p. 361.

[413] Briedenthal diary, p. 344.

[414] Cotten, "The Williamson County Cavalry," p. 111.

[415] Mathes, *General Forrest*, p. 125.

[416] Mitchell, "How Forrest Won over Streight," *Confederate Veteran,* vol. XX, p. 380.

[417] Briedenthal diary, p. 344.

[418] Ibid.

[419] James Lawson Brown journal.

[420] Ibid.

[421] Wallis letter, May 26, 1863.

[422] Jordan and Pryor, *The Campaigns of Lieutenant General N. B. Forrest and Forrest's Cavalry*, p. 276.

[423] Lytle, *Bedford Forrest and His Critter Company*, p. 175.

[424] Committee of the Seventy-Third Indiana Regimental Association, *History of the Seventy-Third Indiana Volunteer Infantry*, p. 151.

[425] Briedenthal diary, p. 344.

[426] Webb, *Crucial Moments of the Civil War*, p. 264.

[427] Roach, *Prisoner of War and How Treated*, p. 42.

[428] Dinkins, "Pursuit and Capture of Colonel Streight," *Confederate Veteran*, vol. XXXVI, December 1927, p. 17.

[429] *Southern Confederacy* (Atlanta), May 10, 1863.

[430] Wallis letter, May 26, 1863.

[431] Briedenthal diary, p. 344.

[432] Committee of the Seventy-Third Indiana Regimental Association, *History of the Seventy-Third Indiana Volunteer Infantry*, p. 152.

[433] Ibid.

[434] *AOR*, Series II, Vol. V, p. 721.

435 Ibid., pp. 714-715.

436 *AOR*, Series I, Vol. XXIII, Pt. 1, p. 295.

437 *Gadsden Times* (Gadsden, Alabama), July 29, 1909.

438 Agee, "Forrest-Streight Campaign of 1863," p. 10.

439 Cullman County Comprehensive Employment Training Act Personnel, *Cullman County Churches and Cemeteries*, vol. II, p. 23.

440 Dyer, *A Compendium of the War of the Rebellion*, vol. III, various pages.

441 "A Company Made Favor With General Forrest," *Confederate Veteran*, vol. XXII, March 1914, p. 130-131.

CHAPTER 16

442 Spencer journal, pp. 5-6.

443 Hartpence, *History of the Fifty-First Indiana Veteran Volunteer Infantry*, p. 129.

444 Ibid.

445 Ibid.

446 Spencer journal, p. 8.

447 Committee of the Seventy-Third Indiana Regimental Association, *History of the Seventy-Third Indiana Volunteer Infantry*, p. 137.

448 Spencer journal, p. 8.

449 Ibid.

450 Ibid.

451 Ibid., pp. 8-9.

452 Ibid., p. 9.

453 Ibid.

454 Ibid.

455 Hartpence, *History of the Fifty-First Indiana Veteran Volunteer Infantry*, p. 142.

456 Ibid., pp. 144-145.

CHAPTER 17

457 Hartpence, *History of the Fifty-First Indiana Veteran Volunteer Infantry*, p. 141.

458 Committee of the Seventy-Third Indiana Regimental Association, *History of the Seventy-Third Indiana Volunteer Infantry*, p. 153.

459 Ibid.

460 Briedenthal diary, pp. 345-348.

461 Hartpence, *History of the Fifty-First Indiana Veteran Volunteer Infantry*, p. 144.

462 Witham to Morton telegram, August 5, 1863.

463 *AOR*, Series II, Vol. V, p. 946.

464 Ibid., p. 956.

465 Ibid., p. 969.

466 *Richmond Enquirer,* May 21, 1863.

467 Roach, *Prisoner of War and How Treated,* p. 45.

468 Ibid.

[469] Ibid., pp. 44-45.

[470] *AOR*, Series II, Vol. V, p. 590.

[471] Ibid., p. 716.

[472] Ibid., p. 691.

[473] Spencer journal. p. 40.

[474] Parker, *Richmond's Civil War Prisons*, pp. 37-38.

[475] Spencer journal, p. 43.

[476] *AOR,* Series II, Vol. VI, pp. 241-242.

[477] Ibid., p. 279.

[478] Ibid., p. 302.

[479] Ibid.

[480] Ibid.

[481] Roach, *Prisoner of War and How Treated*, p. 92.

[482] Ibid., p. 100.

[483] Funk, "The Great Escape From Libby Prison," *Outdoor Indiana*, vol. VIII, No. 1, July 1964, p. 5.

[484] Roach, *Prisoner of War and How Treated*, p. 103.

[485] Ibid., pp. 117-118.

[486] Committee of the Seventy-Third Indiana Regimental Association, *History of the Seventy-Third Indiana Volunteer Infantry*, pp. 160-161.

[487] Ibid., p. 160; and service and pension records.

[488] Hartpence, *History of the Fifty-First Indiana Veteran Volunteer Infantry*, p. 146.

[489] Bruse letter to his wife, September 25, 1863.

[490] Hartpence, *History of the Fifty-First Indiana Veteran Volunteer Infantry*, p. 167.

POSTSCRIPT

[491] McCash, "Colonel Abel D. Streight's Raid, His Capture and Imprisonment," p. 414.

[492] Cook, "The 1863 Raid of Abel Streight: Why it Failed", *Alabama Review*, October 1969, p. 261.

[493] Ibid., p. 269.

Selected Bibliography

Articles

"A Company Made Favor With General Forrest." *Confederate Veteran* (March 1914): vol. XXII.

Bearss, Edwin. "Colonel Streight Drives for the Western and Atlantic Railroad." *Alabama Historical Quarterly* (1964): vol. XXVI.

Cook, James F. "The 1863 Raid of Abel Streight: Why it Failed." *Alabama Review* (Oct. 1969).

Cullum, Rev J. W. *Confederate Veteran* (Jan. 1899): vol. VII.

Dinkins, James. "Pursuit and Capture of Colonel Streight." *Confederate Veteran* (Dec. 1927): vol. XXXV.

Domer, Ronald G. "Rebel Rout of Streight's Raiders." *America's Civil War* (Sept. 1996).

Funk, Arville L. "The Great Escape from Libby Prison." *Outdoor Indiana* (July 1964): vol. VIII.

Mann, Robert N. "Paul Revere of the South." *History and Heritage: Articles on Cherokee County, Alabama.* Gadsden, Ala.: Cherokee County Historical Museum (1963).

Mitchell, Mrs. C. A. "How Forrest Won Over Streight." *Confederate Veteran* (Aug. 1912): vol. XX.

"Roddey's Old Company." *Confederate Veteran* (May 1905): vol. XIII.

Saunders, Ellen Virginia. "War-Time Journal of a 'Little Rebel'." *Confederate Veteran* (Jan. 1920): vol. XXVIII.

Whitsitt, W. W. "Streight's Raid." *Confederate Veteran* (Aug. 1917): vol. XXV.

Youngblood, G.W. *Confederate Veteran* (Oct. 1894): vol. II.

Books

Addison, Stuart. *Iowa Colonels and Regiments.* Mills, Iowa: 1865.

Ambrose, Daniel Leib. *History of the Seventh Regiment Illinois Volunteer Infantry.* Springfield, Ill.: Illinois Journal Company, 1868.

Aycock, Roger. *All Roads Lead to Rome.* Atlanta, Ga.: W. H. Wolfe & Co., 1981.

Beatty, John. *Memoirs of a Volunteer,* ed. by Harvey S. Ford. New York: W. W. Norton, 1946.

Boatner, Mark Mayo. *The Civil War Dictionary.* New York: David McKay Company, Inc., 1959.

Breidenthal, Henry. Diary. *Rebellion Record–Supplement.*

Brewer, Willis. *Brief Historical Sketches.* Montgomery, Ala.: Alabama CW Centennial Commission, 1962.

Brooksher & Snider. *Glory at a Gallop.* McLean, Va.: Brassey's, Inc., 1993.

Brown, D. Alexander. *Grierson's Raid.* Urbana, Ill.: University of Illinois Press, 1962.

Cluett, William W. *History of the Fifty-Seventh Regiment Illinois Volunteer Infantry.* Princeton, Ill.: T. P. Streeter, Printer, 1886.

Committee of the Seventy-Third Indiana Regimental Association. *History of the Seventy-Third Indiana Volunteers*. Washington: Carnahan Press, 1909.

Crawford, James Gavin. *Dear Lizzie*. Indianapolis: Private Printing, 1978.

Dodd, Donald B. & Wynelle S. *Annals of Northwest Alabama*, vol. IV. Jasper, Ala.: 1985.

Dodge, Grenville M. *Personal Recollections of Abraham Lincoln, General Ulysses S. Grant and General William T. Sherman*. Council Bluffs, Iowa: 1914.

Duncan, Thomas D. *Recollections of Thomas D. Duncan, Confederate Soldier*. Private Printing.

Dyer, Frederick H. *Compendium of the War of the Rebellion*. New York: Thomas Yoseloff, 1959.

Eddy, Thomas M. *The Patriotism of Illinois: A Record of the Civil and Military History of the State*. Chicago: Clarke, 1866.

Fisher, John E. *They Rode with Forrest and Wheeler*. Jefferson, N.C.: McFarland and Company, Inc., 1995.

Fitch, John, ed. *Annals of the Army of the Cumberland*. Philadelphia: J. B. Lippincott and Company, 6th Edition, 1864.

Fleming, Samuel F. Jr. *Sergeant Newton Cannon*. Franklin, Tenn.: The Carter House Association, 1963.

Foote, Shelby. *The Civil War*, vol. 2. New York: Random House, 1963.

Garfield, James A. *The Wild Life of the Army*. East Lansing, Mich.: Michigan State University Press, 1964.

Gibson, Charles Dana. *Assault and Logistics*. Camden, Maine: Ensign Press, 1995.

Griffith, Lucille. *Alabama: A Documentary History to 1900*. University, Ala.: University of Alabama Press, 1968.

Hartpence, William R. *History of the Fifty-First Indiana Veteran Volunteer Infantry*. Cincinnati, Ohio: Author, 1894.

Henry, Robert Selph. *First With the Most Forrest*. New York: Konecky and Konecky, 1992.

Henry, Robert Selph. *As They Saw Forrest*. Nashville, Tennessee: McCowat Mercer Press, Inc., 1956.

Hirschon, Stanley P. *Grenville M. Dodge: Soldier, Politician, Railroad Pioneer*. Bloomington, Ind.: Indiana University Press, 1967.

Hoole, William S. *Alabama Tories: The First Alabama Cavalry, U..S..A., 1862-1865*. Tuscaloosa, Ala.: Confederate Publishing Company, Inc., 1960.

Hubert, Charles F. *History of the Fiftieth Regiment, Illinois Volunteer Infantry*. Kansas City, Mo.: Western Veteran Publishing Co., 1891.

Hurst, Jack. *Nathan Bedford Forrest*. New York: Vintage Books, 1994.

Jordan, Thomas and J. P. Pryor. *The Campaigns of Lieutenant General N.B. Forrest and Forrest's Cavalry*. New Orleans: Blelock & Co., 1868.

Lindsley, John B. ed. *The Military Annals of Tennessee: Confederate*. Wilmington, N.C.: Broadfoot Publishing Company, 1987.

Long, E. B. *The Civil War Day by Day*. Garden City, N.Y.: Doubleday and Company, Inc., 1971.

Longacre, Edward G. *Mounted Raids of the Civil War*. Lincoln, Neb.: U. of Nebraska Press, 1975.

Lytle, Andrew Nelson. *Bedford Forrest and His Critter Company.* Nashville, Tenn.: J. S. Sanders & Co., 1931.

Mathes, J. Harvey. *General Forrest.* New York: D. Appleton and Company, 1902.

Morrison, Marion. *A History of the Ninth Regiment Illinois Volunteer Infantry.* Monmouth, Ill.: John E. Clark, Printer, 1864.

Morton, John Watson. *The Artillery of Nathan Bedford Forrest's Cavalry.* Nashville, Tenn.: Publishing House of M.E. Church, 1909.

Nowland, John H. B. *Sketches of Prominent Citizens of 1876.* Indianapolis: Tilford and Carlton Printers, 1876.

Phisterer, Frederick. *Statistical Record of the Armies of the United States.* New York: The Blue & The Gray Press, n.d.

Pruitt, Wade. *Bugger Saga.* Columbia, Tenn.: P-Vine Press, 1976.

Ridley, Bromfield L. *Battles and Sketches of the Army of Tennessee.* Dayton, Ohio: Morningside Bookshop, 1978.

Roach, A.C. *The Prisoner of War and How Treated.* Indianapolis: Robert Douglas, Publisher, 1887.

Scribner, Theo. T. *Indiana's Roll of Honor.* vol. II. Indianapolis: A. D. Streight, Publishers, 1866.

Society of Survivors. *History of the Ram Fleet.* St. Louis: 1907.

Starnes, H. Gerald. *Forrest's Forgotten Horse Brigadier.* Bowie, Md.: Heritage Books, 1995.

Starr, Stephen Z. *Jennison's Jayhawkers.* Baton Rouge, La.: LSU Press, 1973.

Sykes, E.T. *Walthall's Brigade.* Private Printing, 1916.

Tennessee Civil War Centennial Commission. *Tennesseans in the Civil War: A Military History of Union and Confederate Units.* vol. 1. Nashville: Tennessee Civil War Centennial Commission, 1964.

Thompson, Wesley S. *The Free State of Winston.* Winfield, Ala.: Pareil Press, 1968.

Webb, Willard, ed. *Crucial Moments of the Civil War.* New York: Bonanza Books, 1976.

Willett, Robert L. *One Day of the Civil War.* Dulles, Va.: Brassey's, Inc., 1997.

Wills, Brian Steel. *A Battle From the Start.* New York: Harper Collins Publishers, Inc., 1992.

Wilson, Charles Dana. *Assault and Logistics.* Camden, Maine: Ensign Press, 1995.

Womack, Ben. *Call Forth the Mighty Men.* Bessemer, Ala.: Colonial Press, 1987.

Wyeth, John Allan. *That Devil Forrest.* New York: Harper and Bros., 1959.

Young, Bennett H. *Confederate Wizards of the Saddle.* Dayton, Ohio: Morningside Bookshop, 1979.

Government Publications

Adjutant General's Office. *Official Military History of Kansas Regiments.* Topeka, Kan.: State of Kansas, 1870.

Beers, Henry Putney. *Guide to the Archives of the Confederate States.* Washington: U. S. Government Printing Office, 1968.

Illinois Military and Naval Deptartment. *Report of the Adjutant General.* Springfield, Ill.: Phillips, 1901.

_____. *Report of the Adjutant General*. Springfield, Ill.: State of Illinois, 1878.

Indiana Adjutant General. *Indiana Volunteers, 1861-1865*. Indianapolis: State of Indiana, 1898.

Indiana Adjutant General. *Report...1861-1865*. vol. 2. Indianapolis: Samuel L. Douglas.

Munden, Kennth W., and Henry Putney Beers. *Guide to Federal Archives Relating to Civil War*. Washington: US Government Printing Office, 1962.

Ohio Roster Commission. *Official Roster of the Soldiers of the State of Ohio in the War of the Rebellion*. Akron, Ohio: Werner Printing and Manufacturing Co., 1888.

_____. *Official Roster of the Soldiers of the State of Ohio in the War of the Rebellion*. vol. 2. Cincinnati: Wilstach, Baldwin, 1886.

Parker, Sandra V. *Richmond's Civil War Prisons*. Richmond, Va.: State of Virginia, 1963.

Record of Deaths by Regiment. Washington, D.C.: U. S. Government Printing Office, various dates.

Regimental Records. National Archives, Washington, DC.

Reid, Whitlaw. *Ohio in the War: Her Statesmen, Her Generals and Soldiers*. vol. 2. Cincinnati: Wilstach, Baldwin, 1872.

War of the Rebellion: Official Records of the Union and Confederate Armies. 127 vols. plus index. Government Printing Office, 1880-1901.

Diaries and Journals

Anonymous. Journal. Alabama Department of Archives and History, Montgomery.

Barnard, Job. Diary. Indiana State Library, Indianapolis.

Brown, James Lawson. Journal. Centralia, Ill.. Loomis Collection.

Brown, John Preston Watts. Diary. Tennessee State Library and Archives, Nashville.

Brumfield, Staunton. Diary. Indiana State Archives, Indianapolis.

Du Bose, John Witherspoon. Manuscript. Alabama Department of Archives and History, Montgomery.

Duncan, John A. Journal. Civil War Miscellaneous Collection, United States Army Military History Institute, Carlisle, Pa.

McKee, John J. Diary. Civil War Miscellaneous Collection, United States Army Military History Institute, Carlisle, Pa.

Norton, Reuben S. Journal, typed manuscript. Rome, Georgia, Public Library.

Pomeroy, Fletcher. Diary. Dave Paul Collection.

_____. Diary. David Habura Collection.

Spencer, William. Journal. Indiana Historical Society Library, Indianapolis.

Letters and Telegrams

Anonymous. Letter, August 5, 1863, *Indianapolis Daily State Sentinel*.

Anonymous. Letter to Governor Morton of Indiana, August 5, 1861. Indiana State Archives, Indianapolis.

Bruse, James Van Cleve. Letter to his wife, September 25, 1863. Stephen Loomis Collection.

Cohen, J. C. Letters to the *Jewish Messenger*, April 10, 1863 and May 6, 1863. Corinth website, internet.

Hathaway, Gilbert. Telegram to Governor Morton, April 22, 1863. Indiana State Archives, Indianapolis.

Kibee, Amos W. Letter to his cousin, May 9, 1863. Civil War Miscellaneous Collection, United States Military History Institute, Carlisle. Pa.

McHolland, D. A. Telegram to Governor Morton, April 14, 1863. Indiana State Archives, Indianapolis.

Saunders, John. E. Letter to John A. Campbell, May 9, 1863. National Archives, Washington, DC.

Stratton, George P. Letters to his folks, April 10, 1863 and to his sister, May 2 and 3, 1863. Indiana State Archives, Indianapolis.

Streight, Abel. Telegram to Governor Morton, April 8, 1863. Indiana State Archives, Indianapolis.

Wallis, William W. Letter. Stephen Loomis Collection.

Witham, Simon. Telegram to Governor Morton, August 5, 1863. Indiana State Archives, Indianapolis.

Wunderlich, John N. Letter to his brother, May 8, 1863. Civil War Miscellaneous Collection, United States Military History Institute, Carlisle, Pa.

Newspapers

Gadsden Daily Times-News.
Gadsden Times, (Gadsden, Ala.).
Indianapolis Daily State Sentinel.
Indianapolis Journal.
Memphis Commercial Appeal.
Nashville Union.
Richmond Enquire.
Southern Confederacy, (Atlanta).
Tri-Weekly Courier, (Rome, Ga.).

Pamphlets and Manuscripts

Agee, Rucker. "The Forrest-Streight Campaign of 1863." Milwaukee: Civil War Round Table of Milwaukee, 1958.

Blount County Historical Society. "The Forrest-Streight Raid: A Blount County Viewpoint." 1963.

Cotten, Michael. "The Williamson County Cavalry." Goodlettsvelle, Tenn.: Michael Cotten, private, 1994.

Cullman County Comprehensive Employment Training Act Personnel. "Cullman County Churches and Cemeteries." Cullman, Ala., 1974.

Kniffin, G.C.Y. "Streight's Raid." Washington, D.C.: Military Order of the Loyal Legion, 1910.

McCash, William Barton. "Colonel Abel D. Streight's Raid, His Capture and Imprisonment." Athens, Ga.: University of Georgia, 1956.

Streight, Abel D. "The Crisis of Eighteen Hundred and Sixty-One in the Government of the United States and How it Should be Met." Indianapolis: Author, 1861.

Service Records

Washington, DC. Service Records & Pension Records of: Allen, E. Thomas; Bird, Henry; Cameron, James A.; Carley, Albert A.; Cornyn, Florence; Crandal, Robert; Farris, James J.; Forrest, Nathan B.; Forrest, William B.; Hathaway, Gilbert; Jones, James C.; McCullock, Thomas D.; Oates, H. C.; Reed, B. C. G.; Sansom Rufus F.; Sheets, James W.; Smith, David; Spencer, William; Strafford, Charles; Streight, Abel D.; Welton, John A.

APPENDIX - KNOWN CASUALTIES

Name and Unit	Force
Hazard, John S. 10th MO Cav DOW Bartons Sta	Dodge
Klaine, M. B 10th MO Cav WIA Leighton	Dodge
Nicholson, W.L. D 10th TN KIA Days Gap	NBF
Martin, T. F. E 11th TN WIA Days Gap	NBF
Smith, D. M. E 11th TN WIA Tuscumbia	NBF
Ransom, Whit G 11th TN MIA Days Gap	NBF
Stewart, J. W. K 11th TN WIA Leighton	NBF
Gilman, Tom I 15th IL Cav KIA Bartons Sta	Dodge
Day, Richard R. I 1st AL US MIA Moulton	Streight
Forsythe, Thomas J. I 1st AL US MIA Moulton	Streight
Hightower, Marion I 1st AL US MIA Days Gap	Streight
Powell, Joshua I 1st AL US MIA Days Gap	Streight
Powell, Tilman I 1st AL US MIA Moulton	Streight
Williams, Riley I 1st AL US MIA Days Gap	Streight
McCullock, James C. I* 1st AL US WIA Days Gap	Streight
Campbell, John R. K 1st AL US MIA Days Gap	Streight
Cock, Charles K 1st AL US MIA Days Gap	Streight
Funderburk, Christopher C. K 1st AL US MIA Days Gap	Streight
McCullough, Thomas B. K 1st AL US WIA & MIA Days Gap	Streight
Noles, John K 1st AL US WIA & MIA Blountsville	Streight
Russell, John T. K 1st AL US MIA Rome	Streight
Smith, David D. K 1st AL US MIA Rome	Streight
Cameron, James C 1st AL US KIA Bartons Sta	Dodge
Unknown 1st AL US KIA Bartons Sta	Dodge
Taylor, T. * 3rd Ohio DOW Days Gap	Streight
Riley, Benjamin A 3rd Ohio KIA Days Gap	Streight
Stafford, Charles B 3rd Ohio KIA Blounts Plan	Streight
Swaney, Solomon F* 3rd Ohio KIA Days Gap	Streight
Curry, Wm A. G 3rd Ohio POW & DIP Rome	Streight
Haughey, Frank A. H 3rd Ohio DOW Days Gap	Streight
Reed, E. N. I 3rd Ohio DOW	Streight
Haskill, James M. I* 3rd Ohio WIA Days Gap	Streight
Forrest, Wm H. C 3rd TN WIA Days Gap	NBF
Bodie, M. V. F 4th AL CSA MIA 4/17/63	Roddey
Thompson, Aaron A 4th TN KIA Days Gap	NBF
Turner, Robert P. A 4th TN KIA Gadsden	NBF
Hunt, Hartwell 4th TN Cav CSA KIA Blount's Farm	NBF

* Left with Spencer at Days Gap

Sheets, James W. * 51st IVI DOW 6/21/63 Days Gap	Streight
Clark, Samuel B 51st IVI KIA Days Gap	Streight
Coshow, John B 51st IVI KIA Days Gap	Streight
Wonder, Adolphus B 51st IVI MIA Days Gap	Streight
Hosier, Jacob B* 51st IVI WIA Days Gap	Streight
Lowthain, Cyrus B* 51st IVI WIA Days Gap	Streight
McDaniel, Tilman C 51st IVI MIA Days Gap	Streight
McWilliams, Charles A. C 51st IVI KIA Blountsville	Streight
Osborn, Silas C 51st IVI KIA Days Gap	Streight
Jelf, William F. C* 51st IVI WIA Days Gap	Streight
McCall, J. C* 51st IVI MIA Hog Mtn	Streight
Owens, Harrison C* 51st IVI WIA Days Gap	Streight
Dickinson, Floyd C* 51st IVI MIA Hog Mtn	Streight
Wilson, John A. E* 51st IVI WIA Days Gap	Streight
Kendall, Ethan F 51st IVI KIA Days Gap	Streight
Parker, Washington F 51st IVI DOW Days Gap	Streight
Rhodes, Enoch F 51st IVI KIA Crooked Cr	Streight
Moroney, James F* 51st IVI WIA Days Gap	Streight
Pyle, Andrew J. F* 51st IVI WIA Days Gap	Streight
Stafford, J. A. F* 51st IVI WIA Days Gap	Streight
Stafford, W. E. F* 51st IVI MIA Hog Mtn	Streight
Turner, Washington F* 51st IVI WIA Days Gap	Streight
Williams, William H. H* 51st IVI WIA Days Gap	Streight
Farris, George W. I* 51st IVI WIA Days Gap	Streight
Kells, James I* 51st IVI WIA Days Gap	Streight
Kitchen, Jacob B. I* 51st IVI WIA Days Gap	Streight
McCoarte, James I* 51st IVI WIA Days Gap	Streight
McColley, Henry B. I* 51st IVI WIA Days Gap	Streight
Misner, John K* 51st IVI WIA Days Gap	Streight
King, Henry R 51st IVI MIA Days Gap	Streight
Boggs, Theodore F 66th IVI DOW Leighton	Dodge
Leatherman, Christopher 66th IVI Died Eastport	Dodge
Spencer, William ** * 73rd IVI MIA Days Gap	Streight
White, Samuel A 73rd IVI KIA Blounts Plan	Streight
Brown, George A* 73rd IVI WIA Days Gap	Streight
Griffin, Patrick B* 73rd IVI WIA Days Gap	Streight
Huntley, Henry E. ** B* 73rd IVI WIA Days Gap	Streight
Cook, William G. ** D* 73rd IVI WIA Days Gap	Streight
Carley, Albert A. E 73rd IVI MIA Days Gap	Streight
Jackson, Robert E 73rd IVI KIA Days Gap	Streight
Page, William ** E* 73rd IVI WIA Days Gap	Streight
Greeg, Hallen E* 73rd IVI WIA Days Gap	Streight
Crandall, Robert ** F* 73rd IVI WIA Days Gap	Streight
Winters, John F. G 73rd IVI DOW Blounts Plan	Streight

** Reported alive in 1900

Hammerly, William G* 73rd IVI MIA Days Gap	Streight
Seargeant, Lorenzo H* 73rd IVI WIA Days Gap	Streight
Nalley, Sebastian I 73rd IVI Died Tuscumbia	Streight
Foote, Adrian V. H. I* 73rd IVI WIA Days Gap	Streight
Witham, Samuel ** I* 73rd IVI WIA Days Gap	Streight
Bird, Henry K 73rd IVI MIA Days Gap	Streight
Carr, Shannon K 73rd IVI MIA Days Gap	Streight
Farris, Augustus J. (James)** K* 73rd IVI WIA Days Gap	Streight
Hathaway, Gilbert 73rd IVI KIA Blounts Plan	Streight
Porter, Oscar T. 7th KS KIA Salisbury TN	Dodge
Stout, Joshua T. 7th KS KIA Leighton	Dodge
Utt, L. H 7th KS Cav WIA Leighton	Dodge
Jenkins, Walter A* 80th IL Inf WIA Days Gap	Streight
Keeler, Samuel B. A* 80th IL Inf WIA Days Gap	Streight
McIntosh, Francis M. B* 80th IL Inf WIA Days Gap	Streight
Miller, Henry B* 80th IL Inf MIA Days Gap	Streight
Horn, John C 80th IL Inf KIA Days Gap	Streight
Hulls, Reuben D 80th IL Inf DOW Days Gap	Streight
Holm, John F. D* 80th IL Inf WIA Days Gap	Streight
House, William D* 80th IL Inf WIA Days Gap	Streight
Jones, Nicholas B. D* 80th IL Inf MIA Days Gap	Streight
Newhaus, Frederick D* 80th IL Inf WIA Days Gap	Streight
Pavey, Charles W. E* 80th IL Inf WIA & MIA Days Gap	Streight
Davis, John H. F 80th IL Inf MIA Days Gap	Streight
Jones, Edmund R. F 80th IL Inf KIA Days Gap	Streight
Rohn, Charles F 80th IL Inf MIA Days Gap	Streight
Rohn, Philip F 80th IL Inf MIA Days Gap	Streight
Allen, Robert F. F* 80th IL Inf WIA Days Gap	Streight
Gallagly, William W. F* 80th IL Inf WIA Days Gap	Streight
Mackey, John F* 80th IL Inf WIA Days Gap	Streight
McCaughan, James F* 80th IL Inf MIA Days Gap	Streight
Smith, James P. F* 80th IL Inf WIA Days Gap	Streight
Hamsom, James G* 80th IL Inf WIA Days Gap	Streight
Baggs, Absalom I* 80th IL Inf MIA Days Gap	Streight
Jones, James C 80th IL Inf KIA Days Gap	Streight
Krebs, Edward D 9th IL Inf MIA Bartons Sta	Dodge
Cockriff, Jasper G 9th TN KIA Days Gap	NBF
Roach, Pvt 9th TN Cav KIA Blount's Farm	NBF
Oates, H. H. L Julians KIA Days Gap	Roddey

Key:

WIA – Wounded in Action	KIA – Killed in Action
MIA – Missing in Action	IVI – Indiana Volunteer Infantry
NBF – Forrest's Division	

Index